Claiming the Dream

CLAIMING THE DREAM

THE VICTORIOUS CAMPAIGN OF DOUGLAS WILDER OF VIRGINIA

BY MARGARET EDDS
WITH AN INTRODUCTION BY PAUL DUKE

ALGONQUIN BOOKS OF CHAPEL HILL • 1990

Published by
Algonquin Books of Chapel Hill
Post Office Box 2225
Chapel Hill, North Carolina 27515-2225
a division of
Workman Publishing Company, Inc.
708 Broadway
New York, New York 10003

Library of Congress Cataloging-in-
Publication Data
Edds, Margaret, 1947–
Claiming the dream : the victorious campaign
of Douglas Wilder of Virginia / by Margaret
Edds : with an introduction by Paul Duke.
p. cm.
Includes bibliographical references.
ISBN 0-912697-85-7 : $18.95
1. Wilder, Doug. 2. Virginia—Governors—
Election—History—20th century. 3. Virginia
—Politics and government—1951– I. Title.
F231.3.W55E33 1990
975.5'043'092—dc20   90-311
                                 CIP

First printing
10 9 8 7 6 5 4 3 2 1

For Thomas

CONTENTS

ACKNOWLEDGMENTS

This book could not have been completed without the generous assistance of several dozen politicians, political workers, and consultants who shared insights and details about the inner workings of the campaigns of Douglas Wilder and Marshall Coleman. My appreciation to them is great, and I am especially indebted to those who put aside their own causes in the interests of providing an accurate account of a momentous political event. I am grateful for the support and encouragement of my editors at the *Virginian-Pilot/Ledger-Star*: Sandy Rowe, Jim Raper, and Dale Eisman; and to several colleagues whose help and friendship were invaluable: Bonnie Winston, Warren Fiske, Bill Byrd, Tom Boyer, Marvin Lake, and Steven Johnson. Don Harrison saved me from technological catastrophe, and Larry Sabato provided wise counsel. I was indeed fortunate to have Louis Rubin, Jr., and Guy Friddell as my editors. Whatever is of value here bears their mark; any mistakes are my own. I owe most to those who lived with me through this writing —Margaret Simpson, Kate, Adam and, always, Bob.

INTRODUCTION: PRELUDE TO A NEW DAY
BY PAUL DUKE

The Commonwealth of Virginia's new political day arrived bursting with magic moments and incredible ironies.

Here was L. Douglas Wilder assuming office as the nation's first elected black governor and taking command of a statehouse that often had seemed a relic of the old Confederacy.

Here was Wilder, just two generations away from slavery, proudly boasting of his Virginia heritage and dutifully paying tribute to Thomas Jefferson and his founding father kinsmen whose world had been built around the slavery culture.

Here was Wilder proclaiming triumph for the ancient ideas of freedom and opportunity, delivering his eloquent and conciliatory inaugural address a scant few feet from a statue of Confederate knight Stonewall Jackson, who fought and died to restrain those ideas.

But on this trail-blazing day in January 1990, the blend of old and new, black and white, came easily. The 30,000 people crammed into Virginia's lovely old Capitol Square constituted one of the largest throngs ever to attend a gubernatorial inauguration in the United States. Blacks far outnumbered whites, and some suggested it was the largest turnout of blacks in Richmond since Abraham Lincoln walked the city's streets in the final hours of the Civil War.

Sitting near Wilder on the inaugural platform were Oliver Hill and other black pioneers who had made it all possible by courageously and persistently demolishing the state's legal lattice of segregation during the turbulent 1950s. A few rows away were several old enemies from the once-vaunted Byrd Democratic Organization, men who long since had made their peace with the new politics of racial equality. Way back in the crowd was one notable incongruity, the towering charcoal grey statue of the machine's grand patriarch, Harry Flood Byrd, for so many years the state's foremost symbol of racial division. Now, as Wilder spoke proudly of Virginia's "new mainstream," some of the onlookers could be seen hugging the sides of Old Harry to get a better view of the newest Democratic hero.

It was a remarkable tableau, one that would have been unthinkable back in the 1950s when I was a young Associated Press reporter covering the state capitol. In those days blacks regarded this as hostile territory. None held important positions in the state government. The only blacks seen around the capitol building were those who swept the floors or washed windows—indeed, as a young college graduate, Wilder found the only state job open to him was that of cook at a penal institution. When the segregationist storms were at their peak, the benches along Capitol Square's hilly brick walkways were removed to avoid any chance that whites and blacks might sit next to one another.

The most gratifying change for me was the knowledge that my home state had taken the last step in exorcising the reputation it had held for most of the twentieth century as a sleepy Southern backwater—"a political museum piece," in the famed phrase of political scientist V. O. Key. It seemed fitting, too, that Wilder would be wielding more administrative power than any other elected black leader in American history. And, that the great breakthrough had come in the state that introduced slavery into the English colonies in the sixteenth century.

This valuable chronicle by Margaret Edds draws a vivid contrast between that old Virginia and the new Virginia that emerged to enable Doug Wilder's dream to come true. Clearly, as she says, an important threshold has been crossed, one that none of us on the front lines of the civil rights wars of three decades ago would have prophesied. For whites, the Wilder victory was a redemptive act that meant Virginians were free at last of their historic bondage to racial politics. For blacks, it meant one more crucial milepost had been reached on the treacherous road to equal justice.

The new day had been more than a hundred years in coming. Appomattox may have ended a civilization, but it did not end a way of life. The cherished dream of Southern independence might be gone and the institution of slavery with it, but the Civil War did not destroy a society founded on the premise of white superiority. The plantation legacy of a strictly defined social order with an aristocratic concept of liberty lived on. Blacks might be free, but the fruits of that freedom would be sparse indeed. The South would be everlastingly white man's country.

The conventional wisdom is that Reconstruction hardened these attitudes, and it is certainly true that Northern-imposed rule had its harsh and vindictive side. But there also was a brighter side frequently obscured by the stereotypical view. Radicals in Congress pushed through the Fourteenth and Fifteenth Amendments to the Constitution guaranteeing blacks the rights of citizenship and the ballot. Northerners gave generously to help alleviate hunger and malnutrition in Southern areas devastated by the war. New industries were launched. Schools and welfare agencies were established to serve blacks and whites alike. A Yankee general raised funds to start a training school for young blacks, the Hampton Normal and Industrial Institute. The Reverend Henry Ward Beecher took the lead in funneling emergency aid to Lexington's struggling Washington College, whose new president was Robert E. Lee.

The hope was that a new egalitarian society could be induced to rise from the ashes of chaos. The crusading *Harper's Weekly*, urging that blacks be brought into the political process, noted that "if ignorance is the difficulty, why intrust the states to ignorant white men?" The more enlightened carpetbaggers tried to do their bit for democracy, too. Henry H. Wells, the military-appointed governor of Virginia, emphasized in his 1868 inaugural address the need for fundamental changes to assure the blessings of freedom for all. "The law must rise entirely beyond any and all discrimination on account of color," he said.

Indeed, there was important progress on the racial front. Blacks began to vote in large numbers in Virginia elections. Many held elective and appointive offices in both local and state govern- ment over a twenty-five year span. The General Assembly, the world's oldest legislative body, included black members in every session from 1869 to 1891. Partly because of these advances, Henry Grady and other moderate voices began to predict a "new South" that would be a full partner in the nation's exploding industrialism.

It was all wishful thinking. In their hearts and minds, white Southerners had never surrendered. The nostalgia for past glory was aptly illustrated in the Richmond *Enquirer*'s assertion that Virginians must "keep green the graves of our noble dead." Besides, the racial gains had been achieved with a federal bayo- net at the South's back. When Reconstruction ended, the care- fully framed safeguards for equal rights began to crumble every- where and blacks started to drift backward into serfdom. New laws were hastily enacted to require separate schools and col- leges, and to ban blacks from restaurants, hotels, parks, and other public places. In Washington the Supreme Court turned a deaf ear to black cries for help, refusing to halt the gathering tide of discrimination, even sanctioning a wave of new voting restrictions despite the Fifteenth Amendment's injunction. The social reformation was over. The South had resumed its romance with evil.

By the turn of the century, white rule was firmly reestab- lished in Virginia and race-baiting was back in style. A 1902 convention called to overhaul the state constitution roared its approval of harshly tightened voting standards that all but dis- enfranchised blacks. They might be deprived of their pride and self-respect but the new feudalism would at least provide soci- ety with the overall benefits of security and stability. The white man obviously knew what was best for the black man, and what was best was that he have little or no role in public life, perform the menial tasks of society, subsist in economic peonage, and live totally to himself. The master-slave relationship had reap- peared in a new system of paternalistic despotism.

This world of Jim Crow would last more than fifty years, insur- ing that the South would remain, in Allen Tate's phrase, "Uncle

Sam's other province." It was the world of my boyhood, and one that all of us who grew up in the Virginia of the 1930s and 1940s remember all too well. Blacks were our cooks, janitors, and gardeners. They cleaned our homes and were the day-care custodians of our children. But they always came in the back door and never ate at our tables. At lunchtime, I could walk a block from my Richmond office to Murphy's downtown five-and-dime store and order a hot dog, but no black could do so. In nine years of covering Virginia affairs, I never once encountered a black reporter or had any significant relationship with blacks. The news business was as segregated as any other business.

Most of us accepted this apartheid uncomplainingly. This did not mean that we harbored any hostility toward blacks, only that ancestral persuasion had left its mark. It was comfortable to live with the delusion that blacks were content with their lot, even if they did dwell on the far side of the tracks.

The mythology, however, faced serious new clashes with reality. A band of young lawyers headed by Thurgood Marshall of the National Association for the Advancement of Colored People (NAACP) had decided to return to the federal courts in an effort to overcome voting and education inequities. This time the response was more sympathetic. The new, more liberal judges named by Franklin Roosevelt and Harry Truman started lowering some of the barriers, including those making state law schools off limits to blacks; one entered the University of Virginia in 1950 to a minimum of protest. Paralleling the legal action was a rising political assault from the North. Democrats began promoting anti-discrimination legislation in Congress and the party's 1948 national convention adopted a far-reaching civil rights plank over the furious opposition of Dixie delegates. The South was under siege once more.

Virginia soon confronted two crises. One was the celebrated case of the Martinsville Seven in which seven young black men were sentenced to death for the brutal rape of a white woman. As electrocution neared, worldwide protests developed and thousands descended on the state capitol to voice outrage at the severe penalties. Although no white man had ever been sentenced to death for rape alone in Virginia, Governor John Battle permitted the executions to proceed in February 1951. The other problem occurred two months later when a group of Prince Edward County farm children went on strike to dramatize their school's substandard conditions, including lack of a cafeteria and gymnasium. This gave Oliver Hill and other black lawyers the opening they were seeking to attack segregation as inherently wrong because it perpetuated a system of inequality.

Despite these troubles, few were prepared for the thunderbolt of Monday, May 17, 1954: the announcement by the Supreme Court that segregated schools were unconstitutional. The bulletin clattered over the AP wire at 1:20 P.M., and I still recall racing to the third floor office of Governor Thomas B. Stanley in pursuit of comment. To my amazement, the reaction was one of sensible, almost submissive restraint. No criticism of the Court, no threat of defiance, no stirring call to arms. The decision, said the unruffled Stanley, called for "cool heads, calm study and sound judgement." He promised to consult with leaders of *both* races to devise accommodations "which will be acceptable to our citizens and in keeping with the edict of the Court."

The counsel of patience and sanity came from all quarters. Attorney General J. Lindsay Almond, who had handled the state's courtroom defense, said he hoped for "some rational adjustment." State education chief Dowell Howard dismissed all thought of defying the decision. "We are trying to teach school children the law of the land and will abide by it," he said. The *Richmond News Leader*'s brilliant young conservative editor, James J. Kilpatrick, warned against any resort to extremism that might endanger public education. "This is no time for rebellion," he wrote. "We are not about to return to some dark, medieval night of tutors and private schools for the well-to-do and illiteracy for everyone else." In Washington, Senator Harry Byrd said that the state faced "a crisis of the first magnitude," but he, too, struck a temperate tone.

For a few brief shining days, it appeared that Virginia would be a peaceful complier. It was the deceptive calm before the hurricane. Within a month, the atmosphere had dramatically changed as opposition forces mobilized to meet the gravest threat to Southern life since the Civil War. Politicians from the Southside, rural Black Belt country and the heartland of the Byrd Organization, united in expressing "unalterable opposition" to the ruling, a position that the senator himself now began to take. Lindsay Almond hinted at revised policies to sidestep compulsory integration and militants started pushing an even more drastic measure—turning over public schools to private agencies.

The pressure was too much for Tom Stanley, a well-meaning, friendly man who unfortunately was not one of the Organization's keener intellectual lights. A poor boy who made a fortune in the furniture manufacturing business, Stanley had methodically worked his way up through Democratic ranks, first serving in the legislature, then in Congress, and finally winning the governorship in 1953. His style was that of the gracious gladhander and, to those of us who covered his office, he seemed woefully unprepared to cope with the awesome burden thrust upon him. Hence, it was not surprising that six weeks after his plea for moderation the sixty-three-year-old governor began buckling, telling associates that he had erred in his original pledge to take the statesmanship path. From now on, the Commonwealth would fight with all its legal might, perhaps even discarding the state constitution's requirement for free public schools. Stanley did keep his word to consult with black leaders, only to insult them with the request that they agree to continue segregation on a voluntary basis. Thus did the Old Dominion reverse course and begin moving toward a fateful rendezvous with resistance.

What followed was like a page from the antebellum past. Every resource at the state's command was marshalled in defense of the status quo. The merest suggestion of token desegregation was discouraged, with a diehard private group, the Defenders of State Sovereignty and Individual Liberties, set up to carry the no-compromise banner. In the legislature, hard-liners assailed the integration drive as the handiwork of outside agitators, some of them Communist. The state's twelve-man Congressional delegation unanimously joined eighty-nine other Southern legislators in unanimously excoriating the Supreme Court for "a clear abuse of judicial power," a political exercise that some hoped might persuade the justices to soften their mandate. All of the folklore arguments from pro-slavery days were trotted out —that there would be intermarriage, mongrelization of the races, and destruction of the culture. Southside congressman William Tuck condemned "this effort to distort the minds, to pollute the education and to defile and make putrid the pure Anglo-Saxon blood that courses through the innocent veins of our helpless children."

To all such emotionalism, black leaders responded that they only wanted their constitutional rights. "We are not trying to be white," said the Reverend Charles L. Evans of the black-affiliated Baptist Association of Virginia. "We want an opportunity to be better Negroes." However laudatory that aspiration might be, it made no dent with white Virginians who were still wedded to the old ways, what Douglas Southall Freeman once called "a deliberate cult of the past."

The first move in the attempt to save the past was appointment of a carefully stacked commission to study the possibilities. The thirty-two members, all white, all male, and all state legislators, were predominantly from the ultra-conservative Black Belt region. The chairman, Garland Gray of Sussex County, was a confirmed segregationist. There seemed little doubt that the manifest purpose was to put into practice what was being so resoundingly preached. Accordingly, the panel's report a year later proposed a series of complicated legal maneuvers to sidetrack integration, primarily through a scheme of channeling public funds to parents to send their children to private, nonsectarian schools if they so desired. Somewhat surprisingly, though, the commission left the door ajar for local community leaders to decide for themselves whether to permit some degree of desegregation. Governor Stanley, receiving the recommendations in late 1955, pronounced them "splendid."

By now, however, the flag of rebellion was flying higher than ever. Senator Byrd informed visitors to his Capitol Hill office that the Gray Commission's formula was too weak. The moment had come for a tougher battle cry, which he proceeded to give on February 25, 1956. "If we can organize the Southern states for massive resistance to this order," he declared, "I think that in time the rest of the country will realize that racial integration is not going to be accepted in the South." There would be no armistice. Local option was forgotten as the legislature turned more strident and voted to suspend public money to any white school that admitted blacks. In his newspaper office a few blocks up the street from the statehouse, Jack Kilpatrick egged on the lawmakers. The *Richmond News Leader*'s editor had long since ended his flirtation with restraint and clamored to meet the issue head on. "The answer lies in establishing one policy, unyielding, for the state as a whole," he wrote. "No integration in Virginia's public schools, now or ever."

If Harry Byrd was the father of massive resistance, Jack Kilpatrick was its patron saint. Day after day in his fiery, pungent editorials he prodded the legislators to boldly uphold the noble cause. To Kilpatrick, the Supreme Court had come to represent "jurisprudence gone mad" and now, in his search for stronger ammunition, he resurrected a daring weapon—interposition.

Most of the legislators had never heard of the word, but they soon learned that it was a close relative of John Calhoun's discredited doctrine of nullification a century earlier. The theory, dating back to the 1790s and early 1800s, was that a state had the right to "interpose" its sovereignty and to challenge federal action which it believed exceeded constitutional authority. Most legal scholars regarded the concept as a fantasy, an unreal dream left over from the early National era. Lewis F. Powell, chairman of the Richmond School Board and a man destined for a seat on the Supreme Court in 1972, dismissed it as "legal nonsense." Kilpatrick was undeterred, seeing interposition as a device whereby Virginia could rally the South against the federal onslaught. In a series of crusading commentaries, he slugged away, imploring the legislature to approve a motion asserting the state's claim: "Whether or not such a resolution may be expedient, whether or not we are derided by centralists and scorned by the advocates of federal supremacy, Virginia once more should enunciate the sovereignty of states; we should recur to fundamental principles. This is our heritage. This is our tradition. This was the philosophy of the great men who walked the halls of our own Capitol."

With the defiant mood in full sway, interposition generated much sound and fury at the General Assembly's winter session of 1956. Few legislators believed the artifice would do any good. Many privately ridiculed it as a futile gesture, a kind of patent medicine remedy. Most of the critics, however, were reluctant to speak out lest they be labeled soft on segregation. One who did was Robert Whitehead, a canny and astute country lawyer from the Blue Ridge foothills. Whitehead was no advocate of integration but, as a moderate, he believed that interposition amounted to a call for insurrection. An anti-Byrd Democrat, he nonetheless was popular with his colleagues and respected for his political savvy and oratorical skills. His speeches, laced with colorful similes, always drew big crowds. On the climactic day of debate in the House of Delegates, the public gallery was a standing-room-only overflow and the main chamber was jammed with relatives and friends of the delegates. Whitehead scoffed at interposition as "a rusty relic of archaic assinity" and jibed at Kilpatrick as an intruder who led the Assembly "around by the nose." For two hours, he lectured his fellow lawmakers on Constitutional history, pointing to Patrick Henry, James Madison, and John Marshall as exponents of federal supremacy. "It was John Marshall of Virginia, the great Chief Justice, who first established the right of judicial review in this land," he said. "It was he who laid the foundation for the truism accepted today by all legal scholars and courts that the Constitution of the U.S. means what the Supreme Court of the U.S. says it means."

It was the most memorable address of the time. The legislators knew that Whitehead was right, but the uncontrollable interposition bandwagon rolled on as the 140-member Assembly climbed aboard with only seven dissenting votes. In its final form, however, the declaration was toned down so that it was little more than a boisterous protest, prompting Whitehead to chuckle: "The thunder roared, the lightning flashed and a chigger was killed."

While the political rite of interposition was being carried out, the dreaded federal encroachment was accelerating. The courts, tired of the state's foot-dragging, ordered the admission of black children to schools in Charlottesville and Arlington. In July

1956, Governor Stanley drove a hundred miles to Washington for an emergency conference with Senator Byrd and Southside congressman Bill Tuck and Watkins Abbitt. There would be no capitulation; the counterattack would go full speed ahead. Stanley called the legislature back for an extraordinary fall session that produced twenty-three additional defensive laws, many of them giving the governor's office dictatorial powers to shuffle students, operate classrooms, and, if need be, to close schools.

It did not work. Nothing worked. Not even the harassment of the NAACP and efforts to censor school books deemed tolerant of race-mixing. Nor the proliferation of subsidized white-only private academies, including one in Norfolk which proclaimed as its creed the retention of "great traditions such as respect for God, the nation, the white race and western civilization." Nor the unrestrained bombast of Lindsay Almond who followed Stanley into the governor's mansion, vowing in his 1957 campaign to "cut off my right arm" before permitting a single black child to enroll at a white school.

By September 1958, the judiciary's legal hammering had substantially reduced Virginia's options. It could obey the law or close its schools. Still refusing to concede the inevitable, state officials permitted closure to proceed in Front Royal, Charlottesville, and Norfolk. With 13,000 children locked out, the enthusiasm for defiance began to ebb, with public sentiment shifting from intransigence to accommodation. The conservative Virginia press, including Kilpatrick's *News Leader*, began beating a retreat with calls for a recognition of reality. Business leaders, fearing the state's inviting economic atmosphere would suffer, quietly passed word that closing schools was too damaging.

Senator Byrd was unswayed. He insisted that the legal warfare go on, contending that if the pro-integration forces won in Virginia, "they can march through the South singing hallelujah." Much to Byrd's dismay, however, Governor Almond was ready to call it quits, particularly after state and federal courts handed down rulings on January 19, 1959—Robert E. Lee's birthday—declaring that the school laws were unconstitutional. A week later, after one more tirade of defiance, Almond stunned hard-liners by asking the legislature to start dismantling the massive resistance barricades and to chart a new course with more benign policies. In February, the closed schools reopened and the first integrated classes began. After almost five years, the containment charade was over.

It is often said that Senator Byrd and his lieutenants seized upon the racial crisis to shore up the Organization's political support at a time of mounting challenge. There may be some truth in this, but it strikes me as too facile. For one thing, the Byrd machine was never a machine in the usual sense of the word, but rather more like a gentleman's club for conservative government, with the only qualification for membership an unswerving allegiance to the club's political philosophy. That philosophy was rooted deeply in the doctrine of state's rights, which the senator had consistently supported since going to Washington in 1933, voting against the New Deal and almost all other extensions of federal authority. It is also true that Byrd spoke for the vast majority of Virginians in trying to retain segregation. After all, race had long shaped the cultural landscape and here, as elsewhere in the South, whites had grown accustomed to being the master race.

Looking back today, it is hard to believe that the world of the 1950s ever existed—that so many otherwise intelligent people were so willing to embrace the old suppressions. What lingers in the mind are all the vignettes in absurdity: The priority given the Commonwealth flag over the Stars and Stripes at the state capitol; the decision by an editor at the *Richmond Times-Dispatch* to drop several Pogo comic strips because they lampooned the school closures (thereby prompting the joke that some newsmen were worried about their daughters marrying a possum); the picture of genteel ladies from the United Daughters of the Confederacy beseeching the legislature to forever preserve as "hallowed ground" the site of a Confederate widows' home.

The segregation surrender in 1959 ended Virginia's long love affair with the Civil War. What is truly astonishing, though, is how quickly the old order collapsed and a New Dominion rose from the rubble. Within five years, some of the most fervent opponents of integration were energetically pursuing the fast-growing black vote. The Byrd oligarchy, its domination shattered by a burgeoning urbanization, began losing power to a new generation of younger, more flexible Democrats much less wedded to the conservative orthodoxy.

By 1969, the renaissance had produced a brand new state constitution devoid of the last vestige of racism and prohibiting discrimination in any form. In the elections that year, Virginians chose Republican Linwood Holton, a man who genuinely believed in civil rights, to be their new governor. And, in Richmond, the voters decided to send to the legislature a young upstart named Douglas Wilder.

Claiming the Dream

PROLOGUE: A SON OF VIRGINIA

On a cold, sparkling day outside the state capitol in Richmond where the Congress of the Confederate States of America once met, Lawrence Douglas Wilder placed his left hand on a family Bible, raised his right hand, and in measured, solemn tones took an oath of office as the sixty-sixth governor of the Commonwealth of Virginia. Children perched on the bare branches of dogwood trees or their parents' shoulders, and elderly men and women, some of them leaning on canes and walkers, strained to see as the largest crowd ever assembled on the capitol grounds in modern times ushered in what many hoped would be a new era in American politics. The man they had come to watch, who lifted a radiant face to the crowd, was different not only from the Virginia governors who preceded him, but from every previous governor elected in any American state. All the rest were white; Douglas Wilder was black.

The moment was especially poignant for those who had listened thirty-two years earlier as another Virginia governor took the oath of office, pledging to stand firm against a rising tide of racial integration. "Against these massive assaults, we must marshal a massive resistance," thundered J. Lindsay Almond, Jr., a courthouse orator from Roanoke who served as governor from 1958 to 1962, and who as attorney general had worked to block the entrance of black children into white public schools. "I cannot conceive such a thing as a little integration," Almond had declared, "any more than I can conceive a small avalanche or a modest holocaust."

1

Three decades later, the rhetoric of the dignitaries who lined bleachers three stories high to witness Douglas Wilder's swearing-in reflected a changed world. "It's a great day for Virginia," said retired U.S. Supreme Court justice Lewis F. Powell, Jr., the eighty-two-year-old white lawyer who had chaired the Richmond school board with a calm hand during the racial turmoil of the 1950s, and so was chosen to administer Wilder's oath. The election of a black governor in the state where black slaves first set foot in America "is a great American story. It's a great world story," commented the Rev. Jesse Jackson, the nation's preeminent black political leader during the 1980s. And Wilder, who called his victory the triumph not of a person or a political party, but of the ancient idea that all men are created equal, added a moving benediction. "I am," he said at the conclusion of his inaugural speech, "a son of Virginia."

Since 1970, when the Joint Center for Political Studies in Washington, D.C., began keeping track, the number of black elected officials in the nation had spiraled from about fifteen hundred to seventy-two hundred. But the ranks had included no state governors and only one U.S. senator. Californians came close to electing a black governor in 1982 when Los Angeles mayor Tom Bradley missed by just over a percentage point. But the lustre of Bradley's showing dulled four years later in a landslide defeat that, once again, left P. B. S. Pinchback of Reconstruction times as the only black American ever to occupy a governor's chair. Pinchback, whose mother was a slave and whose father was a Georgia slave owner, served thirty-six days in 1872 and 1873 as acting governor of Louisiana during impeachment proceedings against Republican governor Henry Clay Warmoth.

It was no "small avalanche" of votes on November 7, 1989, that allowed Douglas Wilder to become the nation's first popularly elected black governor. A fifty-eight-year-old Richmond lawyer, Wilder climaxed a twenty-year political career in the state senate and as lieutenant governor by winning 896,936 votes, the largest number cast for a gubernatorial candidate in Virginia's history. But there was a cascade of ballots for his Republican opponent as well. Former attorney general J. Marshall

Coleman, a white Northern Virginia lawyer generally viewed as a racial moderate, amassed the second highest vote count on record. The miniscule 6,741-vote margin between them made the governor's race one of the closest ever held in Virginia. The outcome was not validated until completion of a time-consuming recount.

For many voters in a state that spearheaded the Confederate war effort and led the South in massive resistance to public school integration in the 1950s, the election of Douglas Wilder was a cathartic event, allowing the state at long last to resume its eighteenth century role as a force of political enlightenment for the nation. The results were, to them, all the more remarkable because New York City on the day of Wilder's victory elected a black mayor with white support that was far more meager than Wilder's, and because California twice had failed to do what Virginia had now achieved. Where New York mayoralty candidate David Dinkins won the backing of 30 percent of the whites who voted in his election, Wilder received 41 percent of the white vote in Virginia, a stunning statistical comparison for those who grew up in a segregated South. California and New York, after all, were supposed to be the symbols of America's future, and Virginia, by reputation, the embodiment of its past.

For a watching South, the victory was the latest and most powerful signal that those who had labored for equality in the political vineyards for decades had not done so in vain. As black candidates contemplated races for statewide office in Georgia, South Carolina, North Carolina, and elsewhere, the election held out the hope of success and a model for achieving it. To the white majorities, who would be asked to nominate those black candidates, Wilder's election suggested that there was less to fear and perhaps more to gain in supporting blacks than many had imagined. Southerners too were gratified that the region that had long been castigated for its treatment of African-Americans might now be leading the way in race relations.

For a nation perplexed by new evidences of racial strains as the 1980s ended, the Wilder victory was welcome news. The civil rights era, when good and evil were as distinguishable for many as black and white, had passed. The new racial challenges came in confounding shades of gray. In many ways, relations between blacks and whites were more integrated and routine than they had ever been. But 1989 was also the year when a white gang's attack on black youths in the Bensonhurst section of Brooklyn, New York, made national headlines. It was a year of continued setbacks for affirmative action programs before the U.S. Supreme Court, of Spike Lee's provocative racial film *Do the Right Thing*, and of black teenagers wearing T-shirts with the message, "It's a black thing . . . You wouldn't understand." In Virginia, it was the year of Greekfest, a shocking weekend of racial violence in Virginia Beach. Against that backdrop, the elections of Wilder and Dinkins—as well as of black mayors in the majority-white cities of Seattle, Washington; Durham, North Carolina; and New Haven, Connecticut—were reminders of how much has changed in the last three decades, and of how profound, if not universal, the alterations are.

Nationally, Douglas Wilder's election also signaled the advent of a new type of black politics in which fiery rhetoric and emotional appeals gave way to discussions of mainstream issues. As blacks who have come up through the ranks of state legislatures and the Congress move to the fore, those black leaders such as Jesse Jackson who emerged from the crucible of the civil rights movement, and have never held elective office, may find their influence eclipsed. "Jesse runs to inspire; I run to win," Wilder once said. He repeatedly urged voters to take race out of the election, and to a remarkable extent, they did. Only in the final days of the campaign, with Coleman trailing in the polls, did the Republican candidate inject racial innuendo, and then in an oblique way that bore no resemblance to the race-baiting of Old South segregationists. His complaint, tailored to an age in which quotas and affirmative action are the focus of public policy debates involving race, was that Wilder was being treated by a double standard, presumably—although Coleman stopped short of saying so—because he is black. Personal problems in Wilder's background that might have eliminated a white candidate from the contest were being ignored by the press and the electorate, Coleman charged, while an international contingent of reporters seemed bent on portraying the Democratic candidate in the most favorable light.

There is no doubt that at least some of those who voted saw Wilder's past indiscretions as less important than the opportunity to make history by electing a black man governor. But neither was there any doubt that an older double standard—one that was once massive and overwhelming, in which whites were judged by their abilities, and blacks by their skin color—was at work in the election, too. There is evidence of racial sentiment in both preelection and exit polls, which consistently showed Wilder much further ahead of Coleman than the final count revealed. In the last analysis, political scientists believe, many voters who before the election had listed themselves as undecided simply could not pull the voting machine lever for a black man.

While the racial focus was expected, what few anticipated was that the Virginia gubernatorial contest would also become a very vocal referendum on another issue of national significance—abortion rights. When the election campaign had gotten under way, neither Marshall Coleman nor Douglas Wilder had any inkling of how critically the outcome would be affected by a U.S. Supreme Court ruling in July 1989 allowing states to place limited restrictions on abortions. Yet by election day many believed the decision in *Webster v. Reproductive Health Services* was the pivotal development of the campaign. Wilder, who approached the abortion question from a libertarian perspective, was the first gubernatorial candidate in the nation to center a campaign around support for freedom of choice on abortion. In a shrewd strategy tailored to a moderate-conservative state, Wilder put his emphasis not on whether abortion is right or wrong, but on who makes that decision, the government or individual women. His victory prompted soul-searching from the top of the Republican party to its grassroots. During much of the 1970s and 1980s, Republicans had enjoyed extensive benefits and few liabilities from wholeheartedly adopting the agenda of the right-to-life movement. As the 1990s began, Wilder's election posed the question of how best to respond to the changed dynamic.

Thus, while political contests are an everyday occurrence in American life, the 1989 Virginia race for governor stands apart as a barometer of public attitudes involving two of the most personal and emotional issues of our time, race and abortion. Some 2.7 million registered voters were asked to weigh those issues, and what that diverse group of people said and did in the months leading up to the election offers powerful, and sometimes unexpected, insights about the national consciousness. The campaign itself gave birth to an array of theories and strategies involving the politics of race and abortion, many of which were certain to be used and tested in other political contests in the 1990s. That the election was set in a state whose heritage is rich with conflicting symbols, both of the American dream extended and of promises denied, only made the debate more poignant. It was a Virginian, Thomas Jefferson, who framed the national ideal that all men are born equal, and it was another, Robert E. Lee, who commanded a Confederate army dedicated in part to the principle that they were not.

The Virginia election also highlighted anew major pitfalls in American political campaigns. To an astounding degree this $23 million extravaganza—the most expensive race in Virginia's history, and one of the most costly in the nation's—revolved around the impact of thirty-second television commercials prepared by political consultants who had little ongoing stake in the governments they proposed to create. While nastiness has long been an element of politics, the ability to manipulate emotions with sound and visual images has taken negative campaigning to new depths in the television age. Few campaigns better demonstrate this principle than the Wilder-Coleman matchup and the Republican primary that preceded it. But the election also showed that years of planning cannot insulate candidates from the press of unexpected events, and that many of the most telling moments in campaigns remain those unprogrammed instances when the day's news and a candidate collide.

The Virginia campaign showed also the enormous limitations of public opinion polls as prognosticators of election results, and the perils of attaching too much credence to them. In both the governor's race and the contest for lieutenant governor between Democrat Donald Beyer, Jr., and Republican Edwina "Eddy" Dalton, most polling results bore little resemblance to the election outcome.

Aside from campaign strategies and political messages, however, the Virginia gubernatorial contest of 1989 was foremost a climactic moment in the long march of a man, Douglas Wilder, and a people toward full participation in the American dream. "We mark today not a victory of party or the accomplishments of an individual, but the triumph of an idea," Wilder said as he looked out over the faces of the thousands who streamed to his inaugural. "An idea as old as America, as old as the God who looks out for us all. . . . The idea that all men and women are created equal; that they are endowed by their Creator with certain inalienable rights, the right to life, liberty, and the pursuit of happiness."

The election that made that triumph possible would not be forgotten soon. Those interested in the political process would see it not only as a significant historical milestone in the long struggle of black Americans to make the idea of equality a reality, but as a case study of the impact of momentous changes in American social and economic experience upon the fabric of community life. How it came about, how the forces involved in such changes were translated into the practicalities of a hard-fought battle between professional politicians striving to use every social, technological, and moral resource available to them to gain public office, makes the political campaign that led to the inauguration of Douglas Wilder as the first black person ever to be elected governor of an American state worthy of the closest scrutiny.

1

THE JOURNEY BEGINS

Southside Virginia is a region of red clay and scrub pine, the Commonwealth of Virginia's nearest geographical equivalent to the Deep South. The people of this tobacco-and-cotton-growing country traditionally were less prosperous than their fellow Virginians to the north and east. Harry Flood Byrd, Sr., the conservative champion of states' rights who ran Virginia politics for four decades, centered his organization in the region's courthouses. And in the 1950s and 1960s, following the *Brown v. Board of Education* decision of the United States Supreme Court that ended legal separation by race in public schools, the most vocal resistance to racial integration came from the Southside, where there was a sizeable black population.

Today, however, January 26, 1989, a man named Joe Alder, a sheriff's deputy in the town of Kenbridge in Lunenburg County, was up before daybreak, preparing for the ninety-minute drive to the state capitol in Richmond, where a black lawyer, Douglas Wilder, was about to announce his unopposed candidacy for the Democratic party's nomination for governor of Virginia.

Four years earlier Joe Alder had become an instant celebrity when he lent his drawl, his badge, and—most important—his white skin to a campaign commercial that some said won Wilder the state's number two job of lieutenant governor. If the stereotypical Southern cop could make the leap, so the thinking went, how wide could the racial abyss be?

Now Alder was heading to Richmond to stand at Wilder's side as the lieutenant governor launched a campaign to become the first black man to be elected governor of any state in the union. "I will do anything in my power to get him elected," said Alder, who had been captivated by the politician's charm since their first chance encounter in 1985. Alder's description of Wilder was the quintessential Southern compliment: "He's down home. He doesn't think he's above everybody. . . . He's a hometown boy."

Ninety miles north in Richmond, the staid but gracious former capital of the Confederacy, Buford Scott was also scurrying to make the 10:00 A.M. kickoff. Scott was chairman of the board of Scott & Stringfellow, a leading brokerage house in the city that for decades had been the spiritual and financial hub of the state, a status only recently challenged by the booming Northern Virginia suburbs. A soft-spoken scion of Richmond's genteel upper crust, Scott seemed at first glance to be as unlikely a Wilder supporter as Alder. For different reasons, he was also equally crucial to the campaign. "Generally, I knew them as servants," Scott once said when asked to describe his links to blacks while growing up in Richmond in the 1940s. One of Scott's enduring memories is of a 1950s train ride from New Haven to Richmond with a Yale classmate, a swim team member from Hampton who was black. When the train reached Washington, that era's racial line of demarcation, Jim Crow laws took effect, and Scott's traveling companion was forced to move to a separate car in the rear of the train.

Buford Scott got to know Doug Wilder when their children were classmates at a prep school in Richmond's West End. His admiration for the politician, though not unqualified, had grown with the years, and in December 1988, he was the host for the first major fund-raising event of Wilder's still-unannounced gubernatorial campaign, a glittering affair that brought some seventy-five guests to Scott's Pennsylvania-granite home overlooking the James River. The canapés-and-cocktails message was direct. Wilder would prove to be the best man running for governor, Scott said. His election would "send a wonderful message around the country" about the open-mindedness of the Old Dominion. And once elected, Scott told his guests, Wilder was smart enough to know that the nation's eyes would be trained on his performance. "He understands that it would be a terrible thing for minority candidates if he blows it," Scott declared.

As 10:00 A.M. neared, Scott bolted from a round of morning appointments and dashed onto Main Street, hoping to catch a trolley to the city's gleaming new convention hall, the Richmond Centre. None was in sight, so Scott sprinted uphill several blocks to Wilder's event.

When Oliver Hill walked into the January kickoff, saw the flags and balloons, the integrated crowd, the technician monitoring the live television hookup to sites in Norfolk, Harrisonburg, Roanoke, Abingdon, and Fairfax County, his mind skipped back four decades to 1948. That was the year Hill was elected to the Richmond City Council, becoming the first black Virginian since Reconstruction to hold so prominent an elective post. Hill, who ran citywide, may also have been the first black Southerner to win an election in which the majority of the voters were white. "I did a whole lot of breaking the ice," said Hill, tall and still distinguished-looking at eighty-two.

Unquestionably the Virginia of the 1980s was a world apart from the state in which Hill held office for two years, until his defeat in 1950. Then, Hill's political rallies were held at black churches. An integrated crowd would have been unthinkable. Speaking invitations from white groups were almost nonexistent. To campaign citywide, which Hill insisted on doing, he had to scour Richmond newspaper notices to find out where white organizations were holding political forums, and then show up unannounced. Forty years later, even with Wilder's clear path to the Democratic nomination and all the attention surrounding his announcement, Hill had no illusions about the candidate's prospects in a state that is more than 80 percent white. "He's got to be an underdog," Hill said. "There's no way he's not, just on the racial issue alone. . . . You can have tremendous change and still not have a good situation."

For a moment, however, on that January morning, most in the audience seemed willing to suspend disbelief. As the loudspeaker blared a martial tune, two dozen dignitaries—the governor, the attorney general, wealthy Democratic campaign contributors, the head of Richmond's largest black voter group, local officials, Hill, Alder, and Scott among them—mounted portable risers and led a pulsating tribute to the short, silver-haired man who followed. With a broad mountain accent and the verve of a sideshow barker at the State Fair, state senator Virgil Goode invoked a parade of Virginia giants. First, he said, there was Patrick Henry, crying out for individual liberty; then Thomas Jefferson, proclaiming the rights of free men. Conveniently leapfrogging Robert E. Lee, commander-in-chief of the Lost Cause, and Harry Byrd, Sr., who in the 1950s rallied a frenzied South to massive resistance against public school integration, Goode arrived at the 1980s. Two Democratic governors, he said, would be followed by a third—Doug Wilder. The crowd roared its approval.

Flanked by two of his children, arms held high in a thumbs-up show of confidence, his pear-shaped face lit by a grin, Wilder appeared briefly to savor the moment. He stood at the brink of a nine-month journey—one that would not only focus national and international attention on the Old Dominion, but turn conventional wisdom about abortion politics on its ear and break a hitherto impassable barrier for any black American who aspired to so high an elective office as governor.

In the speech that followed, there were only brief allusions to the poignancy of the day, a mention here of the nearby ghetto where Wilder grew up, a reminder there of the "sense of fairness" of Virginians. A man whose fanciful oratory could take audiences soaring, or leave them mired in convolution, Wilder stuck to a printed text. What the politician offered was a colorblind recital of his twenty years' experience in state government and a campaign blueprint that wrapped even populist ideas in a mainstream mantle. Fifteen years earlier, when Norfolk lawyer Henry Howell—"Howlin' Henry" to his critics—proposed taking the sales tax off food, the idea was branded radical. But Wilder, the first gubernatorial candidate since Howell to spotlight the plan, presented a different slant. He described the proposal as "long-term tax relief for all Virginians," and coupled it with a pledge not to propose new taxes. He promised to fight drugs and, reaching out to an audience that might be particularly skeptical of a black candidate, to create jobs and housing for rural Virginians. Extending yet another olive branch, he pledged: "Every governor of this state has relied on the keen insight of the Virginia business community. I intend to follow this tradition."

Later, at a press conference, for the first time that day Wilder spoke directly about race. It was ten minutes into the conference before a reporter for the *Washington Post* raised the subject. Wilder, in a relaxed and confident mood, quickly fielded it. To some, he said, his candidacy was viewed as a unique, potentially historic event. As for himself, however, "I will devote absolutely no time nor effort to that, or discussing that. . . . As far as I'm concerned, it plays no part at all in my evaluation of the fall and the operation that I have in store for Virginia."

Within hours, Wilder was talking to audiences about equality and history—and, indirectly, race. The remarks surfaced during a whirlwind announcement tour that over the next two days took the candidate to the three corners of Virginia. He reserved the largest block of time for the Southwest, a mountainous, coal-bearing region of isolated hollows, independent people, and fiercely partisan politics. Wilder had surprised pundits in 1985 by capturing the sympathies of many in the Southwest's "Fightin' Ninth" congressional district. Black voters in the Ninth are about as plentiful as coal tipples in Virginia Beach. But a kinship sprang up between the political underdog and mountaineers who view themselves as outcasts from the state's establishment. On a gamble, Wilder had launched a statewide tour in the Southwest in 1985, and his warm reception was a crucial early signal that his campaign would have to be taken seriously.

Reporters had watched wide-eyed that year as local Democrats braved rain and a thick mountain mist to shake the hand of an urban stranger. By 1989, Wilder was embraced like an out-of-town nephew who had made good. This time the weather cooperated. February had not yet arrived, and already the forsythia and japonica were budding, and bulbs were pushing green shoots through the soil as Wilder drove into the town of Lebanon for a breakfast rally.

At the Western Sizzlin' steakhouse, Trinkle Phillips, the Russell County Democratic chairman and a local furniture store operator, directed latecomers toward a steaming buffet and shook his head at a mention of Wilder's race. "We're just common folk, and he's more or less our type," said Trinkle, noting that Wilder carried neighboring Buchanan County, "and there's only one colored voter in the county." Christine Eldreth, a Democratic committee member in neighboring Washington County, was more cautious. "I've had people tell me they wouldn't vote for him, because, well . . . " Because of race? Eldreth and her husband, Richard, nodded their heads.

Within moments, Wilder himself touched on the racial theme. Looking out at tables lined with the faces of coal miners, mountain farmers, small-town lawyers, and shopkeepers, Wilder stilled the clinking of forks and coffee cups as he spoke of the Virginia constitution's promise of equal rights. Softly at first, and then warming to the words and the setting, Wilder recalled reading as a boy the constitutional guarantee that "all men are by nature equally free. . . . That means all of us. We can be whatever we want to be." Pausing, he added, "I don't know any place in this country that I could run and be elected governor, [other] than Virginia. I believe that."

Two hours and a winding drive later, Wilder was repeating the message for a noontime crowd in Norton, a town of about five thousand people whose fortunes fluctuate with those of the coal industry. "Some forty years ago, when I was a young boy running around, wondering what might be my life . . . oh, I never dreamed that one day I'd be there in the shadow of the Capitol raising my hand to take the oath of office as the lieutenant governor of the Commonwealth," he said. "But the possibility was there for me. And I've tried to say, if it's there for me, it can be for others. . . . As I view the landscape of our country, and as I view those states and those persons from near and far, and as I see the political machinations and the things that take place all over the world, as I see how people write and what they say, and what can be and what may not be, I don't know any other place in our country that I might be governor of a state than in Virginia."

Throughout a long campaign, Wilder would seldom if ever repeat those words. Although a racial message was implicit in slogans like "We've come too far to turn back now," he would make few direct statements on race and opportunity. He was running as a politician, not as a black politician, he preferred to say. Yet, from the start, the implication was clear. Whatever else it might become, the 1989 race for governor would also be a referendum on racial tolerance in Virginia. History to the contrary, Wilder and his strategists believed that was a winning proposition.

Their optimism was grounded in Wilder's reception during his race for lieutenant governor four years earlier, and in the changing demographics of a state of six million people that ranks twelfth in population and ninth in per capita income in the nation. Particularly in its eastern corridor, the Virginia of the 1980s was a vibrant place, filled with new jobs and an increasingly diverse blend of people. The combination belied the state's image as a somnolent, aristocratic Southern preserve more committed to the past than the present.

Once Virginia had been a seedbed of political creativity that produced four of the nation's first five presidents. But during much of the twentieth century, her role nationally seemed primarily to be as a source of history lessons. Both politically and culturally the state has long been identified with an innate conservatism. It takes three Virginians to change a light bulb, according to a popular joke, one to screw in the new bulb and two to praise the old one. Out-of-state reporters who wanted to juxtapose Virginia's 1989 gubernatorial race against her history never needed to look far for a statue or a battlefield linking past to present. Along Richmond's Monument Avenue, the heroes of the Confederacy—Robert E. Lee, Stonewall Jackson, J.E.B. Stuart —sit timelessly astride their chargers. At Manassas, Fredericksburg, Petersburg, and dozens of other sites, schoolchildren and history buffs roam battlefields where thousands of soldiers in blue and grey fell. More blood was shed on Virginia soil during the Civil War than in any other state, and perhaps more than in all others combined.

The state's dominant political figure in the twentieth century was Harry F. Byrd, Sr., a forward-thinking governor from 1926 to 1930, who became increasingly resistant to change as a U.S. senator under five presidents from Franklin D. Roosevelt to Lyndon B. Johnson. A courtly, rosy-cheeked apple farmer and newspaper publisher from Winchester, near the state's northern tip, Byrd built a political organization grounded in a pay-as-you-go philosophy of government. His theory of government left the state fiscally solvent, but lagging in services such as education and transportation. His Democratic fiefdom, distinguished by an aura of financial integrity, was sustained by a devoted network of local officeholders and by a severely restricted electorate. Stringent voter registration laws, limits on the number of officials who were popularly elected, and such devices as scheduling statewide elections in nonpresidential election years combined to keep voter participation at a minimum. Democratic primaries, in which elections were almost always decided because Republican opposition was so weak, between 1925 and 1945, routinely attracted less than 12 percent of the voting age population, according to the political scientist V. O. Key. Blacks, hampered by a poll tax, literacy tests, and frequently hostile election officials, participated hardly at all.

As the 1950s began, Byrd Organization dominance was being challenged by dissidents demanding improved state services. But the U.S. Supreme Court's 1954 school desegregation decision breathed new life into the Organization's ranks. For the remainder of the decade, Byrd's cry for massive resistance to school integration rallied sufficient support to suppress political opposition. But the resurgence, like the issue that spawned it, was temporary. With the arrival of the 1960s, power began to shift away from Harry Byrd toward a diverse, expanded electorate that, for the first time, included large numbers of blacks.

While men aligned with Byrd continued to occupy the governor's office during the 1960s, the forces of both Republicans and liberal Democrats were growing. In 1969, following a rending Democratic primary and runoff in which a moderate candidate, William C. Battle, prevailed, liberals left the party en masse and helped elect the state's first Republican governor since Reconstruction, A. Linwood Holton. A Roanoke attorney, Holton was steeped in an independent and often progressive political tradition that had characterized the Virginia Republican party west of the Blue Ridge Mountains, separating it from the Byrd Organization. True to the mandate from the blacks who helped elect him, Holton devoted himself to improving race relations in the Old Dominion.

Four years later, however, his party set out on a different course. With liberals newly in control of both the national and Virginia Democratic parties, prominent Democratic conservatives forged an alliance with members of the Republican party's right wing. For the remainder of the 1970s, the coalition would be the dominant political force in the state, electing two Republican governors and a host of other GOP officials. At the group's high-water mark in 1981, the governor, the attorney general, one U.S. senator, and nine of ten congressmen from Virginia were Republicans.

It was Charles S. Robb who rescued the Virginia Democratic party. Robb's credentials as a ramrod-straight former Marine and the son-in-law of former president Lyndon Johnson made him an almost overnight sensation when he emerged as an aspiring state politician in the mid-1970s. The party had retained a lock on the General Assembly during the 1970s, but a twelve-year absence from the governor's office and steady gains elsewhere by the GOP had left many commentators predicting that Republicans would command the state's future. Moderate in philosophy and conservative in bearing, Robb managed in 1981 to do what no Democrat had accomplished since 1965—preside over a Democratic sweep of the state's three top offices: governor, lieutenant governor, and attorney general. As governor, Robb succeeded in positioning the Virginia Democratic party closer to the state's moderate-conservative mainstream. His successes in improving teacher salaries and holding down taxes paved the way for a second Democratic sweep in the 1985 elections. In 1988 Robb was elected to the U.S. Senate. As Doug Wilder began his quest for the governorship in 1989, Democrats held one of Virginia's U.S. Senate seats, five of ten congressional slots, and 95 of 140 seats in the state legislature.

* * *

The state in which Wilder launched his political bid is a richly variegated one, with a resplendent mix of geography and tradition. Economically, there are increasingly two Virginias. One is an eastern corridor, stretching from the high-rise havens outside Washington, D.C., to the bustling Tidewater cities of Hampton, Newport News, Norfolk, and Virginia Beach. This is the slice of the state known as the "Golden Crescent," the center of population and finance. To the west and south of Richmond is another, more traditional Virginia where the economy is still tied to small industries and to the land in many places, and where the problem with growth is likely to be that there is too little instead of too much of it.

Within those two divisions are a half dozen geographic regions that have traditionally defined the state and its people. Starting in the east is the low-lying Tidewater, where broad estuaries from the Potomac River in the north to the James River in the south feed into the Chesapeake Bay, creating scenic shorelines and thousands of maritime jobs. The region contributed much to the nation's early history, and it is here that Jamestown and Williamsburg are located. Here, too, are one of the nation's largest shipbuilding operations, the Newport News Shipbuilding and Dry Dock Company, and dozens of military facilities, including the headquarters of the U.S. Navy's Atlantic fleet. Roughly one million people live in the region, and politically a strong showing among them is usually considered essential to a statewide Democratic victory. A few decades ago the Byrd Organization had powerful lieutenants in the Tidewater, but there was also an independent streak in the region's voters that at times produced support for opposition candidates.

To the west of Tidewater is the Southside, sometimes described as a state of mind as much as a region. Generally, the Southside encompasses the land beyond Tidewater that is south of Richmond and east of the Blue Ridge Mountains. The area, once the center of a thriving plantation economy, particularly in the eastern counties, today is still largely agrarian. It has the largest black population of any section of the state, and the most persistent tradition of racial separation. It was here in Prince Edward County that officials closed public schools for four years beginning in 1959, rather than integrate, denying black school children local access to education. Here, also, in an era that predated one-man, one-vote requirements for forming state legislative districts, resided a host of influential lawmakers who revered and sustained Harry Byrd. Today, in state and federal elections Southside voting patterns are still defined to a substantial degree by race. Blacks vote overwhelmingly for Democratic candidates; whites often vote Republican.

Just north of the Southside is Richmond, an uncommonly pretty state capital, noted for its renovated Fan District town homes and leafy parks, and surrounded by suburbs that are perhaps the most conservative in Virginia. Long considered a spiritual and financial mecca for the state, the Richmond area usually produces heavy Republican majorities in state and federal contests. The city itself is substantially Democratic and majority-black, a development that local officials tried to forestall with annexations a few decades earlier. A famous court case growing out of a 1969 annexation reached the U.S. Supreme Court, and had the effect of halting city council elections for seven years until the matter was decided.

As both population and money shift toward Northern Virginia, Richmond is already losing some of its status as the philosophical center of Virginia. The emergence of Northern Virginia as a political force is one of the major developments in the Old Dominion in the 1980s. Forty years ago the counties outside Washington were wide rural expanses and the population was clustered in a few spots such as Alexandria, adjacent to Washington, D.C. Today, many of the outlying counties are overflowing with affluent suburbanites who think little of paying $250,000 or more for a home and who demand services and political attention to match. One out of every seven voters in the state lives in Fairfax County, the most populous of several Northern Virginia counties, and statewide candidates devote ever-larger blocks of time to wooing them. The region, in which per capita income is one of the highest in the nation and more than double that in some other areas of the state, has also emerged as a lode of campaign contributions. Often transitory, and more focused on Washington than Richmond, Northern Virginia voters traditionally have been influenced less by state than national trends. The region felt little loyalty to the Byrd Organization. In the 1980s Democrats who won statewide contests usually counted on carrying Northern Virginia. But the area's two congressmen are Republicans, and many Democrats fear a growing trend in the wealthy suburbs toward the GOP.

Although the geographic definition differs, politically, the Piedmont is viewed as the land north and west of Richmond, leading up to the Blue Ridge Mountains. Largely a region of small towns and rolling countryside rising gradually toward the mountains, the Piedmont is conservative territory that once supported Harry Byrd. Today, residents generally view Republican candidates as the proper philosophical heirs to the Byrd tradition. A few localities are exceptions. Charlottesville, site of the University of Virginia, is the home of some of the most liberal voters in the Commonwealth.

West of the Blue Ridge is the Valley of Virginia, stretching from Roanoke in the south to the Maryland–West Virginia borders in the north. Sustained in the eighteenth and nineteenth centuries by a farm—rather than a plantation—economy, the region had relatively few slaves and was a site of substantial pro-Union sentiment before the Civil War. Today the population of the area is only about 10 percent black. Politically, during the Byrd years residents of the southern end of the Valley, around Roanoke, practiced a brand of progressive Republicanism that put them at odds with the Organization. The upper end of the Valley, including Byrd's hometown of Winchester, was Democratic and conservative. Today Democrats often receive substantial support in the Roanoke area, while Republicans consistently do well in the northern part of the Valley.

Finally comes the Southwest, whose ridges and ravines Daniel Boone traversed before he discovered a passageway to the west at the Cumberland Gap. At its farthest tip, the region is farther west than Detroit, Michigan, and residents are closer to the capitals of nine other states than to Richmond. It is little wonder that they often complain of being treated like political stepchildren. The economy is sustained by coal mining, small farms, and a smattering of industry, an unstable blend that keeps the region one of the poorest in the state. Politically the Southwest is legendary for a fierce partisanship that produces raucous elections and, not infrequently in past decades, ballot fraud. Harry Byrd was never a regional favorite. In statewide elections, the Southwest often favors independent and even maverick politicians with an affinity for ordinary working people. The combination in the Southwest seemed made to order for Douglas Wilder, and so, on the weekend after announcing his candidacy for the Democratic nomination for governor, Wilder spoke more freely about the constitutional promise of equality in the Southwest than in any other region.

Back in Richmond that night, a sequinned, black-tie crowd swayed to the sounds of the Lonnie Liston Smith Jazz Ensemble at an elegant downtown hotel. Democratic operatives sized up the ticket sales, the new faces, and the upbeat mood, and called the kickoff a success. Arlington County board member John Milliken, musing over Wilder's prospects, noted that major fundraisers for two Republican candidates for governor had approached him within the last week to say, "If my man loses I'm with you."

"I think," said Milliken, weighing his words, "that Doug's got a shot at it."

Victory might not be likely. It certainly was not guaranteed. But it was not impossible. The campaign was under way at last.

2

FROM CHURCH HILL TO CAPITOL HILL

From the intersection of Twenty-eighth and P Streets in Richmond's Church Hill neighborhood, the route downtown slices a world fallen on hard times. Small bungalows border on deteriorating rowhouses and vacant lots strewn with cheap wine bottles and yesterday's trash. Poverty, drugs, and a middle-class rush to the suburbs have taken their toll on what was once a thriving black neighborhood. At Broad Street, the path turns west past St. John's Episcopal Church, where Patrick Henry cried for liberty or death, then dips into Shockoe Bottom, where the acrid scent of warehoused tobacco once filled the air. Several hundred yards beyond, the road rises abruptly toward Virginia's seat of government, Capitol Hill.

From the corner lot at Twenty-eighth and P where Robert and Beulah Wilder raised their eight children who lived past infancy, to the statehouse that Mr. Jefferson designed, it is two miles on the odometer. "It's a short distance to walk," Doug Wilder, the seventh of those children, was fond of saying during his campaign for governor, "but it's a mighty, mighty mountain to climb."

In the fifty-eight years of his ascent, Wilder traveled far. By 1989 his childhood home, a two-story frame house with chickens, geese, and homing pigeons in the backyard, had given way to a stately brick home across town, with formal gardens and two Mercedes-Benzes in the driveway. The lad who shined shoes and hawked newspapers door-to-door, who as a young man waited tables at downtown hotels, and whose first law office was over a shrimp house, had become the millionaire senior partner in a law firm that did work for General Motors, Chrysler, K-Mart, and Chevron. The boy who attended segregated schools with hand-me-down textbooks, and who was strongly discouraged from attending law school in his home state because he was black, had risen to the pinnacle of political power in Virginia and the threshold of national influence.

He had reached those heights largely by his own timetable and in his own way. Those who try to fit Wilder into the mold of a traditional black politician—evangelical, a fire-and-brimstone orator, passionate about poverty and justice, grounded in the civil rights movement—will be disappointed. While others were marching on Selma and Washington in the 1960s, Doug Wilder was building a law practice and amassing a small fortune. He is not untouched by the experiences of his youth, and he speaks eloquently of his regard for all those who struggle against enormous odds. But emotional causes are not his priority. "I don't think you'd see Doug leading a mission to impoverished areas," says Leonard Lambert, a Richmond attorney who shared a law office with the politician for twenty years. Wilder's message to black youth remains, "Work hard. Go the extra mile." He speaks of education and economics, not government, as the great social equalizers of our time. Of the Rev. Jesse Jackson, he says: "Jesse runs to inspire. I run to win."

Those who see Wilder as cut from a new mold of nonconfrontational black politicians also miss the mark, however. Although he is no zealot, he has spent his entire political career bobbing and weaving between confrontation and conciliation. Named for the nineteenth century political figure Frederick Douglass and the poet Paul Laurence Dunbar, Wilder has touches of both the fiery abolitionist and the contemplative poet in his soul. His twenty-year political career has been a balancing act between a black constituency and a white power structure. Along the way, he has become a master of hardball politics. Wilder has humbled Virginia's white establishment, tweaked even Democratic governors, and audaciously redefined himself as the need arose. But when it suited his purposes, as in the months leading up to his 1989 gubernatorial bid, he could become the most reassuringly conciliatory of politicians.

Throughout his sixteen years in the state senate, and again in 1985 when he became the first black Southerner since Reconstruction to win a statewide executive post, Wilder was sometimes described as the ultimate insider. But the description overlooks his frequent flashes of independence. What Wilder is, first and foremost, is a consummate politician, standing apart from the political establishment at times, embracing it at others. His handling of race is an example. In 1989 Wilder downplayed racial identification. But at other points in his career, he has not hesitated to play a racial trump card.

Longtime acquaintances say there are several keys to Wilder's personality. He is enormously confident about his own abilities, and about the likelihood that events will work together for the good of Doug Wilder. "He sees a damn silver lining in every cloud," says his longtime senate aide, Judy Anderson. She and others recall numerous instances when Wilder was totally unfazed by adverse headlines or conventional wisdom that he had erred. During the dark days of August, 1989, when his campaign was being riddled with bad publicity, aides and family members say Wilder remained a fount of optimism.

Like a seasoned prizefighter, Wilder also thrives on competition, laughing uproariously at the notion of infighting among key aides, or the prospect that his recent running mates, Lt. Gov. Donald Beyer, Jr., and Atty. Gen. Mary Sue Terry, may spend the next four years battling it out for the 1993 Democratic gubernatorial nomination. Nor is he averse to the darker side of power, remembering both favors and slights. He can be intensely loyal, but "he's not afraid of stepping on or over people," says Leonard Lambert. "Doug's philosophy has always been, 'I don't get mad. I get even.'"

Critical to Wilder's success is a quick mind and skill at debate, a talent honed as one of Richmond's most successful criminal lawyers. He is glib—critics say unprincipled—enough to explain away any shortcomings, and to justify easily his philosophical evolution from liberal to moderate. During the campaign, when striking miners or liberals complained that his positions on issues were too close to Marshall Coleman's, Wilder urged them to remember his past. When conservative audiences complained about that past, Wilder urged them to remember that times and people change. Taken to task for introducing several controversial bills and resolutions in the Virginia senate, Wilder insisted that he "didn't do a thing" for the legislation once it was introduced. Asked about specific liberal votes, Wilder was never at a loss for a rationale that coincided with his more moderate campaign views.

If all else fails, Wilder can usually dismiss a question with an answer that includes a mind-boggling array of twists and turns. For example, asked during an interview just before the nomination about his position on the racially and politically sensitive issue of statehood for the District of Columbia, Wilder replied, "I have to be convinced of certain legal situations in terms of what the constitution was and in terms of what the land was originally supposed to have been, for what purpose it was originally ceded to the federal government, where the capital is to reside. I likewise have concerns for any group that feels disenfranchised.

"It's no decision for me to make at this time," he concluded.

Of all Wilder's political assets, the greatest is an easy warmth and obvious zest for life. The divorced father of three children, Wilder has interests far beyond politics. He is a pool shark, jazz devotee, accomplished bridge player, amateur artist, sports fan (the Washington Redskins in football, the Detroit Pistons in basketball), chef at his own dinner parties, and more. Although U.S. senators John Warner and Chuck Robb offer competition, on a one-on-one basis Wilder is the most personable campaigner on the Virginia political scene.

Marshall Coleman's staffers came to view Wilder during the campaign as an unprincipled, even dangerous politician. They pointed to a litany of failings, including a 1978 Virginia Supreme Court reprimand for poorly representing a legal client, incomplete financial disclosures, late payment of taxes in some past years, and a long-running dispute with neighbors and city officials over the condition of an unoccupied investment rowhouse that Wilder once owned. When it surfaced during the campaign that Wilder had placed the house in a personal trust, rather than selling it as he had implied, critics charged him with outright deception. But one of the great shocks of the campaign came when voters responded to advertisements on those issues not with dismay at Wilder, but with anger at Coleman. Wilder's standing in polls was largely unaffected by the television assault, while the number of voters who blamed his opponent for negative campaigning skyrocketed.

Part of the explanation may well have been the difference between the figure whom voters saw described on GOP television spots and the man they met at shopping centers, campaign rallies, and other public occasions. The latter was warm-eyed and relaxed, quick with a laugh, a hug, a pat on the back, or a double-clasped handshake. In the image of his father, who often wore a coat and tie at home, Wilder was usually immaculate, his mustache trimmed, his shirt collar starched, a white handkerchief peeping out of the breast pocket of an expensive, well-cut suit. His only concession to hot days or informal settings was to unbutton his collar and loosen his tie. There was little that was threatening about a grey-haired man who stood only 5 feet, 9 inches tall in his Bally loafers, and who worked a crowd like everyone was family. "Hello pretty little lady," he would greet youngsters. "Good to see you. God bless you," he would tell retirees. "You are b-aaaad. You are s-o-o-o bad. You are *terrible,*" he would say, jiving with a Northern Virginia yuppie. With an actor's range, his voice often soared an octave in seconds, from a rich, sympathetic baritone to a cackling, high-pitched laugh.

Given the constraints of history, the strength of his Republican opponent, the racial animosity unearthed by the Greekfest riot, and labor unrest throughout the summer and fall in the southwest Virginia coalfields, Wilder's election "had no business happening by all objective measures that I can find," said state Democratic chairman Larry Framme a few days after the victory. "That's why I come back to the belief that Doug won this by sheer force of personality as much as anything else."

At the core of his psyche, says Wilder, is an abiding faith that all things are possible. "It's faith first of all in God, and I don't talk about it, but you have to have that. If you didn't have that, all else would be failing." And then, he adds, it is also faith in the individual, especially himself. "There's a purpose to living, and I think it's to exalt the highest possible potential of the individual. I've always believed in self-reliance. I endorse Emerson wholeheartedly in that. Rather than look to others for complaints about why, you have to look to self. My sustaining faith is that most of the things that I've ever tried, I've been successful at."

It is a few weeks before election day and Wilder is sitting in his state government office, surrounded by award plaques, photos of the rich and famous, and framed bits of wisdom reminiscent of his favorite poem by Langston Hughes: "Hold fast to dreams / For if dreams die / Life is a broken-winged bird / That cannot fly."

"I don't go to bed too many times being angry about the failures of the day," he insists. "I count each day as a life, each day, and say, 'What will life be like today?' Life to me is a verb, not a noun. You have to use it, say, 'Okay, I'm willing.'"

Asked if he ever wished to have been born white, Wilder laughs, then admits to conversations on the topic. "I guess when others have discussed it, you know, sit around in groups and say, wouldn't you rather be such and such a person, [I've said] no, because I've always considered I was fortunate to have been born me. . . . I never, absolutely never had any regret, or any feeling of, oh my goodness, if I had been born another way I would have been this." He smiles again. "Because I always thought I could rise to the top as me."

That strong sense of self-worth is attributed by friends to the supportive environment into which Wilder was born on January 17, 1931, in Richmond. His Church Hill neighborhood was strictly segregated and poverty was widespread, but there were demanding teachers at George Mason Elementary School and dozens of positive role models among the neighbors who ran their own family businesses or simply worked hard. "It gave us a sense of worth and community spirit that helped to build character," says Allen Roots, a Richmond accountant and boyhood friend. Describing his home, Wilder once remarked to a reporter for the *Washington Post* that "We were a large family and poor as Job's turkey but it was gentle poverty. By that I mean we had music. The vases would have flowers from the yard."

Indeed, there is a Norman Rockwell–like quality to the descriptions of Wilder's growing up in a family where discipline, hard work, love, and laughter were the mainstays. Agnes Wilder Nicholson, a retired school secretary and the second oldest of Wilder's four living sisters, recalls their home as a gathering spot for the neighborhood. Scarcely a day went by when some relative or friend did not visit. The kitchen door was never locked, and the room was a haven for games and gossip.

The house, which was torn down a few years ago, was located across the street from Fourth Baptist Church, and although the Wilders were members of First African Baptist downtown, both churches figured in their lives. On occasion, Nicholson recalls, when Fourth Baptist was giving a play and a member of the cast failed to show up, someone from the congregation would knock on the Wilders' fence and call out, "We need to borrow one of your children." Sundays were a day when the Wilder children either sat through church or were ordered to remain indoors.

Robert J. Wilder, Sr., was a disciplinarian who set rigid rules for his children and expected them to be obeyed. There were chores to do in the afternoons, curfews to be met, manners to be obeyed. Jean Miller, Wilder's youngest sister and an educational consultant in Michigan, recalls that even so minor an infraction as passing a neighbor without saying hello might have its penalty. If one child was out of line, their father occasionally disciplined the siblings as well. His rationale was that "if you did it, probably others were thinking about doing it," Miller said.

A salesman for Southern Aid Insurance Company, the oldest black-owned insurance company in the United States, the elder Wilder was also a church deacon, respected in the community, and notoriously tight with a dollar. On Sundays, the children were each given a dime when they left home for First African—a penny for the Sunday School collection plate, two cents for church, and seven cents for the streetcar ride downtown. They were expected to find a way home on their own. Once, when young Douglas won a week's trip to New York for selling the *Richmond Planet*, the city's black newspaper, his father gave him five dollars to take along. When Wilder returned, even before he could report on the wonders he'd seen his father wanted a financial accounting. "You threw it all away," he complained upon hearing that only a few cents were left.

Both of Robert Wilder's parents were born in slavery, and a few tales of that era have survived in family folklore. Doug Wilder's grandfather, James W. Wilder, and grandmother, Agnes Johnson Wilder, were married on a Henrico County farm north of Richmond on April 25, 1856. A copy of their marriage certificate is pressed into a family Bible maintained by Nicholson for the clan. The couple were later sold separately, and Agnes and the children were taken to neighboring Hanover County. James was considered so trustworthy that he was allowed to visit his wife each Sunday. According to family legend, if he ever returned late, the white overseer would beat on a saddle to make it sound as if the slave were being punished. Agnes Wilder worked in her owner's house and learned to read while listening to the lessons of a handicapped child for whom she cared. The family was reunited at the end of the Civil War. Wilder also recalls being told that his grandfather hid in a silo when Gen. Ulysses Grant, commander-in-chief of the Union forces, captured Richmond. James Wilder apparently had been frightened by his owner's tales of likely atrocities at the hands of Union soldiers. He told his children that he almost smothered in the silo.

Less is known about the family of Wilder's mother, Beulah. Beulah never knew her father, and she was raised by a grandmother and aunt in Richmond after her mother and stepfather died. A strong and compassionate woman, revered by her children, Beulah Wilder is widely credited with being the single most dominant force in developing Doug Wilder's considerable self-esteem. "They were the best of friends," Nicholson recalls. Beulah and Douglas, as his family calls him, would spend long hours together working crossword puzzles, reading, or simply talking. As a child, Wilder says, he used to delight his family by telling them that he was the son of rich people and had been mistakenly left on the wrong doorstep. "'Oh yes,'" he recalls his mother saying, "'you're a special little boy.' And I would say, 'Tell me about it.' And she always would."

In later years, when Beulah Wilder was ill and dying, her politician son would visit regularly, regaling her for an hour at a time with chitchat and gossip from the old neighborhood. When she was worried about legal or business matters, "he would always tell her, 'Don't worry. I'll take care of it,'" remembers Agnes Nicholson, unknowingly quoting a phrase that Wilder still uses when political problems arise. "He may not have taken care of it, but with that, she would leave it."

Wilder thrived in that self-contained environment. He was a constant tease to his sisters, good in school, and aggressive at sports, though too small to make the varsity. He was also allowed a bit more leeway in bending rules than older siblings had been. In free moments he could be found practicing his shots at a nearby pool hall, or holding forth on some issue at one of several neighborhood barber shops and shoe shine stands. "He was the arguingest little man I ever saw," said Arthur Burke, seventy-six, as he whiled away the hours at one longtime Church Hill institution—Billy's Barber Shop—on election day. In Wilder's youth, Billy's was an unofficial courthouse square where men gathered to discuss baseball, politics, and other heavyweight topics. It was there that Wilder first sharpened his debating skills, and Burke recalled a high compliment once paid the youngster by another patron: "He said, 'You should be a lawyer. You argue too much and you tell the biggest lies in the world.'"

Wilder's first real encounters with whites came as a teenager when he ran an elevator in a downtown office building. Before that, there was no occasion for mixing. School, church, and home were as segregated as the restrooms and drinking fountains at downtown department stores. Whites sat in the front of streetcars, blacks at the back. Train station ticket lines, restaurants, courtrooms, libraries, and playgrounds all were divided by race. He was interested to find, Wilder recalls, that he shared an easy rapport with the white boys who worked with him that summer.

After high school graduation in 1947, Wilder toyed with the idea of joining the navy, then wound up at Virginia Union University across town from Church Hill. Virginia Union was founded at the end of the Civil War with help from the Freedman's Bureau to offer a liberal arts education for newly emancipated blacks. It was less prestigious than Hampton Institute to the southeast or Howard University to the north, but the one-hundred-dollars-a-semester tuition was right, and there was free room and board at home. His mother scraped together the first twenty-five dollars, and he was responsible for raising the rest. The future politician majored in chemistry, specialized in partying, and graduated a semester behind his class after repeating a calculus course. Nights and weekends he waited tables at private country clubs and fancy Richmond hotels, including the John Marshall, the Jefferson, and the William Byrd. In 1985, the same John Marshall ballroom where he had once filled water glasses and removed plates would be the scene of one of his greatest triumphs, the victory party that followed his election as lieutenant governor.

Still uncertain of his goals in life, Wilder held odd jobs after graduating in August 1951 and waited to be drafted. The summons came soon after New Year's Day, 1952, and in August army private Wilder and the rest of his company in the Seventeenth Infantry Regiment's first battalion landed at Inchon, Korea. In that fevered setting, Wilder made his first significant stand for equal rights, entertained the most revolutionary political feelings of his life, and won one of the nation's highest awards for valor, the Bronze Star.

President Harry Truman by executive order had desegregated the armed forces, but decades of separation could not be wiped away by the stroke of a pen. Complaints that black soldiers were not receiving promotions were widespread when Wilder arrived in Korea, and he eventually spearheaded a drive to ensure that the dissatisfaction was aired. Maneuvering his way past a difficult lieutenant, Wilder arranged a meeting between a superior officer and several dozen black soldiers. In his first political forum, Wilder apparently performed well. Within days, promotions began arriving, including one for Wilder, who moved up to corporal and later sergeant.

During his days in Korea Wilder and some black army buddies toyed with the notion that armed revolution might be the only way to right America's social ills. They were fascinated by the terrorist Mau Mau revolution against British colonial rule in Kenya, and he and a friend exchanged letters signed with the symbol of the Kikuyu tribesmen, the burning spear. They also contemplated working as waiters once they were back in the States, and using their positions to sprinkle poison on the salads of white oppressors, Wilder once told a biographer.

Wilder later insisted he was only aware of such thoughts and never held them personally. "They were more friends of mine, and one guy particularly. But, no, I never entertained any such nonsense like that," he said, dismissing the idea with a laugh. "Like I said, I've never been unsuccessful." But Wilder also admits that the wartime experience fostered irrationality among many, and that his attitudes during that period were more radical than before or since. "You see, war just takes your senses away from you," he says, noting that some American blacks and whites felt such hatred that he believes they threw hand grenades at each other. "You couldn't prove it," he said. "But you had every kind of suspicion."

Three months before returning to the United States, Wilder performed the heroic act that won him the Bronze Star. While helping remove wounded soldiers from Pork Chop Hill, he and a comrade encountered enemy fire coming from a bunker. Wilder, then a corporal, directed the other soldier, a private, to drop grenades in the rear of the enclosure while he covered the front exit. Expecting that a couple of North Koreans would emerge, Wilder was stunned when, one by one, twenty men scrambled out. With Wilder leading the group and the private bringing up the rear, the party marched for forty minutes through mortar fire to an American encampment. Back at the camp, Wilder discovered that there were only nineteen prisoners, and he believes the private who aided in the capture killed one on their long march. He did not report the matter, nor did he lodge a formal complaint upon learning months later that the lieutenant who met them at the camp won a higher medal, the Silver Star, after writing himself into the report. "I guess he made colonel out of it," Wilder says, shaking his head at the audacity. As he often does in conversation, Wilder lapses into imaginary role-playing. This time, he is the colonel describing to his children the bogus heroism. "Oh yes, I was over there, dead of night . . . ," he begins, dropping his voice to a deep bass before erupting in laughter.

He did not try to rectify the prisoner count, Wilder said, because he had no proof of a misdeed. Nor did he challenge the Silver Star because "it's very difficult to take an award away from someone once they've got it." But, aghast at the episode, Wilder did not tell his family until years afterward about his own medal, and made no public mention of it until deciding in 1985 that it would be a valuable credential with voters. "I couldn't believe it," he said of the lieutenant's actions. "I said if awards are given to people for this reason, people would believe it was given to me for the same reason."

When he returned to the United States, Wilder ran headlong into racial barriers that wartime had temporarily erased. Applying for a job at the state Employment Office, he was told there was only one opening for which he qualified. The job was as a cook, and Wilder turned it down. By 1956 he had decided to go to law school, and Howard University in Washington was his choice. The University of Virginia Law School had technically been integrated in 1950 with the admission of a single black student under court order. But other blacks had not been encouraged to follow, while those who attended law school out of state could count on a state-financed scholarship. As the nation's first black law school, Howard from the 1920s on had been a seedbed for developing the men and women who would man the front trenches of the civil rights movement. Its classrooms were laboratories for sharpening the strategies that slowly were dismantling segregation. Wilder arrived at Howard with a different agenda. He was less interested in saving the world than in succeeding as the first black lawyer on Church Hill. And in a holdover from his Union days, he was still open to having a good time. "In law school he was single and thinking party all the time," says Otis N. "Petie" Paige, a longtime family friend with whom Wilder boarded during part of his law school days. The frivolity ended when Wilder realized he was in danger of flunking out, and reversed his course. By the time he graduated, he had become a solid performer in the classroom. He had also become a husband, marrying Eunice Montgomery, an attractive economics undergraduate at Howard, in October 1958. By the next summer, he was a father as well.

Wilder installed his new family in the parental home at Twenty-eighth and P streets, opened an office above Ike's Shrimp House a few blocks away, and set about building a law practice. Today Wilder heads a seven-attorney law firm that includes his son Larry, who as a graduate of the University of Virginia's law school symbolizes changing times. The current law office is located in a handsomely furnished restored building in a section of Church Hill that, when Wilder was growing up, was occupied only by whites. Although Wilder lives in a comfortable, integrated neighborhood several miles away, it is a point of pride to him that his work remains near his origins.

Over the succeeding decades Wilder built a law practice that included everything from wills, divorces, and traffic cases to sensational murder trials. A promising black attorney arriving in Richmond today would have a range of options, including joining some of the most prestigious law firms in the South. But when Wilder returned to town, black lawyers were still a rare breed, and most had to make their own way. Three of the region's most respected civil rights lawyers—Oliver Hill, his law partner Samuel W. Tucker, and Spottswood W. Robinson III —had settled in Richmond, handling landmark cases out of cramped offices with limited resources. For various reasons, Wilder did not join their practices. Not the least of these was his need for independence.

Although fighting injustice matters to Wilder, many who know him say he is primarily motivated by more worldly goals: personal achievement, acquiring the finer things of life, maintaining a good appearance, and retaining independence. Wilder does not disagree with that list. But, aware of the precedent-setting nature of his legal and political career, he adds: "You fight injustice with every step you take." At the same time, "I never viewed myself as an activist," he says, voicing a phrase that soothed white skeptics during his bid for governor. While others took to the streets to press for equal rights, Wilder says he was convinced by the 1954 U.S. Supreme Court school desegregation decision in *Brown v. Board of Education* that "you could do it from within. Of course, everybody says they marched on Washington now. I was not there. I didn't even participate in the pickets here in Richmond, but I felt I made my contributions in other ways. I wanted to be the best lawyer I could be, so that when I walked into the courtroom, . . . people would listen and could get results. And I think that happened. If I had to do it over again, I'd do the same thing."

Even so, Wilder did make some tangible gains for the civil rights movement. He led in integrating the Richmond Bar Association, local courtrooms, and a golf course, and he broke the color barrier at the Jefferson-Lakeside Country Club in Henrico County, just north of Richmond, by joining it. Defying convention, he refused to sit in "colored" sections of the courtrooms where he appeared, and fellow lawyers recall that he never treated white judges obsequiously. Wilder says he also represented "any number of persons who would be involved in demonstrations, and didn't charge anything." Asked if that was his policy, he chuckles as he admits the dual pulls of practicality and ideals. "Well, no, I tried to, and they just didn't have it. And then it got to be a pattern," he says. The largesse was not without its monetary reward. "Lots of times, the families would use me for other kinds of things," he adds.

Gradually Wilder's clientele, as well as his reputation as a scrappy, flamboyant trial lawyer, spread throughout the state. Among his most notorious clients were William Penn, one of two brothers who left a trail of murders in Richmond in the late 1960s, and Curtis Darnell Poindexter, who gunned down a judge and wounded several other people in a courtroom melee in Louisa County west of Richmond in 1975. The Poindexter case would trail Wilder to the gubernatorial race, as Republicans claimed that land given him in payment for the defense was deliberately left off his financial disclosure form.

A 1970s Richmond magazine article described Wilder as one of the four best trial lawyers in town, and those who watched his work were often impressed with his colorful oratory and his command of witnesses. "The courtroom was his playground," says Lambert, his old office mate. "He had a quick mind, a photographic mind. He'd lead a witness out on a limb as far as we wanted, and then cut the limb off." There were others who felt that it was Wilder himself who was overextended. Privately, some competing lawyers and even court officials grumbled that Wilder often delayed court hearings involving his extensive caseload and did not always show up prepared. "He was very, very busy," acknowledged Philip B. Morris, a Richmond lawyer and one of Wilder's earliest white political supporters. "If he were to do it over again, he probably would have surrounded himself with more help."

The nadir came in 1975 when the state Supreme Court, acting on an appeal by Wilder, confirmed a lower court opinion that Wilder was guilty of "inexcusable procrastination" in representing a New Jersey family over a 1966 car accident. According to testimony, nearly two years elapsed after his hiring as counsel before he brought action for his clients. Then followed a series of misfilings, and the legal time limits for resolving the case eventually ran out. At one point, in what the court said "could obviously have had no effect other than to mislead his clients," Wilder wrote that "your case is proceeding as can be expected at the moment." In fact, no lawsuit was pending at that time. A case filed earlier had been dropped six months before when the driver of the other car could not be located. It was almost two years before Wilder filed a new lawsuit. The judicial reprimand recommended by the Virginia State Bar Association and upheld by the courts is generally described by lawyers as a serious blemish on Wilder's record. However, Alex H. Sands, Jr., the circuit court judge who heard the case, said in court that it did "not reflect upon his character or his legal ethics." Wilder's response to the episode is apologetic. "I did not represent the best interests of my clients," he says. During the campaign, he repeatedly told businessmen and others worried about the incident that it was a mistake he regrets and has not repeated.

The plunge into politics came in 1969. J. Sargeant Reynolds, a rising liberal star, heir to the Reynolds Metals fortune and one of two Richmond state senators, was running for lieutenant governor. The city's population had been steadily moving toward half black, half white, although a controversial annexation was about to tip the racial balance again toward whites. Wilder believed if a black candidate was ever going to win a citywide election, he must act before the annexation was complete. So he filed for election to the Virginia State Senate from Richmond. He had paid fewer dues than some black leaders also interested in the seat. But Wilder moved first, announcing his candidacy several months before Reynolds was elected. His bold action blocked other blacks, and when two whites entered the race, splitting much of the white vote, Wilder was elected. He won a plurality, 15,844 of the 32,718 votes cast, including an estimated 18 percent of the white vote. In his acceptance speech, Wilder said that he had received "a gratifying number of white votes," and that he looked "forward to the time when all men can run on their qualifications and not as a 'Negro candidate' or a 'white candidate.'" The conservative editorial page of the *Richmond Times-Dispatch*, a thorn to Wilder throughout his years in public office, applauded him for a "dignified and responsible campaign." The editorial writer was particularly pleased that Wilder had not "pandered to [blacks]," as evidenced by his endorsement of the controversial annexation.

Actually, what Wilder had done on the annexation question was to chart a centrist course. He could support an annexation that was anathema to many black voters, Wilder said, so long as city officials also adopted a ward system ensuring the election of blacks to the city council. It was an early example of the ability to maneuver among perilous racial and political shoals that would become Wilder's trademark as a politician. The adroit juggling of diverse and even opposing interests would be a key to his winning of the Democratic gubernatorial nomination twenty years later. It would also leave him open to charges of being ideologically unfocused and guided by shifts in political winds.

Wilder arrived in the Virginia Senate in 1970 as the first black to sit there since Reconstruction. Already some Byrd Organization conservatives were infuriated by his victory in the general election over one of their own, former Lt. Gov. Fred Pollard, and their reception was not warm. Wilder's name was mysteriously left off the guest list to a traditional Assembly opening party hosted by one of Pollard's supporters. Wilder fueled the misgivings two weeks later when he made his debut on the senate floor with a tirade against the state song, "Carry Me Back to Old Virginny." The day before, Wilder had walked out of a legislative banquet sponsored by the Virginia Food Dealers Association when the song was sung. Particularly offensive to him were the references to "massah" and lines such as "that's where this ol' darkey's heart am long to go."

Interviewed not long afterwards as part of a Southern oral history project now stored at the University of North Carolina, Wilder recalled the reaction to his speech. "You would have thought I touched the atom bomb. All hell broke loose. I got letters from all over the world . . . from Mexico, Germany, France, Ireland." One said, "Go home. Keep your mouth shut. Why don't you carry your ass back to Africa," Wilder recalled. Another, "you ginger colored skinned nigger. . . . You ought to be proud of the white blood you have in your veins."

Other legislators, however, welcomed him graciously into the senate. Wilder remembers with particular warmth the reception of his deskmate, the late William V. Rawlings, a pig farmer who represented a slice of the Southside, the state's most racially recalcitrant region. Rawlings became Wilder's confidant and unofficial adviser, steering him toward membership on the Committee on Privileges and Elections, for instance. Rawlings correctly predicted that Wilder might one day be chairman of the committee, which for decades had guarded the right to vote as if it were a patrician privilege.

Throughout the 1970s Wilder pursued a liberal, civil rights –oriented legislative agenda. He pushed for fair housing laws and a holiday honoring the Rev. Martin Luther King, Jr. He backed proposals to strip the sales tax from food and nonprescription drugs, and although he later claimed to have done so only as a courtesy, he introduced resolutions calling for voting rights and statehood for the District of Columbia. He opposed the death penalty and fought tough crime legislation, including bills creating a sentence of life in prison without parole and prescribing a separate offense for the use of a gun in committing a felony. In a group known for its sedate conformity, his full Afro haircut and flashy clothes further accentuated his separateness.

The most publicized of Wilder's legislative ventures was the ten-year battle, stretching from 1975 to 1984, to create a state holiday honoring Dr. King. Wilder downplayed the achievement in his statewide campaigns, but his dogged pursuit of the holiday showcased his legislative skills. The proposal was first introduced in 1975 as a resolution, merely suggesting that localities remember King on his birthday, January 15. The idea did not generate enough enthusiasm even for a hearing. Over the next decade, the proposal would take multiple forms. Twice—in 1977 and 1981—King holiday bills passed the legislature, only to be vetoed by Republican governors. After the first of those vetoes, Wilder chastised former Gov. Mills E. Godwin, Jr., using the sort of racial accusations that never passed the candidate's mouth in 1989. "I think the governor has emerged from a cocoon . . . which spelled him out to be a racist," said an angry Wilder. The veto indicated that Godwin, a former segregationist, "hasn't completely erased his previous image," Wilder said. The man who by 1989 said he had never been an activist helped lead a protest rally of several hundred people. Finally, in 1984, in a resolution that is thoroughly Virginian, Wilder succeeded when he agreed to tack the holiday onto another honoring two Confederate generals, Robert E. Lee and Stonewall Jackson.

At some point—the precise date is disputed by Wilder and Republicans—the politician's priorities began to shift toward a more moderate approach. Critics say the change occurred when Wilder began to think of running for statewide office; he says the evolution began much earlier. What is not in dispute is that by 1989 Wilder had taken a host of positions at odds with those of his early legislative days. The list of issues on which he had become more conservative included the death penalty, parental consent for underage abortions, public employee bargaining, life in prison without parole, and an extra penalty for using a gun in committing a felony.

As his priorities were shifting, Wilder was also climbing steadily through the legislative ranks. By the time he ran for lieutenant governor, he had chaired three major committees and had more legislative experience than the five previous lieutenant governors combined. Under Governor Chuck Robb, he had become known as the man to see about black appointments to judgeships and administrative posts. Meanwhile, Wilder's personality was winning an appreciative audience and considerable goodwill among fellow Democrats. Sen. William E. Fears, an Eastern Shore lawyer whose maverick style masks a Yale education, tells one story that he views as vintage Wilder. On a mid-1970s vacation to Venezuela, the pair discovered that contestants in the Miss Universe pageant were staying at their hotel. Hoping to meet them, Wilder impersonated tennis great Arthur Ashe, while the more rotund Fears posed as his coach.

Wilder's senate colleagues say he was successful because he was shrewd, fast on his feet, and regarded as a power broker with the black vote. In the legislature he could be tenacious on matters that interested him, and indifferent on those that did not. "I really felt that Doug had more of an intuitive than a scholarly grasp on issues," says Sen. Joseph V. Gartlan, Jr., an Alexandria Democrat. Gartlan recalled that as chairman of the Senate Rehabilitation and Social Services Committee, which handles welfare matters, Wilder missed more meetings and showed less interest in technical points than expected. "I was surprised," adds Gartlan, who viewed the committee as a good assignment for a Richmond senator. But former Republican senator Ray Garland of Roanoke, a syndicated columnist on Virginia politics, describes Wilder as having "the perfect personality for a legislative body . . . conviviality, humor, energy. He was a person you were always glad to see coming. You knew things would be a little lighter, a little more dramatic. And behind that was the great power of the black vote."

As Wilder's political career flourished, his marriage fell on hard times. In July 1975, Eunice Wilder filed for divorce, charging her husband of seventeen years with "cruelty and reasonable apprehension of bodily harm." Those charges were later dropped, and the divorce was granted in early 1978. Records from the case have been sealed, and both parties refuse comment on the initial charges of cruelty. "My ex-wife has asked me not to speak about that, and I have not," Wilder says. A year after the divorce, Wilder fought a legal effort by his former wife to receive half of all the property acquired during the marriage, then a novel request in Virginia. Eunice was represented in court by Sa'ad El-Amin, a radical black attorney and Wilder critic whose name the politician refuses to speak publicly. There was no basis for the request in Virginia law, a judge ruled, and Eunice eventually settled for fifty-two thousand dollars. "I think we can conclude that there were a lot of raw nerves and bad feelings," says El-Amin.

What is perhaps the pivotal moment of Wilder's political career came in the spring of 1982. Setting the stage for his move to the executive branch, Wilder faced down the state's Democratic hierarchy, showing both his audacity and the futility of alienating the party's most dependable voting block—blacks. A moderate state legislator from Virginia Beach, Owen B. Pickett, stood ready to accept the party's nomination for the U.S. Senate seat held by Harry Byrd, Jr., who was retiring. But Pickett, who four years later would be elected to Congress, ran afoul of black lawmakers led by Wilder. The black caucus, angered at its cavalier treatment by the Democratic majority in the 1982 Assembly, bristled when Pickett launched his campaign by wooing conservative Byrdites. Wilder threatened to run as an independent if Pickett were the nominee, and after several weeks of escalating tension, Governor Robb recommended that Pickett drop his bid. Although he had already collected enough convention delegates to win the nomination, Pickett bowed to the inevitable. Seldom, if ever, had the clout of black voters been demonstrated so vividly. Robb, Pickett, Wilder, and hundreds of party faithful recognized that without black support, the Senate race was lost. It was Wilder who had delivered the message.

That spring also produced one of the memorable racial incidents of Wilder's life. Encouraged by Robb, Wilder agreed to eat lunch with several prominent Democrats to see if they could work out the emerging impasse over Pickett. The guest list included Al Smith, a folksy fast-food magnate and prominent conservative fundraiser for Robb; Alan Diamonstein, then chairman of the state party; and senate clerk Jay Shropshire, a longtime Wilder intimate who also had strong ties to the conservative establishment.

As they left the capitol and headed west on Grace Street, Wilder suggested that they dine at the Commonwealth Club, an all-white bastion that epitomized the racially and politically conservative ethic of Old Virginia. Smith tried to divert Wilder, saying that he'd called ahead and the dining room was full. Fine, replied the senator, he knew most of the waiters in the grill, and they could eat there. After a tense pause, Smith refused. "Life's too short for me to be embarrassed by taking you to the Commonwealth Club," he reportedly said. Shropshire says that Wilder's eyes were watering as he drove away, headed for his own integrated country club across town.

The episode soon made headlines, with Smith claiming that he had been set up. Wilder, who denied the charge, said the episode strengthened his resolve to run for the Senate if Pickett did not step aside. Relations between Smith and Wilder remained cool until mid-1989, when Smith began working vigorously for the campaign. In late 1988 the Commonwealth Club admitted its first black member, a Richmond dentist.

Three years later, Democrats had not forgotten Pickett's fate when they handed Wilder the nomination for lieutenant governor without opposition. There was, they seemed to be saying, no point in crossing the black vote. Few strategists thought Wilder had much, if any, chance of winning, and their certainty increased when the party also nominated a woman, delegate Mary Sue Terry, for attorney general. Amid predictions that Wilder might topple the entire ticket, Robb's press secretary sighed to a *Washington Post* reporter who asked about the black candidate's prospects, "This is still Virginia." Wilder was slipped assurances that he could chair the state party if he stepped aside. Even the perpetually optimistic candidate seemed taken aback when eleven prominent legislators, including the speaker of the House of Delegates and the state Democratic chair, were caught in a secret meeting aimed at discussing their concerns about the prospective ticket. None of those present was black.

The race that followed was a shoestring classic. Adopting an unlikely strategy, the candidate hired a campaign staff of two, set out on a three thousand-mile trek of the state, and began squirreling away money for an eleventh-hour television assault. Once again keeping to his own drumbeat, Wilder seemed oblivious to the complaints of some party elders that the ruling principle in his campaign appeared to be chaos. Wilder's Republican opponent, state senator John Chichester, brought to the campaign an engaging smile, a courtly manner, a lackluster legislative record, and a host of assurances that all he had to do to win on election day was show up alive. At times, as Chichester kept a leisurely campaign pace, even Republicans complained that his primary aim seemed to be waiting out election day.

Wilder never hired a formal campaign manager, keeping to himself overall responsibility for the campaign. But he named as his chief strategist and principal aide Paul Goldman, a quirky northeasterner whose political brilliance would be proven over the next four years. In retrospect, the campaign plan that they devised—operating on a low budget and hoarding every dollar possible for television—looked masterful. At the time, it seemed improbable. The tour, viewed by some as a black hole into which Wilder was about to disappear, turned out to be an ideal showcase for a novel political bid. Instead of being ignored, Wilder was the toast of dozens of small communities, and his warm reception became the focus of numerous stories in major urban dailies. Back in Richmond, the poor-mouthing and scrimping was also paying off. By the end of October, Wilder had a three-to-one advantage over Chichester in dollars spent on advertising. All the money Wilder had saved on staff and literature and supplies was going straight into television.

The message he conveyed, there and on the campaign trail, was soothingly mainstream. It was heavy on experience, moderate on the issues, and mum on race. Wilder turned down offers from Jesse Jackson to campaign, and trumpeted instead his endorsement from the conservative Fraternal Order of Police. He distributed campaign literature that highlighted his antidrug efforts and ignored the King holiday bill. Wilder and Goldman also defused the racial issue early in the campaign. The opening they were seeking came when Chichester's gubernatorial running mate unsuspectingly charged that Wilder might be the most liberal candidate ever to seek statewide office in Virginia. "Liberal," Wilder and Goldman quickly suggested, was nothing more than a code word for "black." Chichester promptly dropped the liberal label. The episode was another example of Wilder's skillful use of race.

Late in the campaign, Chichester succumbed to pressure to use ads featuring the rowhouse and the Supreme Court reprimand, but for most of the campaign he resisted the urgings of numerous advisers to engage in negative campaigning. On election day, voters responded by giving Wilder almost 52 percent of the vote. An estimated 44 percent of the whites who voted backed him, a remarkable showing paralleling support for white Democrats in close elections.

Still, even as he made history in November 1985, there were many who thought that Wilder's star had reached its zenith. Mary Sue Terry had won 61 percent of the vote in her race for attorney general, making her in some quarters the odds-on favorite to be the Democratic nominee for governor in 1989. And besides, it was one thing for a black candidate to be elected lieutenant governor—a largely ceremonial post. To become chief executive in a state that frequently declared there was "no higher honor" than to be its governor, however, was another matter indeed.

State senator Bobby Scott didn't see it that way. The second black member of the Virginia Senate since Reconstruction, Scott was a Harvard-educated lawyer representing a majority-white legislative district. As joyous Democrats celebrated an election-night sweep at the John Marshall Hotel, he was already looking ahead. Eyeing Terry and Wilder, both flush with victory, standing a few feet apart near the podium, he observed: "The race for governor just began."

3

LAYING THE GROUNDWORK

In January 1988, when Doug Wilder invited more than a thousand of his friends to a birthday fund-raising bash, his unofficial campaign for the 1989 nomination for governor still looked like a long shot. His first year as lieutenant governor had been punctuated by well-publicized breaks with former governor Robb and incumbent Democratic governor Gerald Baliles, leaving a bitter taste in the mouths of crucial party fundraisers. His acceptance of in-state speaking fees—a practice halted only in the wake of public outrage—seemed solid grist for the GOP issue mill. And Attorney General Terry, who had outpolled both Baliles and Wilder in her statewide debut in 1985, appeared positioned to inherit the Baliles-Robb mantle in a showdown with Wilder.

Still, the memory of the 1982 Pickett affair hung over the quiet deliberations of Democrats as they looked toward 1989. The expected Wilder-Terry match was not a prospect to warm the hearts of the party faithful. If Wilder won, the moderate-conservative voters whose return to Democratic ranks had fueled the successes of the 1980s might well be disaffected by the defeat of Terry, a favorite of the group. And if Wilder lost, the fear of another 1982—massive defections by alienated black voters —might preclude any hope of victory in the fall.

Against that backdrop, Wilder entered 1988 with his campaign treasury open and his mouth shut. Dozens of Democrats were still shaking their heads in disbelief at Wilder's public tiffs with Robb and Baliles, the two Democratic officials many thought were most crucial to his continued success. Robb, the son-in-law of former president Lyndon Johnson, was viewed by many as the state's most popular politician and a man who might one day be of presidential caliber. Blessed with telegenic looks and an earnest nature, he had salvaged the state Democratic party by regaining the statehouse in the 1981 elections after a twelve-year Democratic drought. He devoted his 1982–1986 term to making much-needed improvements in education, and to proving that a Democrat could govern without raising taxes. Leaving office, he set about trying to prod the national Democratic party away from liberalism. Baliles was Robb's thoughtful and well-regarded, if somewhat bland, successor. A political moderate, he was a Richmond attorney who came up through the legislative ranks, won the office of attorney general on Robb's coattails in 1981, and scored an impressive victory in the 1985 race for governor. A voracious reader and a man with a passion for ideas, Baliles surprised even supporters when he took office calling for a multi-billion-dollar transportation program that had gone unmentioned in his campaign. After pushing the plan through the Assembly, he concentrated on making Virginia part of a global economy. While Baliles was plagued with political problems during 1989, his last year in office, midway in his administration he was being compared to the early Harry Byrd, who was an activist governor.

Wilder's troubles with Robb dated in a sense to the 1982 episode involving Pickett, but they were recharged during Wilder's 1985 campaign for lieutenant governor. In sum, Wilder felt Robb did not do enough to help him, particularly in the early stages of that campaign. For his part, Robb felt Wilder was far too unappreciative of what he did do. One episode illustrated the 180-degree difference with which two men could view the same events. At a December 1984 press conference Robb admonished those carping about the dangers of nominating both a black man and a white woman in the 1985 elections to come up with alternatives, or quit griping. He urged potential challengers not to be intimidated by Wilder's color or Terry's sex, and said he'd stand behind any challengers dismissed as racist or sexist. Robb's interpretation was that the put-up-or-shut-up challenge forced the discrimination issue into the open and cleared the way for

Wilder's and Terry's nominations. Wilder's view was that Robb was virtually pleading for competition.

Throughout 1985 there were strains between the governor's office and Wilder's tight-lipped campaign, but grumbling was generally submerged. Not until the election was over did the dam break. The national media, which repeatedly credited Robb with playing a major role in Wilder's victory, drove home the final wedge. The national view was that Robb's successful tenure as governor had set the stage for a Democratic sweep in 1985. But some Wilder partisans, who saw the Democratic establishment as only one more obstacle on their candidate's way to victory, were livid that Robb was basking in Wilder's glow. A few weeks after the election, Paul Goldman went public with the complaint. Robb was getting too much credit for a victory Wilder had engineered, he said. Wilder would later insist that Goldman had acted on his own, but there was no reprimand. At least two individuals who worked closely with Wilder and Goldman during that period say Wilder knew in advance of Goldman's plans and tacitly endorsed them. Robb's inner circle privately told reporters that they were furious.

A few months later, another salvo was fired, this time by Wilder. His target was the Democratic Leadership Council (DLC), a group of influential Democrats—with Robb at the helm—who were trying to move the national party into a more centrist position. Originally formed by a group that was white, male, and mostly Southern, the council was branded the "Democratic Leisure Class" by Jesse Jackson. Throughout 1986, Wilder seemed equally skeptical.

His first remarks came in April 1986, the day after a National Press Club appearance by Robb. In a newspaper interview, Wilder criticized the Democratic Leadership Council—though not Robb by name—for trying to take credit for the outcome of Virginia's 1985 elections. To the contrary, "they had absolutely nothing to do with it," he said. "And I think that ought to be said rather abundantly." Recalling the behind-the-scenes struggle he faced against many moderate-conservative Democrats in late 1984 and early 1985, Wilder insisted that he would never have been nominated if the council's philosophy had prevailed.

"So now don't come to say that what took place in Virginia is the genesis of the kind of thing that the DLC stands for," he said. In a speech the following July, Wilder continued the drumbeat. Citing the council's goal of moving away from public perception of the Democratic party as a refuge for special-interest groups, he advised: "Some in the DLC have said that the image of the Democratic party is one of being too closely identified with blacks, women, and labor. Personally, I find that kind of talk counterproductive and only to the aid and comfort of the Republicans."

Late that fall Robb finally answered the sniping with a cannonade. He released to the press two letters he had written that left little doubt about the depth of the resentment Wilder had stirred. More damaging, the correspondence from Robb to Wilder also put one of Virginia's most popular political figures on record as challenging Wilder's management skill and basic trustworthiness. Two and a half years later, on the morning after his nomination to face Wilder in the 1989 gubernatorial election, Marshall Coleman confirmed what political strategists had known for months. Chuck Robb, he quipped, is "a man of letters," and Virginians could expect to become intimately familiar with those letters during the course of the GOP campaign.

Some of Robb's choicest lines were included in a six-page, single-spaced letter written on November 30, 1985, twelve days after Goldman's attack appeared in the press. "Friends don't treat friends like you've treated me recently," Robb wrote. "Unless you can find a way to repair the damage you and Paul Goldman did last week, there are some very large numbers of our mutual friends and supporters who just won't be there again for Doug Wilder." At another point, he questioned Wilder's failure to hire a fund-raising chief in 1985 or to "have someone at the office on a day-to-day basis implementing a game plan and at least returning phone calls. . . . We were very lucky reporters never focused on it as a measure of basic management ability in assessing your potential for governor if the need ever arose." Again, he noted: "Your campaign left many of your hardest-working and strongest supporters quite frustrated."

Robb was stunned that Wilder did not respond either to that

letter or to a couple of others written in the year after Wilder's election. Wilder, in turn, says he was shocked that the letters were ever written. He did not respond because "it takes two to argue," he adds.

In leaking to the press the November 30 letter and another dated August 20, 1986, Robb says he was seeking a confrontation and resolution with Wilder. He got what he wanted. The letters hit Virginia political circles like a high explosive. A series of newspaper stories and editorials swept the state. In December the two men held a cease-fire meeting at Robb's home in McLean. A gradual political armistice set in, but as late as mid-1989 some of Robb's closest political allies acknowledged that the personal relationship of the two men appeared to have been permanently altered by the year-long exchange. Politically, each appreciated the necessity of the other; but personally, basic trust had eroded.

Nor was the former governor of Virginia Wilder's only target in the months after he took office. The feisty lieutenant governor also managed to save some of his ammunition for Gov. Gerald Baliles. The first public break came in July when Wilder joined Republicans in criticizing Baliles's support of a policy allowing death row inmates direct contact with visiting relatives. Virginia Republican chairman Don Huffman already had resigned from the state Board of Corrections in protest of the policy when Wilder joined in the opposition. Baliles's staff complained that there was no advance warning of Wilder's decision to challenge his former running mate on a politically sensitive issue. Wilder's chief of staff, Joel Harris, replied that his boss had no obligation to clear his statements with anyone. The feud was on.

A month later Wilder began distancing himself from Baliles on a more critical issue. Taking the state by surprise, Baliles had entered office calling for a sweeping, multi-billion-dollar road-building program. He had even advocated scrapping the state's sacred pay-as-you-go philosophy, if necessary, to foot the bill. He convened a blue-ribbon commission to work out details, and scheduled a special fall session of the General Assembly to approve their work. Baliles named Wilder to be his eyes and ears on the panel.

The first inkling of Wilder's course on the matter came in August at Cumberland Gap in the Ninth District. At a Democratic breakfast, Wilder warned that the $10 billion price tag attached to the road program might be too low. An added $3 billion might be needed to fund all the projects contemplated, and if money ran short, he warned, rural communities like Cumberland Gap could lose out. Back in Richmond, Wilder was quiet as the Assembly passed the record-setting roadbuilding plan, and approved a series of taxes, including a half-penny-per-dollar hike in the sales tax, to pay for it.

Within days of adjournment, Wilder's silence ended. Appearing before the Dulles Area Board of Trade in Northern Virginia, the auto-congested region that had pressed hardest for the highway plan, Wilder dropped another bombshell. He was for new roads, Wilder said, but he did not favor increasing the sales tax to pay for them. The tax package just approved was too regressive. It fell too heavily on those least able to afford the burden, he said. He had remained silent during the debate, he suggested, only because of loyalty to the Baliles administration.

In the governor's office on the third floor of the capitol, there was outrage. Learning from the July episode, Wilder said, he had made sure to inform the governor of the speech before it was delivered. Chris Bridge, Baliles's press secretary, later said the office telephone log showed that a call had been received about 10:30 A.M., noting only that Wilder was speaking that day on transportation in Northern Virginia. The text of the speech, delivered at a noontime luncheon, reached Baliles's office about 4 P.M., well after it had been distributed to the wire services.

The events, coupled with those involving Robb, threw the moderate-conservative portion of the state's Democratic establishment into confusion. Former state delegate Edgar Bacon of Jonesville wrote a letter to the *Richmond Times-Dispatch*, noting his disappointment in Wilder and warning him about the consequences of future rifts. Others followed suit. Kent Jenkins, then political reporter for the *Virginian-Pilot* in Norfolk, summarized the events in an August 31 article. "Lt. Gov. L. Douglas Wilder, a man with a hectic international schedule, seems to save just enough time for politics to keep the Virginia Capitol in an uproar," he wrote.

Wilder's point had apparently been made, although many were confused about precisely what his point might be. With the December meeting at Robb's house in McLean, he fell virtuously silent about anything hinting at controversy between himself and the two men he hoped to succeed. For the next two years, Wilder devoted himself to winning friends, not enemies, within the party. He crisscrossed the state, making dozens of speeches and charming audiences with his wit and warmth. Typical of his determination to avoid controversy was Wilder's enigmatic statement as Virginians approached a referendum on adopting a state lottery in the fall of 1987. Pressed to take sides in the historic decision, Wilder finally issued a statement saying, "I urge the referendum."

On January 17, 1989, he also delivered an unexpected explanation of one of the earlier episodes. In a speech to the Richmond Crusade for Voters, one of the most influential black political organizations in the state, he said he rejected the sales tax for roads because of a promise he made to the Crusade during the 1985 campaign. On a political questionnaire, Wilder had pledged not to support an increase in the sales tax during his term as lieutenant governor. It was the first anyone in Baliles's inner circle had heard of that rationale.

While Wilder offered principle as the motivation behind his early actions, others suggested that he had been positioning himself as the populist, antiestablishment candidate in a nomination race against Mary Sue Terry. The strategy, which Wilder and some of those close to him denied following, had merit. Sales tax hikes have never been a popular platform for political office in Virginia. Nor was Wilder likely to get many votes out of the party's right wing in a convention battle with Terry.

MARCH 18, 1988

As the spring approached, key aides to Attorney General Terry knew that something was afoot. Indeed, a few of those closest to her had sensed throughout 1987 that Terry was being projected routinely into a race she might never make. Press secretary Bert Rohrer cautioned reporters against assuming that his boss wanted to run for governor in 1989. And Anita Rimler, Terry's longtime political aide, later said she felt subconsciously for at least a year what she refused to admit—that all the fiddling over election returns and gubernatorial campaign strategies would probably be for naught in 1989, because her boss was not going to be a candidate for governor.

Mary Sue Terry is as thoroughly Virginian a politician as any of those to grace the governor's chair in the last two decades. The oldest of three girls born to a farming-schoolteaching family, a onetime assistant prosecutor and part owner in a feed store, she is competent, dependable, and cautious to a fault. In the days when she represented rural Patrick County in the state legislature, reporters used to quip that Terry was a vintage Southside good ol' boy in skirts. To be sure, she was modern in her attitudes toward race, but when it came to taxes or law enforcement or any of a dozen other matters, she was part of the predictably cautious bloc in command at the statehouse. In her early days in the legislature, she opposed the Equal Rights Amendment and state funding of welfare abortions, switching only when she began thinking about running for statewide office.

When she started assembling her 1985 campaign for attorney general, Terry set about courting the monied establishment that had financed Republican victories in the 1970s and had been wooed back partially to the Democrats by Robb in 1981. Quietly, without fanfare, she assembled a list of supporters so broadly based and a campaign treasury so hefty that, in retrospect, her Republican opponent was as good as eliminated before the race began. On election day, while Wilder was winning 52 percent of the vote and Baliles was getting 55 percent, Terry was polling a landslide 61 percent victory. Terry remained to the right of many of the Democratic activists who participate in nominating conventions. But there was every reason to believe she would be a difficult, and perhaps unbeatable opponent for Wilder in 1989.

If Mary Sue Terry had shown a magic touch during her race for attorney general, however, she seemed dogged by trouble throughout her first year in office. Within weeks of the inauguration, a top assistant gave an opinion on legislative conflict of interest that threatened to disrupt the entire 1986 legislative session. In effect, he suggested that no banker could ethically vote on legislation influencing banks, no public school teacher could vote on bills affecting public education, and no lawyer could act on proposals that related to the practice of law. For several days legislative activity was stymied. Worse, from Terry's perspective, it quickly became clear that she had been as surprised by her assistant's comments as anyone. Editorial writers wanted to know who was running the ship. As the months passed, Terry was also plagued by personal difficulties: a back ailment, her mother's death, even a speeding ticket that fired numerous jokes.

By 1987 Terry finally seemed to have gained her footing, and the year ran more smoothly. She won some politically important battles against the insurance industry, fought political extremist Lyndon LaRouche in court, and launched an antidrug program that would eventually receive national recognition. Trusted aides began to sense that Terry was carving a niche she would not be satisfied to leave in two years. "She isn't the type of person to go in and do a coat of paint and leave," said Rimler. Terry's shaky start as attorney general also raised questions about whether she was ready to assume the helm of state government. And there was the matter of Wilder. How much, her advisers had to ask themselves, would a nomination be worth if blacks and liberals went away mad?

On March 18, with the gubernatorial election still nineteen months away, Terry summoned reporters to the capitol for a press conference. Members of her staff blinked back tears as they watched her announce that she would seek a second term as attorney general. Earlier she had telephoned Wilder, who was in his Richmond office getting ready to drive to Norfolk to tape a television program. "I can't say Doug expressed any profound disappointment," quipped Terry when asked his reaction to what she had to say.

The seemingly impossible had happened. Doug Wilder had become the undisputed front-runner for the Democratic nomination for governor of Virginia.

APRIL 1988

As Wilder aides rejoiced, members of the party's moderate-conservative wing began scrambling for an alternative. Early speculation focused on two people—Fourth District representative Norman Sisisky, a folksy beer and soft drink bottler who had been elevated from the legislature to Congress a few years earlier, and Norfolk mayor Joseph L. Leafe, a respected moderate little known outside his home region. State senator Danny Bird of Wytheville had already announced that he was seeking the spot, but throughout his year-long bid Bird never achieved credibility as a candidate. Even after he spent twelve days crisscrossing the state by foot, Bird remained essentially an unknown curiosity. He was personally likeable, but had never taken a leadership role in the senate and had never indicated any particular ambition for higher office. When he withdrew from the contest two days before Wilder's formal announcement, the perception was that a minor irritant, not an obstacle, had been removed. Either Sisisky or Leafe, however, was potentially more dangerous.

Norman Sisisky never cracked the inner circle of legislative might in the years he spent representing Petersburg and several surrounding counties in the General Assembly, but he had good relations with the men who ran the legislature, and the money he had made as a businessman impressed them. When he reclaimed the congressional seat in the Fourth District—the most naturally Democratic district in the state—for the party, their gratitude grew. Moreover, in Washington, Sisisky's natural ease with people and with power seemed to flourish. A noted raconteur, he took quickly to the hobnobbing and intrigue that motivate life in Washington. Still, it was south of the Potomac that Sisisky's political roots, and no small portion of his ambition, lay. Throughout 1986 and 1987, he quietly let it be known that he could be counted among those Virginians who viewed the governor's office as the pinnacle of political success.

Joe Leafe was taking a more systematic approach to running for statewide office. An attorney and former legislator noted for a thoughtful, low-key approach to politics, Leafe began thinking about a bid in 1987. Although he had not settled on which office he might seek, Leafe scheduled appointments with Robb and Baliles to discuss the possibilities. Both men immediately began analyzing his prospects in terms of the gubernatorial race. Leafe also began gathering a support team, including many of the traditional Democratic financiers in south Hampton Roads as well as such political activists as Norfolk treasurer Joe Fitzpatrick, former delegate Robert Washington, and school board chairman Tommy Johnson. That fall and winter, he scheduled meet-and-greet activities around the state.

By the spring of 1988, Leafe was convinced that he could very quickly raise $500,000 to $1,000,000 for a gubernatorial bid. He set a midsummer deadline for deciding whether to run. Leafe had been heartened by Mary Sue Terry's decision to abandon the contest, and felt confident that moderate-conservatives would be looking for a candidate of their political stripe. It was not until later that Leafe began to sense the dilemma that Terry's departure had actually created. Because of it, instead of looking like a man interested in running for governor, Leafe was beginning to look like a man interested in stopping Doug Wilder. "It became an issue of running against 'the black candidate,'" he said.

Governor Baliles's first public entree into the gubernatorial fracus came in late April when he was an ocean away from Virginia, traveling in Israel. Baliles and those close to him knew that back home some party workers were intent on finding an alternative to Wilder. Talk could be heard of a behind-the-scenes quest for a Great White Hope, someone to save the party from the certain ruin of running a black candidate. On the last night of the gubernatorial visit, when the topic of state politics came up at a dinner at the Jerusalem Hilton Hotel, Delegate Robert Ball, a Richmond-area hotel operator traveling with Baliles, was quick to cite Wilder's liabilities. His fellow Richmonder's chances of being elected governor of Virginia were slim and none, he suggested bluntly. As the conversation continued around the table, Baliles surprised aides by jumping in. Quietly but distinctly, Baliles let it be known that he felt confident Wilder could be elected Virginia's next governor.

Not surprisingly, word of the comments beat Baliles back to the United States. A more public endorsement would follow a few days later.

MAY 1988

May 10 was election day in Norfolk, and Joe Leafe, as expected, won another term as mayor. In Leafe's mind, the pieces were falling into place for a statewide bid. Clearly, there would be obstacles, but they did not seem insurmountable. One of the chief problems was the nagging fear that a race against Wilder might damage the good relations he had built over the years with Norfolk's black voters. But Leafe had talked with local black leaders about his deliberations, and he had convinced himself that Wilder did not have as fanatical a following as someone like Jesse Jackson. The day after his reelection, Leafe left on a six-day trip to Las Vegas, combining work and pleasure. Before departing, his secretary scheduled a meeting a few weeks down the road with Baliles. Leafe expected to have the final word on his political plans by then.

Before the mayor was back from Nevada, however, Baliles helped make Leafe's decision for him. As Gordon Morse, Baliles's chief speechwriter, began drafting a commencement address for May 15 ceremonies at predominantly black Norfolk State University, it occurred to him that the setting might be perfect for sending a signal about Wilder. Morse, a former newspaper editorial writer and director of Common Cause of Virginia, looked favorably on Wilder's candidacy, and he knew that the governor did as well, despite their disagreements on policy questions. Two days before the speech, Morse caught Baliles's attention as they were leaving a meeting in the governor's conference room.

"Why don't we do a little hit for Doug and Jesse?" Morse asked.

"Do it. Let me see it," Baliles replied without hesitating.

Morse went to work at his typewriter. On Sunday afternoon, as Norfolk State's graduating seniors and their families crowded into the Scope coliseum, few knew that the words they were hearing were intended for a much larger audience.

"Four years ago in 1984, Jesse Jackson ran for president of the United States, and he was humored and tolerated because he was a leader of black America. In 1988, Jesse Jackson is running for president of the United States, and he is honored and respected in America, period," Baliles began.

"Three years ago, Doug Wilder ran for lieutenant governor of Virginia. Many told him he could not win. He politely ignored them. He drew his resources and took his case to the voters. He relentlessly debated the issues. He talked not of the past, but of the future. And, he won," Baliles continued.

"Now, Doug Wilder has his sights on a new office—a higher office—an office with which I have some familiarity. Again, some will tell him he cannot win. Again, he will politely ignore them. Again, Doug Wilder will draw together his resources and take his case to the voters. Again, he will address the future. And, again he will have a chance to make history in Virginia.

"Perhaps more to the point, Virginia will have the chance to make history, once again demonstrating that enduring values have a home in Virginia—but also establishing that Virginia does not have the time to waste on the old fears, the old habits, and the old divisions."

The lines consumed one page of a six-page speech. They were Baliles's most potent message.

Press secretary Chris Bridge spent the next few weeks haggling with reporters over whether the words constituted an outright endorsement. Bridge said no, but at least two sets of ears, Leafe's and Sisisky's, heard the message differently. "I don't have to interpret it," said Leafe of Baliles's intent. "I think everybody else has interpreted it for me."

To Gordon Morse, the rationale for Baliles's words was obvious. "We needed to send a signal that we needed to rally around this man, that there wasn't going to be a Great White Hope as an alternative to Wilder," he said a year later. Baliles, he added, was simply stating the obvious—that Wilder was lieutenant governor, that no one else of his statewide stature was talking about running. "The only way you come to the conclusion that you need someone else is that you decide Wilder can't win because he's black, and that was the thinking we were determined to cut off," Morse said.

As Wilder partisans began calculating their increasingly apparent lock on the nomination, Leafe also confronted the emerging reality. His reasons for running had nothing to do with Wilder's color, Leafe insisted, but he was increasingly convinced that the message would be ignored. "I don't believe anyone could have gotten in that race and not been damaged longterm as the 'Stop Wilder' candidate," Leafe said later. "Even if you get in the race and lose, you're tagged long-term as creating the damage if he loses in November."

As Democratic delegates gathered in Norfolk in June 1988 to nominate Chuck Robb for the U.S. Senate, the last obstacles to Wilder's nomination a year away were evaporating. If some party activists worried about Wilder's electability and his erratic dealings with Robb and Baliles, a growing number argued that his charisma and willingness to take risks might appeal to a changing state. Wilder, too, sensed the shift and applauded its direction. Seated a few days before the convention at an office desk already adorned with a Wilder-for-governor mug, the unannounced candidate shared his delight in Baliles's actions and in the growing acceptance of his candidacy. Baliles's Norfolk State speech was "historical in my judgment," he noted. And he added softly, the reception as he traveled the state "is really uplifting. . . . You don't feel the hysteria that was associated with [me] four years ago. It's a tribute to the people of Virginia who are prepared to move."

As delegates to the Democratic presidential nominating convention were debating nuclear weapons policy on the floor of Atlanta's Omni on the afternoon of July 19, Doug Wilder was elsewhere, sampling salmon and other delectables at a reception for the Alaska delegation. Some saw the episode as a metaphor for Wilder's overall approach to politics in the summer of 1988. He was, they said, willing to go any distance to avoid controversy and to court potential donors. Wilder, who was not a convention delegate but could have been for the asking, steered a wide berth around nominating and platform fights. During the four-day convention, he did not meet with Jesse Jackson. He did not endorse Jackson's bid for president. He did not even support Jackson's relatively innocuous platform proposals. "He's a scared man. He wants to be governor more than he wants to be humane," fumed Mary Cox, a Jackson organizer from Virginia.

Unquestionably Wilder wanted to be governor, and he left Atlanta bolstered in the confidence that he would be. Based on pledges "from Mississippi to Texas to Florida, Kentucky and Alabama—from all sections, all sectors, and all stripes of our party," the amount of money he could raise for the race was unlimited, Wilder proclaimed. "What do you need? That would be what we can raise."

Back in Virginia, the initial structure for Wilder's gubernatorial bid was taking shape. Months earlier Wilder had met with David Doak, a nationally prominent media consultant who worked for Baliles in 1985 and Robb in 1981. The pair had reached an informal understanding that Doak would make it three in a row in consulting in Virginia governor's races. In early July a "Friends of Doug Wilder" committee set up shop in a two-room office about ten blocks from the capitol. And a small group of advisers began holding strategy sessions. Among the dozen or so people who attended several meetings through the spring, summer, and fall were Doak; Goldman; Joel Harris, Wilder's top aide; Robert Gray, a prominent black attorney and partner in one of Richmond's leading law firms; Bobby Watson, one of the state's best-known Democratic operatives; Marian Tucker, aide to house majority leader Tom Moss; Muriel "Moo" Murray, a longtime party activist and executive director of the state agency that guarantees student loans; and Rhett Walker, the first "Virginians for Wilder" employee.

Much of the attention of the group, which met until early 1989, focused on fund-raising. The belief that Wilder could raise a great deal of money out of state was widespread. In-state giving, however, was less certain. Fund-raising eventually proved to be one of Wilder's strengths, but throughout 1988 "everybody thought that would be his Achilles' heel," recalls Doak. Still, by fall there were some positive signs. Paul Edwards, vice-president of public affairs for Virginia Power, the state's largest power company, and Charles Davis, vice-president of state relations for the giant CSX Corporation, were only two of several corporate representatives who had approached the Wilder campaign to indicate support. Their overtures did not preclude helping a Republican candidate as well. But it was clear that some major players in Virginia's corporate structure were not threatened by Wilder and, to the contrary, did not want to be seen as working to stop a black gubernatorial candidate. "I personally was very concerned that we never be perceived as part of any wide business cabal against Doug Wilder. It would be bad for the state," recalls Edwards, who once worked as press secretary to Republican governor John N. Dalton, who served from 1978 to 1982.

Lee Middleditch, a Charlottesville lawyer and president of the state Chamber of Commerce, had similar feelings. Middleditch was unaligned with a political party, but had cochaired Virginians for Dalton a decade earlier and usually voted Republican in national elections. Still, he was intrigued by the historic possibilities of Wilder's candidacy. Middleditch set up a September meeting with Wilder, and after clearing his decision with the board of the state chamber, openly endorsed Wilder. "I have felt that Jackie Robinson did more for integration in the United States than all the court-ordered programs," he says, explaining his decision. "This was an opportunity to show the nation what a state could do with a governor who is black."

Not everyone wanted to know. Key members of the Baliles-Robb fund-raising circle still thought Wilder was too unpredictable to be trusted. As November arrived, their complaints intensified. Terry staffers were besieged with requests for their boss to reconsider running for governor, and complaints cropped up anonymously in the press. "At this point, I just don't see it for Doug. . . . I think he's going to have a tough time winning," said a prominent Northern Virginia businessman aligned with Robb and Baliles. "I'm a businessman and a constituent before I'm a Democrat," echoed a Richmonder who held a key fund-raising job for Baliles. "And I'm not sure I want him [Wilder] running my state."

The sights of those looking for alternatives turned to the Republican party.

4

THE REPUBLICANS BATTLE IT OUT

DECEMBER 3, 1988

Until Byrd Organization conservatives began switching their allegiance from the Democratic to the Republican party in the early 1970s, the GOP had not been a force in Virginia since post-Reconstruction days. But in the 1970s, as part of the breakup of one-party Democratic rule in the South, that changed. The fusion of conservative ex-Democrats and right-wing Republicans produced a state party that, for a while, was the dominant force in statewide Virginia politics. In 1981, the governor, attorney general, one U.S. senator, and nine congressmen out of ten were Republicans.

By no means, however, did the GOP's sovereignty approach that of the old Organization in its heyday. Democrats retained control of the state legislature and most local offices, and they continued to contest strongly in each statewide election. Finally in late 1981 under the leadership of Chuck Robb, they succeeded in winning back the state's three highest offices. As had been true of the Democrats in the 1960s and 1970s, the Republican party in Virginia had become vulnerable to factional and ideological rifts.

When the Democrats had enjoyed one-party rule, the party primary had been the state's real election; the general election in November was only a formality. So long as state election laws had restricted voting to a very small percentage of the citizenry, the dominant Byrd Organization was immune to having divisiveness from primary contests spill over into the general election. But the end of legal segregation and the curtailment of the power of thinly populated rural counties because of the U.S. Supreme Court's one-man, one-vote ruling helped to produce a greatly expanded electorate. The November general election that pitted Republican versus Democratic candidates became the key to winning office.

Until the 1989 election, the Virginia Republican party had chosen its statewide candidates in state conventions rather than primaries. Democrats had also switched to conventions in 1981 after their disastrous showings in statewide elections during the 1970s. By condensing the audience and reducing public squabbling, the parties hoped to enter general elections with a minimum of damage to their candidates from the nominating process. By the late 1980s, however, the consensus on the part of the GOP leadership that rival candidacies should be adjudicated within a nominating convention was breaking down. The maneuvering in some past conventions had proven so cutthroat that rival factions had failed to coalesce around the winner in the general election. And, politically, in the race for governor several strong candidates were vying for the chance to challenge Douglas Wilder. Each camp was evaluating potential nominating procedures in light of what would best aid their candidate.

So, for the first time in forty years, the distinct possibility existed that members of the state GOP central committee, scheduled to meet on December 3, 1988, would opt for a primary. A primary might open up the nominating process to thousands of newcomers and eliminate much behind-the-scenes backstabbing. But such a move could also result in far more public exposure of rifts and weaknesses, the spilling over of the impact of negative campaigning into the general election, and the stirring of rivalries and passions too incendiary to be put aside once the primary was over.

Even before state Republicans began gathering at the sprawling Ingleside Inn outside Staunton in western Virginia, the word went out. The straw vote on the party's four candidates for governor, scheduled for Saturday night, was canceled. Emotions simply were running too high. Some believed the whole gubernatorial election might turn on the decision of whether to nominate an opponent to Doug Wilder by convention or by statewide primary. Party elders were afraid any misstep, even bickering over a straw poll, might ignite an already explosive situation.

To many on the seventy-seven-member Virginia GOP governing body, the seemingly technical decision about how to pick a candidate had more to do with politics than philosophy. Republicans had nominated a gubernatorial candidate via a statewide primary only once, forty years earlier. The results of that 1949 experiment were hardly a persuasive reason for change. In fact, most Republican voters wound up deserting the party that year and aiding an embattled Byrd Organization candidate in the Democratic primary. Prior to the late 1960s, Republican opposition in most statewide contests was so weak that victory in the Democratic primary was tantamount to election. The 1949 Byrd candidate for governor, John S. Battle, was under fierce assault in the primary from anti-Organization Democrats when Major Henry A. Wise, a Robert Taft Republican and former national committeeman, urged Republicans into the Democratic fray. With only one candidate in their own gubernatorial primary and no party registration requirements to stop them, Republicans followed Wise's recommendation en masse. Fewer than nine thousand people voted in the Republican primary, and Francis Pickens Miller—who lost to Battle in the Democratic primary by twenty-four thousand votes—believed for the rest of his life that the GOP had denied him the Democratic nomination.

It was clear from the outset that the 1989 intraparty battle was of a different stripe. Many expected that the Republican nominee would assume the same mantle worn by the 1949 Democratic primary winner: shoo-in for governor. Party members gathering at Ingleside confronted a four-candidate field. The generally acknowledged favorite of party activists was Marshall Coleman. A tall, gaunt former attorney general with a quick intellect and a tart tongue, Coleman was not yet fifty, but he had been running for governor for almost as long as anyone could remember.

A native of Waynesboro, a blue-collar town just over the Blue Ridge Mountains from Charlottesville, Coleman was not long out of the University of Virginia law school in 1972 when he was elected to the General Assembly from Staunton. A few miles from his childhood home, Staunton is a Republican stronghold, best known as the birthplace of former president Woodrow Wilson. Coleman arrived in Richmond as a reform-minded Republican, eager to do battle with the remnants of the Byrd Organization. Witty and articulate, he was an activist on matters ranging from lobbying to judicial reform, and was quickly named "the most effective young legislator" by a group of capitol reporters. In 1977 he gambled on a race against Democrat Ed Lane and, after highlighting Lane's segregationist past, wound up at thirty-five as the youngest attorney general in Virginia history.

Pitted against Robb four years later in the 1981 governor's race, Coleman was forced to reposition himself philosophically. Robb's tie by marriage to Lyndon Johnson gave him credibility with blacks and other members of the Democratic left, while his cautiousness appealed to moderates and some conservatives. Seeing that he could not siphon off liberal votes from Robb, as he had done with Lane, Coleman decided to move further to the right. He began courting some of the members of the former Byrd Organization that his earlier campaign had so infuriated. The anything-to-win seesaw between progressivism and conservatism hurt him, factoring into defeats that year and again in 1985, when he sought the party's nomination for lieutenant governor. But Coleman, who by 1989 had established himself as a wealthy Northern Virginia lawyer, had been undeterred by the political losses. Through a discouraging decade for the state GOP, he had remained the party's vigilant intellectual voice. While others shied from crossing Democrat governors, Coleman rarely missed a beat in exploiting their mistakes or casting their successes in the least favorable light. For years he had also adopted the principle that wherever two or three Republicans were gathered together, there were two or three votes worth pursuing. As 1989 approached, local precinct leaders and county chairs were mindful of his loyalty.

Coleman, who preferred to stake his future on their gratitude, rather than the whims of a less forgiving public, was pressing for nomination by the traditional convention route. Paul Trible, Jr., was leading the push for a primary. A decade earlier, he and Coleman had shared the limelight as the *wunderkinder* of Virginia politics. But the years had added scars to both men. Trible was a Pennsylvania native who had family ties to Virginia's Northern Neck, an estuary-laced region northeast of Richmond where George Washington was born and the ancestral home of the Lee family of Virginia still stands. In 1976 Trible had recently accepted a job in the area as a small-town prosecutor when the district's longtime congressman decided to retire. The Northern Neck is at the least-populous end of the First Congressional District, far from the shipbuilding and maritime centers of Hampton and Newport News where most of the votes are congregated. But Trible, undeterred by geography, launched an aggressive campaign that highlighted moderate positions and concern for women and minorities. At twenty-nine, he was elected the district's first GOP congressman of the century. Running in the wake of Watergate, he was the only Southern Republican to pick up a Democratic congressional seat that year.

Six years later, anticipating that U.S. Senator Harry F. Byrd, Jr., might retire, Trible positioned himself for a Senate race. When Byrd announced that he was relinquishing the seat held by him or his father for fifty years, Trible moved quickly. So well was the groundwork laid that when Byrd thought of revoking his decision, he could not. Too many supporters had already committed to Trible. Benefiting from the Democrats' confusion over Wilder's threats and the Pickett withdrawal, Trible narrowly defeated the eventual Democratic nominee, former lieutenant governor Richard Davis.

In the Senate, where he moved to the right in philosophy, Trible never developed legislative prowess matching his political success. The reaction to his performance as part of a 1987 Senate panel investigating U.S. arms sales to the Iranian government was particularly disappointing to supporters. After first saying that he intended to question Marine Lieutenant Colonel Oliver North aggressively about his role in the arms sale, Trible instead praised the officer. The switch occurred after North had emerged as a folk hero, and prompted one magazine correspondent to tag Trible "Senator Jello." Trible was also hampered by an air of programmed artificiality that in some circles had earned him the nickname "Plastic Paul."

When Trible announced on statewide television in the fall of 1987 that he would not run for a second Senate term, some Republicans were more than shocked—they were furious. And when word leaked out almost immediately that Trible was eyeing a race for governor instead, the incredulity mounted. Dennis Peterson, a top Coleman aide, declared that Trible's game plan was "the approach a weasel would have to running for governor." Few others were as severe in public. But even as some prominent party leaders rallied around Trible, pronouncing him the most electable candidate for governor, his name continued to produce icy silence and even occasional boos at party enclaves. Worried that the resentment would be magnified in a convention, Trible opted to cast his lot with the larger public in a primary.

Eighth District U.S. Representative Stan Parris joined him. Popular in his home district just south of Washington, D.C., yet little known outside Northern Virginia, Parris knew he would likely be swamped by Coleman and Trible in a convention. A primary seemed more promising. An Illinois native whose father went broke during the Depression and died of a heart attack when the future congressman was fourteen, Parris had developed a scrappy, swashbuckling approach to life. He was a pilot and war hero in Korea, and at fifty-nine still flew an open-cockpit biplane. After a twenty-five-year political career, including posts at the local and state level, plus eleven years in Congress, Parris was perhaps best known for his frequent criticisms of government in the District of Columbia and his sparring with Washington mayor Marion Barry.

Years of investing in his region's lucrative real estate market and operating a Lincoln-Mercury automobile dealership in Woodbridge had also made Parris a wealthy man. That money, coupled with the bank accounts of a friendly circle of developers and investors, could finance a high-profile media campaign in a statewide primary, he believed. With luck, Parris might emerge as the seasoned alternative to two men who some voters felt they knew all too well. While opponents were arguing the relative philosophical merits of a convention or a primary, Parris was forthright. "I'm too old and dumb not to tell the truth," he said, seizing on the candor he hoped to make his campaign trademark. "I supported the primary because I believe it dramatically improves my chances."

The fourth Republican candidate was state representative Raymond "Andy" Guest of Front Royal. A wealthy farmer and investor, Guest proved as immaterial in the convention-primary debate as he would eventually be in the election. Guest, whose bid ended quietly four months later, did not take sides. In retrospect, Guest did have one quality that might have dramatically altered the general election campaign. He was the only GOP candidate who was pro-choice on abortion.

As delegates began arriving at Ingleside, the politicking was as heavy as the fog that often cloaks nearby Afton Mountain. At Friday night's executive committee meeting, U.S. Senator John Warner gave an inkling of the tension, as well as a brief respite from it. Warner is a former secretary of the navy whose divorce from his first wife, Catherine Mellon, left him a wealthy man, and whose second marriage to actress Elizabeth Taylor made him an instant celebrity when he first ran for the Senate in 1978.

Initially dismissed as a dilettante by some, Warner had by 1989 long since shed both the image and his marriage to Taylor. He had proven to be a diligent senator, and had emerged as a leading Republican voice on the Armed Services Committee. He had also taken a limited role in party affairs, and typically, was steering clear of the internecine battling over the Virginia gubernatorial nomination. So Warner was surprised when, a few days before the Ingleside meeting, the Trible camp began mailing out copies of complimentary remarks about the junior senator inserted by Warner in the *Congressional Record*. At the executive committee meeting, Warner sounded gruff and grandfatherly as he turned to Trible's campaign manager and admonished: "Judy Peachee, if you send out anything else with my name on it, I'm going to drop kick your butt over the Blue Ridge Mountains." There was a moment of stunned silence before laughter erupted in the room.

By Saturday night, the rumor mill was churning. Trible and

Parris operatives compared notes in corners of the bar, while Coleman supporters were quietly passing the word, "We've got it." Wandering Republicans found Brunswick stew and apple cider in Trible's hospitality suite, and gift bags filled with date books, rulers, and maps of Virginia in Parris's. For central committee members, Parris offered rows of neatly wrapped white boxes, labeled in calligraphy and filled with china paper-clip holders. Coleman distributed a twenty-five-page position paper, "Agenda for the 90s," detailing dozens of positions at a time when the competition had scarcely mentioned issues.

Sunday morning, Coleman forces were predicting a one-or two-vote victory. "Close, but we win," ventured Betsy Davis, Coleman's finance director, as she watched committee members filing into a meeting room for the vote. Weldon Tuck, Trible's convivial organizational manager and a distant relative of a former Byrd Organization governor, William Tuck, would prove a more accurate counter. Over two weeks before the Ingleside conclave, Tuck told intimates that the Parris-Trible forces would muster forty-four votes. The remark later seemed prescient.

As the Sunday debate began, politics were on most minds, but arguments focused instead on the merits and liabilities of primaries and conventions. Activists opposed to switching from a convention recalled the fractious Democratic primaries in 1969 and 1977, when wounded Democratic nominees went on to lose to fresh, unscathed Republican candidates. Largely because of those results, Virginia Democrats had switched to nominating by convention in 1981. They had won every contest for state office since. "Which is better—for a candidate to spend $1 million next June comparing himself to other Republicans, or to spend the same $1 million in November, comparing himself to Doug Wilder?" asked party treasurer William Hurd, a Coleman backer.

But supporters of a primary argued that the open balloting would attract large numbers of new voters to the Republican party. And they talked about the bitterness left by complex convention rules and the inevitable attempts to manipulate them. Virginia's Fifth District, stretching along the North Carolina border, recently had undergone just such a contest in a U.S. House race. Republicans had left their district convention so divided that wounds were still not healed by the election date, and a Democrat won. The most emotional appeal of the morning came from Virginia Hall, a committee member from Danville who lived through that race. "People are turned off by the mechanisms which blunt the voices of hard-working Republicans," she said. "How do you go back to a hard-working person who was cut out of the system and ask them for support again?"

When the ballots were collected, a three-person committee was sent to count them. As the trio reentered the room, the first thing state party operative Mike Salster noticed was a frown creasing the brow of Dave Johnson, a party vice-chairman who favored a convention. "We've got ourselves a primary," concluded Salster. The vote was forty-three to thirty-three. Tuck's mid-November prediction had been one vote off the mark.

Trible forces, believing they had as good as nominated their man, wasted no time celebrating. "Today was Marshall Coleman's last hurrah," proclaimed Bob Weed, a Trible strategist who had worked furiously for the primary. But Coleman, ever oblivious to others' predictions of his doom, was shifting gears without slowing his pace. Within moments, the victorious Trible-Parris alliance had evolved into a Coleman-Parris union between two underdogs taking on a newly emerged front-runner, Trible. Immediately after the vote, a key Coleman backer, putting Plan B into action, called for the candidates to make joint debate appearances in each of Virginia's ten congressional districts. A weary central committee agreed unanimously. In securing the primary rather than convention vote, Trible had won a round, but Coleman and Parris were far from ready to concede the match.

DECEMBER 15, 1988

As the campaign's first financial reporting deadline approached, Douglas Wilder moved into action. On the Democratic front, party critics were grumbling about his alleged inability to raise money, and the report, due January 15, would indicate whether they were correct. After months of what some saw as a lackadaisical approach to collections, Wilder commissioned a telephone solicitation firm to contact middle-class blacks nationwide for funds. He scheduled his first major fund-raising event, the affair at the home of Richmond stockbroker Buford Scott. And he began pressing for checks from those who'd indicated support.

In an interview, Wilder also ridiculed the notion that his fledgling campaign was in disarray. The lieutenant governor noted that he'd "already obtained the services" of David Doak (a claim which later proved inaccurate), and had hired the Washington polling firm of Donilon and Petts. "I have people who will be, in the event I announce, moving into positions of campaign manager on a day-to-day basis," he added. Shaking his head in mock amazement, he added: "I find it the most amusing scenario that I've not even announced, and the campaign is dead."

A month later, Wilder proved that his organization was very much alive. He reported donations of almost $850,000, well above the $500,000 threshold that Democratic moneymen had set as an arbitrary indicator of success. To be sure, he had collected close to half of the money in the forty-five days before the report was due. The sum was boosted by an eleventh-hour, $100,000 check from Bahman Batmanghelidj, an Iranian-born Fairfax County developer. And the numbers looked better because of Atty. Gen. Mary Sue Terry's deliberate decision to keep her finance totals below Wilder's. But once again, acting in his own time and his own way, Wilder had proven the political experts wrong.

JANUARY 9, 1989

At Marshall Coleman's headquarters, the new year's first poll scarcely brought tidings of joy. Boyd Marcus, a balding, bespectacled consultant who had run president-elect George Bush's Virginia campaign with a steady hand, surveyed the tally soberly.

Bush had coasted to victory in Virginia, but the campaign Marcus had just been hired to manage was going to be sledding uphill all the way. In a head-to-head matchup among Republican voters, according to the Arthur J. Finkelstein polling firm, Trible pulled 44 percent support. Coleman had 15 percent; Parris trailed with 10 percent.

Benchmark polls recently delivered to the Parris and Trible campaigns looked even grimmer for Coleman. V. Lance Tarrance & Associates, Parris's pollster, in late December showed Trible capturing 50 percent of a sample of eight hundred GOP voters. Coleman had 16 percent, Parris 11. Meanwhile, Texas pollster David Hill was bolstering Trible's morale with a December poll showing him favored by 39 points ahead of Coleman and 44 over Parris.

If the early results seemed devastating to Coleman, the Finkelstein firm was trained to detect a silver lining. Based in Irvington, New York, the company is known for fiercely competitive work for conservatives, including North Carolina senator Jesse Helms. No stranger to long odds, Finkelstein was widely considered to have been the mastermind behind Sen. Alfonse M. D'Amato's upset victory over four-term incumbent Jacob K. Javits in the 1980 New York state Republican primary. Finkelstein detected voter unease over Javits's advancing age, seventy-six, and D'Amato rode that weakness to victory.

With the GOP primary election still six months away, Finkelstein's consultant to the Coleman campaign, John McLaughlin, saw three reasons for optimism. First, the firm did not detect any deep commitment to Trible among voters. The former senator seemed to be leading largely because his name was familiar. Second, although statewide totals showed Coleman and Parris fairly close overall, regional breakdowns revealed that Coleman was actually a dominant second choice. Parris's 10 percent showing statewide was due almost exclusively to his strength in Northern Virginia, where he led even Trible. In the Richmond area, Parris was favored by only 4 percent of voters, and he did worse in Tidewater and western Virginia. And third, Coleman's name identification was still down. About 28 percent of those polled said they'd never heard of Coleman, suggesting that a large segment of GOP voters had an open mind on his candidacy.

The formula for success would be a freewheeling, aggressive campaign, one that highlighted Trible's pale image and reinforced mounting doubts about the former senator's toughness and strength of character. For Marshall Coleman, laying out that strategy was like inviting a duck to water. Through an eighteen-year political career, Coleman had established a reputation for being fiercely competitive. Privately he was witty and amiable, but almost every former political opponent described him as a vicious campaigner.

JANUARY 11, 1989

As Lt. Gov. Doug Wilder gaveled the Virginia Senate into order for its 1989 session the thoughts of many of those present focused on the governor's suite and Gerald Baliles's soon-to-be-delivered opening day address. Already Wilder had announced that he intended to press his longstanding fight to remove the sales tax on over-the-counter medicines. A favorable nod from the governor was probably essential if the proposal was to enjoy any happier fate than in the seventeen years since Wilder had first proposed the idea to a skeptical Assembly.

This winter, however, more was at stake than $30 million in tax relief for Virginia citizens. There was also the matter of Wilder's political reputation. Democrats stood ready to nominate him for governor, but questions persisted about his ability to persuade Baliles or the Assembly's Democratic majority on policy. Sensing Wilder's vulnerability, Republicans were poised to leap on the sales tax question as a test of his legislative clout.

Before the day was out, Baliles had sealed the fate of Wilder's pet project once again. Even though Virginia was armed with a record $500 million surplus, Baliles, who privately viewed the drug tax removal as a token gesture, at best, could find no room in the budget for his former ticket mate's idea. Baliles tried to soften the blow by describing his proposal for a one-time windfall tax credit of $35 for each taxpayer as relief from the sales tax on food and nonprescription drugs. In a press announcement the next day, Wilder gamely referred to the refund as the governor's "food and nonprescription drug sales tax credit proposal." Few listeners were persuaded. And when the senate refused to lift the drug tax three weeks later on an eighteen to twenty-one vote, with prominent Democrats hammering shut the coffin, Wilder's embarrassment was complete.

A mid-January appearance before a dinner meeting of statehouse reporters—billed as the opening of the governor's race—had a brighter outcome for the lieutenant governor. With Trible off on a skiing vacation in Utah, the spotlight focused on Coleman and Wilder. Stan Parris, Andy Guest, and Danny Bird—who would drop his bid for the Democratic nomination a few weeks later—were little more than a sideshow to the main event. Coleman was in fine form, jabbing at his opponents with pointed wit. "Paul didn't have to go all the way to Utah," he chided. "We've got a long downhill slide waiting for him here in Virginia." When capital punishment was raised, he tweaked Wilder: "For him, capital punishment means receiving another letter from Chuck Robb."

Wilder fought back. The impression was that of a seasoned bulldog rebuffing a scrappy terrier. Wilder bided his time patiently, waiting to strike until Coleman labeled him a "gutsy, liberal [former] member of the Senate." What is a liberal? Wilder asked softly. "Is it a person who would say that marijuana is not a serious crime and should be decriminalized?" he said, referring to all-but-forgotten comments attributed to Coleman in a yellowed newspaper clipping. "Is it a person who would say the state should spend one percent of all construction money for prisons to decorate it with art, as he did?" Wilder pressed. More than one reporter came away from the exchange with an unexpected conclusion: Coleman had been sharp; Wilder had been sharper.

Coleman lost no time in taking the attack to Paul Trible. While Wilder was celebrating the official launching of his campaign with a foray into mountainous southwest Virginia, the four candidates for the GOP nomination were holding their first joint appearance before a Republican Women's Club meeting at an all-white country club in the Richmond suburbs. Trible used part of the session to sign a pledge against negative campaigning that Coleman had proposed at the Ingleside enclave two months earlier. Coleman used his time to needle Trible over a bogus claim that the former senator intended to raise taxes.

The tax issue provided the first skirmish in the Republican campaign, and its handling was vintage Coleman. Armed only with a smidgen of evidence, Coleman did not hesitate to inflate the facts into a full-blown charge. Trible, also typically, seemed caught off guard by the broadside, and unable to match Coleman's cool mastery of nuance and logic. At his formal campaign kickoff a few days earlier, Trible had suggested that a 1 percent income tax surcharge, applied on a local-option basis, might be an alternative of last resort in funding pressing transportation needs. Governor Baliles had proposed such a tax to the 1989 Assembly on its opening day. A transcript of the Trible press conference, later released by his staff, showed that the candidate suggested user fees, bonds, and special taxation districts as ways of paying for new roads. The Baliles idea might be tried, he said, "if all that is not enough."

The remark was the only opening Coleman needed. Seizing the offensive, Coleman blithely insisted to the GOP audience that, when it comes to raising taxes, "a maybe is a yes." A Republican, he added, "is not going to win this fall by running as the high-tax alternative to Doug Wilder." Trible replied that he had "no intention of raising taxes," but for the Coleman campaign, it was as if the words had never been spoken. Within days, Coleman announced a $50,000 advertising salvo hammering Trible's alleged tax hike plan. Adopting a line from an editorial in the

Richmond News Leader, the ad asked whether Trible had been "Mondale-ed," a reference to the 1984 Democratic presidential nominee who lost in a landslide after pledging to raise taxes.

Coleman's language, retorted Trible, was the mark of a man "willing to say or do anything to get elected." It was a potent counter; Trible's words would shadow Coleman in the fall campaign, much as the Robb letters dogged Wilder. To those with the Trible campaign, what made the Coleman allegations particularly outrageous was the similarity between Coleman's and Trible's positions on taxes. Coleman had issued a firm pledge not to sign into law any new taxes in his administration. But he had left one loophole: taxes approved by voters in a referendum were all right. The income tax surcharge proposed by Baliles —and allegedly endorsed by Trible—could also take effect only if approved by voters in a referendum.

Precision in advertising was a nicety that Marshall Coleman could not afford. A Finkelstein survey soon showed that the tax-baiting had paid dividends. The tax ad was shown only in Richmond and Roanoke, the two areas of the state where Coleman had a sufficiently high positive rating to sustain a negative advertising campaign. Although the poll-taker found that Coleman and Trible lost support about equally in the Richmond area after the tax ad ran, the results in the Roanoke area were more to Coleman's liking. Coleman's support went down a trifle, but Trible's fell by several percentage points. So the long battle of attrition had begun.

FEBRUARY 3–10, 1989

Republican activists at Ingleside had urged their candidates to debate each other. The opening round of negotiations on a format was set for February 3. GOP chairman Don Huffman came from Roanoke to chair the afternoon session at state party headquarters, and it was apparent almost as soon as the negotiators began gathering in the conference room that high-level supervision would be needed. It would take about twelve hours of often tense discussion stretching over a week, as well as the threat of a walkout, to bring off the series of face-to-face encounters that finally emerged. The chief negotiator of the Trible campaign, consultant Bob Weed, threw down the gauntlet when the meeting opened. Only one candidate was more than 25 points up in the polls, he said, and if the others expected a public shot at him, it would have to be by Trible's rules, of which there were plenty.

Political "debates," frequently amounting to no more than two candidates standing side by side on the same stage and answering similar questions, have become a staple of American political campaigns in the television age. They are also widely regarded as favoring the underdog, who gets equal exposure with the front-runner. The 1960 presidential debates between Republican Richard M. Nixon and Democrat John F. Kennedy demonstrated the principle, as the lesser-known Kennedy captivated the television audience with his looks and charm.

The Trible campaign wanted the debates to begin on March 1 and end by April 21, almost eight weeks before the June primary. Their candidate was willing to debate in each congressional district, but he wanted the order of the appearances to run numerically, one to ten, through Virginia's districts. Thus the first five debates would be held in Trible territory—either suburban Richmond or sites to the south or east of the capital city. Not until the sixth debate would the candidates hit Coleman's western stronghold, and not until the eighth would Parris get to show his hometown colors. Next, the Trible campaign wanted to take advantage of his presumed wide support by holding the debates in large halls, and awarding tickets on a first-come, first-serve basis. In so doing they hoped to be able to pack the audiences with Trible partisans. The list went on. Instead of forcing the candidates to field questions from members of the press corps, the Trible campaign wanted queries to come from the audience of GOP regulars. And finally, a set rotational order for questions was proposed—first Trible, then Parris, then Coleman, then Guest. The entire package seemed orchestrated to protect Trible from aggressive questioning and from comparison with Coleman, an acknowledged master at debate.

The Coleman, Parris, and Guest staffs were enraged, but it

was quickly apparent that the Trible folks were not in a bargaining mood. Each time someone raised a counterproposal, Bob Weed—a skilled, if somewhat eccentric strategist—would bend over the paper on which he was laboriously taking notes with his left hand, and mutter for a full ten seconds, "No, no, no, no, no . . . " "Look," Weed finally said, "I'm holding all the high cards. You guys are going to have to come to me."

Dropping his restraint, Huffman shot back: "You may be holding the high cards now, but that could change if it looks like you're sandbagging the whole thing." Later, the chairman again signaled his exasperation with a touch of dry, western Virginia wit. "Bob," he drawled, "have you ever heard of a blivett?" Assured that no one in the room knew the term, Huffman added softly: "That's like trying to stuff sixty-five pounds of horse manure into a sixty-pound bag. You just can't do it."

When the opening round finally ended, the disgruntled participants had agreed on little more than to hold a series of hour-long debates—with the terms and format still to be worked out. Grumbling, they agreed to resume the negotiations in five days. By Monday, two days before the appointed meeting, word spread that if Trible persisted in his hard-line views, the Coleman and Parris campaigns were going to boycott future negotiations. There were hints of a press conference to announce the walkout if the Trible campaign refused to budge at the next session.

The Wednesday morning meeting opened poorly. When Trible's aides, Judy Peachee and Bob Weed, walked into the room, they were livid. The day before, Coleman had unleashed his television commercial referring to Walter Mondale's 1984 tax-hike proposal, asking, "Has Paul Trible been Mondale-ed?" The timing of the assault was no coincidence, Trible's managers fumed. In their view Coleman partisans had planned the release to coincide with the debate negotiations. With Weed and Peachee preoccupied by the lengthy discussions, they would be unable to craft a speedy response to the Coleman ad. Well, Weed added, two could play at the game. The Trible campaign was taping a response to the Coleman commercial that afternoon, and he would be leaving before noon, whether or not an agreement had been reached on the debating terms.

Posturing aside, when the actual negotiations began the tone clearly had shifted. The Trible campaign apparently recognized that it was getting on dangerous ground, and as the morning wore on, agreements began to be reached. The threat had worked; Trible had no intention of scuttling the debates. By Friday the plan was set. The agreement would give Virginia a long-running series of debates, from March 1 to mid-May, that seemed likely to anesthetize voters. And the ground rules were still designed to minimize risk to Trible. Even so, Stan Parris and Marshall Coleman had what they wanted: eleven chances to overtake a front-runner whom few viewed as invincible.

MARCH 3, 1989

The GOP's traveling roadshow made its debut at Nandua High School in the hamlet of Onley, on the Eastern Shore. One of the state's most strikingly beautiful spots, the Eastern Shore is a seventy-mile-long peninsula unconnected by land to the rest of Virginia. It is bordered by barrier islands and wetlands on its eastern, Atlantic side, and by the Chesapeake Bay on the west. The peninsula is home to small towns with fanciful names such as Birdsnest, Temperanceville, and Bullbegger, to an annual wild pony roundup at Chincoteague, and to fewer than fifty thousand residents. Many are independent folk who feel less attuned to state government than to local politics.

About three hundred people attended the first Republican debate, but the setting was so remote that even the *Richmond Times-Dispatch*, the closest thing to a statewide newspaper in the Old Dominion, used wire service copy the next day instead of sending a correspondent to the event. That was just as well, because little worth noting occurred. The most memorable moment came when Paul Trible held up a piece of Parris literature picturing Virginia without the Eastern Shore attached, and pledged: "My friends, I will never forget the Eastern Shore of Virginia."

To insiders, however, the biggest surprise of the night was a fact that went unnoted in news accounts. Trible had orchestrated the debate schedule to begin in the First District, a shipbuilding, fishing and timbering region he had represented for three terms in Congress and in which he remained enormously popular. But Coleman, and to a lesser degree Parris, turned out bigger cheering squads on opening night. That pattern, an early sign of the shallowness of Trible's support and the determination of Coleman's, would continue in later debates.

Over the next two and a half months, the candidates met weekly for a series of encounters that became increasingly vituperative as they developed. The exchanges between the candidates kept the GOP campaign in the headlines and set a tone for the closing month. Coleman was ever the aggressor, needling, prodding, poking at Trible's vulnerable points. Although Trible responded at calculated moments, generally he tried to remain above the fray. His favorite response to Coleman's gyrations was a disdainful dismissal: "As long as I can stay 25 points ahead, I'm willing to listen to Marshall Coleman." Parris, who adopted a relaxed, grandfatherly aura which was in sharp contrast to the pit-bull image he usually evoked in congressional races, ran as the seasoned alternative to two brash young men. "I really regret it when Marshall does a commercial and says something nasty about Paul and Paul does a commercial and says something nasty about Marshall," Parris noted piously during one debate, held several weeks before his own negative commercials began.

The debates did little to establish philosophical differences among the Republican candidates. The three—reduced from a quartet when Guest abandoned the race after the fourth debate —were united in opposition to taxes, abortion, a state-mandated family-life education program, and assorted other programs. They were also uniformly appalled at the performance of recent Democratic governors in handling such matters as roads and prisons.

But if the exchanges produced few substantive differences, the debate series nevertheless had a considerable impact on the GOP primary contest. First, Coleman managed to generate headlines by pushing a new issue or angle at every debate. After each encounter, aides stood by with copies of press releases detailing Coleman's newest charge or program. For example, in Chesterfield County, a Republican stronghold of strip shopping centers and suburban tract homes along Richmond's southern border, Coleman unleashed a diatribe attacking Trible's claim to being Ronald Reagan's best friend in the Virginia congressional delegation. Waiting until the closing moments of the March 9 debate, Coleman unveiled his evidence—Trible's opposition to Ed Meese's nomination as attorney general, his signing of an Iran-Contra report critical of the president, and his last-place finish among Virginia's congressmen in presidential support during (in Coleman's words) the "critical" year of 1982, when Trible had been in the House of Representatives. Trible, in closing comments moments later, responded: "We've seen Marshall Coleman slash and attack and say or do anything in order to win."

When the lights came on, Dennis Peterson quickly handed out packets of information documenting Trible's alleged incompatibility with Reagan, a serious charge in a locality that had given Reagan solid support. When headlines were written for the next day's newspapers, Coleman commanded them. Not until later did anyone have time to scrutinize the actual statement itself. Coleman's claim that Trible had been less supportive of Reagan than any other GOP congressman from Virginia was technically correct, since Coleman counted Trible's record only during the years 1976–1982, when Trible was in the House of Representatives. Trible's voting record in the U.S. Senate from 1983 to 1988, when he led the Virginia delegation in presidential support, was completely ignored in the Coleman analysis.

The debates fostered an image of Trible as a politician who was not quick on the uptake and who tended to shy away from a fight. To be sure, there were flashes of anger on Trible's part, particularly during the seventh debate in Alexandria. There, in one of the campaign's memorable moments, Trible held aloft a blank index card that he said contained a list of Coleman's accomplishments. "Your campaign is 99 percent promises and one percent performance," he said, as boos and hisses from Coleman supporters confirmed that Trible had landed a blow. But more often Trible was on the defensive, and his reminders that he was ahead and the others weren't rapidly turned stale.

The Coleman campaign believed that the debates made at least one other contribution to the primary's eventual outcome. When the former attorney general began his negative advertising, the hard edge of the commercials was softened slightly by the fact that Coleman was not saying anything that he and Parris had not already said in the debates. The main difference was that by June more people were listening.

MARCH 9, 1989

While the Republican candidates were pounding away at each other, the Democrats were settling their differences. The long-awaited public reconciliation of Doug Wilder and Chuck Robb came on a train ride north to Philadelphia, the City of Brotherly Love. Mounting an Amtrak Metroliner, the pair joined a rolling cocktail party of congressmen and staff headed for a weekend meeting of the Democratic Leadership Council. It was to this group that Wilder had been invited to speak four years earlier, in the wake of his election, when he incensed Robb by turning down the invitation. The implication then was that Wilder, who at about the same time had accused some council members of wearing "Reagan masks," did not want Robb or the group assuming any credit for his victory.

By 1989, however, Wilder was insisting that his various remarks on the council had been misinterpreted, and that he and the group had each reached a better understanding of the other. The failure to show up in 1985 had not been a snub, he said, but the mark of a campaign-weary man who had finally found time for a vacation. By speaking of Reagan masks, he had simply been suggesting that Democrats could not out-Reagan Reagan. His fear was that the Democratic Leadership Council on the right and Jesse Jackson on the left would polarize the party. "I want to learn more about this organization," added Wilder as the caravan rolled north. "I may have been wrong in some of my assessments." "He understands what Virginians are looking for in their leaders," responded an approving Robb. Even so, there were limits to the accord. Reporters covering the event noted that Wilder and Robb spent almost the entire trip at opposite ends of the train.

MARCH 17, 1989

Perhaps the single most important thing Wilder had done in 1988 to allay fears among Democratic party professionals about his campaign management ability was to announce that his campaign consultant would be David Doak, who had managed Robb's 1981 race for governor. Doak had also been the media consultant for Gerald Baliles in 1985, and his firm, Doak & Shrum, had cemented its name nationally by producing what many thought was the best ad of the 1988 presidential primary season, Richard Gephardt's Hyundai commercial, which contrasted Japanese tariffs with American ones. His "hiring" was seen as proof that moderate Democrats would have a voice in the Wilder campaign, and that the strategy would be more traditional than in 1985.

However, at Wilder's January 1989 campaign kickoff, political workers, ever attuned to hints of change in the palace guard, had noticed one curious fact. David Doak was not on the platform. He was at the back of the audience, and he was saying very little. A few weeks later, one longtime Democratic worker was surprised when he met Wilder on the street and suddenly found himself being grilled about Doak's credentials. What exactly had Doak done in some past campaigns? the lieutenant governor wanted to know. The man was astounded that Wilder would have such elementary questions about the man he had been billing for months as his campaign consultant.

Robert Squier, a competitor to Doak, first sensed that something was afoot one day when he was talking to Paul Goldman. Irritated at Goldman over another matter, the Washington-based consultant said: "Look, you never even gave me a chance to make a presentation." "How'd you like to do it tomorrow?"

replied Goldman. Squier, who declined, was flabbergasted. His understanding, obviously incorrect, had been that Doak was already hired.

What Wilder had failed to mention when he announced Doak's hiring in 1988 was that they had never signed a contract. When around New Year's the pair began to talk about money, they found themselves poles apart. Both senate clerk Jay Shropshire, a Wilder intimate, and Bill Wiley, his campaign treasurer, recall that Doak wanted to receive somewhere in excess of half a million dollars for his services. (Doak says he wanted a $60,000 base fee, plus 15 percent of the media billing.) At their last meeting in early March, Doak later recalled: "Doug said, 'Here's the top I can pay, $220,000 plus a win bonus.' We said, 'Here's the bottom we can accept, $325,000 to $350,000.' We shook hands and walked away."

Wilder dropped the bombshell at a $500-a-plate fundraiser in McLean. His media adviser would be Frank Greer, not Doak. Greer, who had helped upset three incumbent Republican U.S. senators in 1986 and was just off a winning governor's race in West Virginia, was one of the hottest young advertising executives in the county. But the dominant reaction south of the Potomac was, "Who?"

Few Democrats even noticed an entry on Greer's resume that would prove critical to the campaign. Among the clients of Greer, Margolis, Mitchell & Associates was a group soon to be propelled into the national spotlight—NARAL, the National Abortion Rights Action League.

An uneasy sense settled in on some Robb-Baliles Democrats that Wilder's 1989 campaign might be as disorganized as they believed the 1985 one had been. It was mid-March, and Wilder had not yet named a campaign manager. When he corrected that deficit a week later, the man he picked was Joe McLean, a pleasant young Tennesseean who had recently been named executive director of the state party. Not only was McLean new to Virginia, but he had never managed a statewide campaign anywhere. Greer was an unknown. The role of Goldman, who was still being kept under wraps because of the controversy with Robb, was unclear. Once again, Wilder seemed bent on proving the obvious: the drumbeat he marched to would be his own.

For Republicans, the gubernatorial primary campaign seemed to be in a holding pattern, with Trible soaring high. Neither Coleman nor Parris had managed to surpass Trible—or to escape the other's shadow. Conventional wisdom held that unless one of the underdogs established himself as the principal alternative to Trible, the pair would split the opposition vote and Trible would win. Throughout a cool, wet April, as three seasoned staffs strove for advantage with press releases and the debates, little changed. Coleman and Parris worried about money and continued to search for a fatal weakness in Trible. Trible likewise worried about money and tried to perform the delicate feat of keeping two opponents at bay, but both of them still in the race. Throughout the campaign, a prime fear of Trible strategists was that, by attacking one opponent too successfully, they might create what they least wanted: a two-man race.

Aiding the Republican candidates were numerous political veterans, many of whom had worked together in past elections and knew each others' strengths and weaknesses intimately. There was Charlie Black, a kingpin of GOP consulting, whose firm has included such power brokers as GOP National Committee chair Lee Atwater. A friend of Parris's for two decades, Black was chief consultant to the Parris campaign, and he brought with him inside knowledge of and some distaste for Paul Trible's political instincts. It was Black who had helped engineer Trible's successful 1982 Senate nomination, but he had left before the general election after losing a power struggle with Judy Peachee. Dick Leggitt, a crusty former reporter, had spent a decade as Parris's press spokesman, but in the spring of 1989 he was on the Coleman staff, providing all-purpose consulting and ample information on Parris. Trible's Peachee and Kenny Klinge, who advised Parris, were fellow architects of the right-wing takeover of Virginia's Republican party in the 1970s and longtime friends. Dennis Peterson, Coleman's press secretary during the primary, in 1985 had managed John Chichester's winning campaign against Coleman for the GOP nomination to run against Doug Wilder for lieutenant governor.

Filling out the rosters were some of the party's premier consultants. With no congressional races to help direct in 1989, and only the states of Virginia and New Jersey holding gubernatorial elections, top consultative talent was available. Ironically, given Trible's lead, the team he assembled was probably the least high-powered. Parris had Black and Lance Tarrance, one of the GOP's leading pollsters. In addition to the Finkelstein firm, Coleman signed on Robert Goodman, an extroverted Maryland media consultant who over the last decade had worked for eighteen Republican senators, including Robert Dole of Kansas, Pete Wilson of California, and Mississippians Thad Cochran and Trent Lott. Sometimes called "Dr. Feelgood" in the trade, Goodman is known for glowing portraits of his candidates and insight in capsulizing the weaknesses of opponents. "Love, hope, hate, and fear are four words that inspire voting," Goodman is fond of saying. Successfully tapping such emotions, he adds, is more important to winning elections than right or wrong.

Against that array, Trible pitted David Hill, who had split from Tarrance to form his own firm, and Ian and Betsy Weinschel of Mount Airy, Maryland. The Weinschels, who began as film editors in the 1970s and launched their own firm in 1981, had handled Trible's Senate race in 1982 and several gubernatorial contests. But they had not attained the reputation commanded by Black, Goodman, and a handful of other consultants. Their television work was recognized for technical merit: flashing lights, multi-layered applications of the candidate's name on screen, and other visual ploys. But they were not known for capturing the essence of a candidate on film.

While the Parris and Coleman operations depended on a host of people, the Trible campaign seemed more insular, at times resembling a one-woman show. Power often appeared centralized in a single pair of hands—campaign manager Judy Peachee's. Through a decade and a half at the center of GOP politics, the

soft-spoken, chain-smoking Peachee had acquired faithful supporters, and also some equally intense enemies. At times, some
in the rival camps seemed as interested in dethroning her as in
beating Trible.

The array of GOP strategists saw April as a month for creating good feelings about their candidates and shoring up weaknesses before the negative media blitz of the final days began. In
advertising lingo, the phase was "warm and fuzzy." Coleman's
most memorable television ad during the period showed him
horseback riding with his sons, Billy and Sean. The voice-over
was that of Sean, a nineteen-year-old Princeton freshman, who
mused: "He's more than a father to us; he's a friend." With viewers who had come to regard Coleman as the slasher of GOP
politics, and who knew little more about his personal life than
that he was twice divorced, the ad gave Coleman a needed dose
of humanity. Goodman also managed to work an anti-Trible
barb into the thirty-second spot, having Sean say of his father:
" . . . he's taught us—never quit. Finish the job." The remark
was playing on Trible's early retirement from the U.S. Senate.

"Quit"—the "Q-word," as it was quickly dubbed—also found
its way into Parris's principal April television ad, a biographical
spot focusing on his rags-to-riches rise. Reminding voters that
Parris was more than a millionaire pal of developers and real
estate magnates, the commercial showed the future congressman flying fighter missions in Korea and earning his way
through law school by washing dishes. "Decorated for courage
as a fighter pilot, he was shot down but flew forty-three more
missions. Stan Parris would not quit," said an announcer in awed
tones. The spot, which provided many Virginians their first look
at Parris, came to be widely regarded as one of the two best
political ads of the GOP primary. The distinction of worst ad
also went to the Parris campaign, however. In a spot unveiled
some weeks later, Parris appeared to be trading on racial ill-will
as he chided Trible for voting in the 1970s to grant statehood to
the District of Columbia. A bit too obviously the ad featured a
picture of the District's embattled black mayor, Marion Barry.

Meanwhile, Trible was running a series of unmemorable ads
that were more fuzzy than warm. A typical one showed the

Trible family walking along a riverbank while an announcer offered generalities about his accomplishments in Washington: "More health care and housing for seniors . . . more funding for education and transportation . . . tougher drug laws," and so forth. The most appealing of the Trible ads used film borrowed from the 1982 Senate campaign. It showed the grinning candidate strumming a mandolin with a group of old-timers at the Galax Fiddlers' Convention, while an announcer spoke—again in generalities—about Trible's dreams for Virginia. The effectiveness of the ad was mitigated, however, when the *Washington Post* pointed out that Trible does not play the instrument. Once again, Trible seemed more illusion than substance.

While television audiences were sampling such tame fare, TV advertising consultants were planning a May repertoire that they hoped would strike at the core of their opponents' credibility. There was no doubt that the attacks would come. The only uncertainty was the form. Goodman acknowledged as much in a mid-April interview. "We have twenty-five things that are not flattering to Paul Trible," he said gleefully. "There's a whole picture here, and we're still trying to figure out how to paint it."

The would-be artists in the Coleman and Parris campaigns got a boost on the morning of April 21. An article in Norfolk's *Virginian-Pilot* by political reporter Warren Fiske provided startling new evidence that when Trible announced his departure from the Senate in 1987, he was already contemplating a race for governor. Unbeknownst to the public, Trible had paid a pollster $5,500 to gauge reaction to his statewide televised withdrawal announcement, which cost $70,000. A twelve-person focus group had been assembled in Richmond to watch the performance and answer questions about their reaction to it. Creating such a focus group was, at best, an unusual step for a man who had just told Virginians that he was leaving office because he wanted to spend more time with his family. At worst, it signaled a calculated deception of Virginia voters. Judy Peachee defended the polling exercise as being a historical tool for future GOP campaigns, but admitted that she had no idea what had happened to the report.

For the Coleman campaign, there was another bright spot a

few days later. As Robert Goodman reviewed Trible's career, the media consultant became intrigued by reports that Trible, who never served in the military, had run a campaign ad in 1982 showing himself in a flight suit climbing into a military aircraft. The shot had been taken several years earlier when Trible, as a member of the House Armed Services Committee, had been given a demonstration flight in an F-15. To Goodman, the notion that for campaign purposes Trible had tried to create an image of himself as a military man, but had sought a medical deferment during the Vietnam War, was telling. It might be the perfect metaphor, he thought, for persistent doubts about Trible's strength of character. The only problem was getting his hands on a picture of Trible with the aircraft.

Dick Leggitt vaguely recalled that a photo taken from the ad had appeared in the *Washington Post* during the 1982 campaign. The article had run in the Metro section, he thought, sometime in October. Goodman dispatched Bruce Mentzer, his firm's media director, to the microfilm room in the Enoch Pratt Library in downtown Baltimore to find the story. After three hours of combing the files, Mentzer's eyes were blurred and he was ready to give up. He had checked numerous 1982 campaign stories referring to Trible, and there was no flight suit photo. Mentzer called Goodman to report. "I don't think it's here," he said. "Try again tomorrow," insisted Goodman.

The next day, Mentzer asked for microfilm for the entire month of October 1982, and began scouring the newspaper, page by page. Several hours later, and by now with a throbbing headache, he stopped. There, on a Metro section front page, was the photograph Leggitt remembered. Excitedly Mentzer telephoned Goodman. "My reaction," Goodman recalled, "was that we had just won the primary."

While Republicans were awash in campaign strategy, much of the rest of Virginia was focusing on a U.S. Supreme Court ruling that had caught state officials napping and threatened to play havoc with the public treasury. If a state exempted retired state employees from paying state income tax, as Virginia did, the court ruled it must also exempt federal retirees from the tax.

The news hit Virginia, with her abundance of federal retirees, like a spring storm. Officials scrambled to project impact estimates—$100 million or more. On April 25 Governor Baliles summoned the Assembly into special session, and Wilder was among a handful of associates taken into confidence on what he planned to propose. The governor would ask the legislature to fully tax pensions for both state and federal retirees with annual incomes over $16,000. Wilder, Baliles's aides later said, gave his approval.

Almost as quickly as the plan was announced to the Assembly, it was in tatters. Too few retirees were exempted under Baliles's plan, critics said. It did not take Wilder long to join the chorus of opposition. In a press release, he called for tax exemptions not only for public retirees but for private ones as well. The statement made Wilder the first statewide candidate to take the debate into the private realm. The legislature soon agreed. When members adjourned on April 27, Wilder had in pocket a claim that would emerge as a major theme on the campaign trail. He had pushed successfully to give all but the wealthiest Virginians pension tax relief. The only price was that he had, once again, stepped on Gerald Baliles.

5

THE RESURRECTION OF MARSHALL COLEMAN

Finally there was a poll with good news for Coleman. On the last day of April, John McLaughlin of the Finkelstein firm called campaign manager Boyd Marcus with numbers suggesting that the hundreds of thousands of dollars Coleman was pouring into television ads were paying off. The latest survey—which was more positive than any other public or private preference poll at the time—showed Trible dropping to 33 percentage points, with Coleman at 29 and Parris at 20. (In contrast, an early May survey for the Parris camp had Trible at 38 points, and Parris and Coleman tied at 22 each.) The Coleman campaign quickly released their figures to the press. The publicity would give Coleman supporters a boost. More important, it would be a tool in refilling a sorely depleted treasury.

Throughout the month, as Democrat Doug Wilder scheduled fund-raising trips to Boston, California, and Washington, the Coleman and Parris campaigns continued their war of attrition against Paul Trible for the GOP nomination. In mid-May, Mason-Dixon Opinion Research, a Maryland firm which regularly polls Virginians for several news organizations, reported that although Trible was still well ahead, he had a "soft" lead—people who said they favored him were showing little enthusiasm—and might be overtaken. Both Coleman and Parris responded as if Trible's death knell had already sounded.

The state press aided the cause by focusing much of its investigative attention on Trible. On May 7, the *Richmond Times-Dispatch* raised doubts about Trible's use of the congressional franking privilege. According to the newspaper, Trible had spent $261,000 of public funds sending out 1.2 million pieces of mail in the year before his retirement announcement. In contrast, in the year after the announcement and just prior to his run for governor, he spent $729,000 mailing 5.2 million items, the report said.

The election seemed increasingly to be a referendum on Trible's performance. "It wasn't any one thing," said Judy Peachee later in assessing the reasons for Trible's loss. "It was the constant pounding from so many directions at one time. They [Coleman and Parris] never, ever took on each other. At some point, we felt like they had to, but they never did. I think they were amazed at our staying power."

MAY 22, 1989

The barrage of negative television advertising began in earnest on May 22. In separate press conferences, Coleman and Parris announced that they were unleashing the long-awaited assaults. Parris's first offering focused on Trible's position vis-à-vis the District of Columbia, an issue of marginal interest downstate and a curious choice for Parris, who was trying to shake his image as a Northern Virginia regional candidate. Opening with pictures of former Democratic presidential contenders Walter Mondale and Michael Dukakis and Washington's black mayor, Marion Barry, the ad began: "Washington, D.C., always votes for liberal Democrats. That's why it's surprising to learn Paul Trible's record on D.C. Fact: Paul Trible voted to give the city of D.C. two U.S. senators and two congressmen, though their votes would cancel out Virginia's." What Parris failed to say was that the vote in question was eleven years old, that Trible had long since disavowed it, and that what a Virginia governor might say or do would have virtually no impact on the stalemated issue of D.C. statehood.

Why Parris singled out the District of Columbia as an issue remained one of the tantalizing questions of the primary campaign. Even some Republicans suggested that his motive may have been to subtly raise the specter of race by referring to Barry, whose administration was drowning in allegations of personal corruption and the city's soaring murder rate. "What was it Doug Wilder said? That liberal was a code word for black," said one GOP state official, speculating on the ad.

Parris's denials of that charge were adamant. "I believe in a classless, raceless, sexless society," he was fond of saying during the campaign. Eighteen years earlier, however, as a new congressman escorting a busload of Virginia lawmakers around Northern Virginia, Parris had told an ill-conceived joke. "The Fourteenth Street bridge is the longest in the world," he quipped. "It stretches all the way from Virginia to Africa." The congressman had long since apologized for the remark. But Parris's insistence—and that of some prominent supporters—on highlighting his tussles with D.C. officials, and on linking Wilder to Barry, was suspect.

Political scientists attuned to the nuances of racial politics say a modern ploy is to equate black candidates with more controversial black figures. Some saw deliberate innuendo in a televised debate in the final days of the 1982 California governor's race when George Deukmejian linked Tom Bradley to California house speaker Willie Brown, a far more flamboyant and polarizing black figure. The same technique seemed at play when Parris told debate audiences, "I'll get in Doug Wilder's face just like I get in Marion Barry's face when I think he's wrong."

While Parris was sidetracked on Washington, D.C., Coleman launched an advertising attack that was more relevant to downstate voters. As the screen turned a stark black and white and a tiny printed disclaimer mentioning the Coleman campaign quickly disappeared, a somber-voiced announcer intoned: "When President Reagan needed us and our support, one man in his own party decided to put self-interest first, to attack and then walk away. His name—Paul Trible. He quit the Senate. He quit the President."

Trible wasted no time in responding. He castigated Parris for "bad votes" against the Gramm-Rudman-Hollings federal spending restrictions and against a 1983 bailout of the Social Security system. And he dredged up the old *Richmond News Leader* story, mentioned in the January appearance of Coleman and Wilder before the capitol press corps, in which Coleman allegedly said that marijuana was no longer a serious problem.

There was one major difference between the attacks by Coleman and Parris and those by Trible, however. The challengers were saturating television screens. Trible was answering via radio. Not until the last week of the campaign would Trible utter a negative word about his opponents on television, and then only in an ad responding directly to one of theirs. Indeed, one potentially devastating ad drafted by Peachee and Weed never appeared. Incensed at the portrayal of Trible as a quitter, they planned a Christian radio spot saying that Trible was "the only one who hadn't quit the most sacred of vows, the commitment to his marriage." Both Coleman and Parris were twice divorced. Trible, however, vetoed the proposal because he thought it tasteless.

The tactical decision to limit negative ads to radio, later singled out as a significant Trible mistake, was dictated by money, Judy Peachee insists. Throughout the campaign, Trible's campaign manager told reporters that she was attacking on radio because she believed voters were offended by having to watch mudslinging from their living room recliners. After the primary, she amended the explanation. "Everybody said, why didn't you go on TV? I didn't have the money. I sat here, and I walked the floor at night, and I said, 'Which one? I've got $200,000. Where do I put it?'" Unsure whether to rebut Parris or Coleman, she decided to opt for radio and attack both. However, the growing suspicion in the Trible campaign was that Parris would prove to be the greater threat.

That view might have been bolstered had Peachee listened in on a May 26 telephone call from pollster McLaughlin to Boyd Marcus at Coleman headquarters. "Don't kill the messenger," McLaughlin said, hoping to lighten the mood as he reported the latest survey results. The crucial final two weeks of the campaign were about to begin, and the leap in preference polls that Coleman had reported in early May had evaporated. The latest numbers looked depressingly similar to those of the winter: among likely Republican voters, Trible was at 35 percentage points, and Coleman and Parris were tied at 23 each. It was the low point of the primary campaign for Coleman's inner circle. In a conference telephone call, the key Coleman strategists glumly reviewed their alternatives. Should they continue to press Trible, or switch their fire to Parris?

"We looked at the numbers and the shifts," Marcus recalled. "In the Roanoke market, we were trading votes back and forth with Trible. In Tidewater we were still the number two choice by a tremendous amount over Parris. In Richmond, Parris had made some gains because the business community was with him. In Northern Virginia, it was clearly Parris and Trible." The group agreed that there was little to gain by switching the focus. "It was an easy decision to make, but a key one," Marcus believes. "If we'd switched our attack to Parris, we'd have lost the thing."

JUNE 1, 1989

As June arrived, the primary election countdown began in earnest. The Trible camp still felt comfortable with their position. By David Hill's count, Trible's lead remained at a solid 10 or so points. Second place was seesawing back and forth between Parris and Coleman. The Parris campaign was also feeling upbeat. Their strategists were convinced that Northern Virginians had more interest in the primary than downstate voters, and that Parris had a strong hold on voter affections there in the Eighth and Tenth Districts. A recently commissioned poll bore out that thinking. With the numbers weighted to reflect a heavy upstate turnout, the latest Parris numbers showed Trible at 34 points, Parris at 29, and Coleman at 20.

Rallying from the recent setback in their own internal poll, the Coleman forces decided the time had come to use the remaining weapons in their anti-Trible arsenal. Armed with the *Washington Post* photograph unearthed at the Baltimore library, Goodman had fashioned a television spot that he hoped would lump the central misgivings about Trible into a single, thirty-second message. "Paul Trible is a study in character," began the litany of complaints. "He condemns the president when he thinks it's a popular thing to do. He quits the U.S. Senate because he's afraid to run against Chuck Robb. He backs a plan to raise Virginia's taxes and blames the press for reporting it." And then, as the flight-suit picture of Trible drifted across the screen, came the kicker: "He even campaigns on television in a uniform he never wore in front of a plane he never flew . . . "

The ad, the most influential of the primary campaign, began running on Thursday evening in the Tidewater area and the next day in the rest of the state. Since weekend air time had to be purchased by Friday, the Coleman campaign calculated that they would have a full three days exposure before Trible could air a response. According to Kenny Klinge, the Parris campaign planned a similar ad, even using the same photograph. The ad, which would have shown contrasting footage from Parris's days as a Korean War pilot, was scripted but never produced, partially because the Parris campaign had learned of Coleman's plans, he said. Apparently, neither candidate viewed as a bar the Eleventh Commandment pledge to "refrain from personal attacks on fellow Republicans" that they had signed a few months earlier.

<hr>

JUNE 4, 1989

Residents of South Hampton Roads awoke Sunday morning to find an endorsement of Coleman on the editorial page of the *Virginian-Pilot/Ledger-Star*. The rhetoric was lukewarm ("On balance, then, the edge in this race belongs to Marshall Coleman," it concluded), but any nod, however slight, was welcomed by a campaign seeking independent confirmation that confidence in Trible was eroding. Three days earlier the *Fairfax Journal* had issued far more stinging rejections of Trible and Parris. The newspaper, published in Parris's backyard, called him a "chronically choleric congressman," "an accomplished windbag," and a "confrontational, doctrinaire Republican" whose "incessant campaign of District of Columbia bashing borders on racism." The newspaper dismissed Trible: "As amiable, as smooth, and as well-rehearsed as any lightweight young politician we have ever met."

In contrast, the *Journal* said, "Coleman belongs to the future, while his two rivals belong either to the distant past or nowhere, depending on which one you are talking about." Bill Wood, editor of the Norfolk-based newspapers, was more skeptical about Coleman, questioning both his reputation for unbridled ambition and his political shifts. But, on balance, Coleman's experience in state government, and lingering doubts about Trible's lack of magnetism and stature, gave the edge to Coleman, Wood said. Earlier, many had expected Trible to win the *Pilot*'s endorsement. Indeed, when the former senator met with the newspaper's editorial board in mid-May, he argued persuasively: "I vote more like you think than any of the other candidates." But Trible was unable to explain convincingly why he had assembled a focus group to watch his withdrawal announcement, and he did not exude gubernatorial presence.

When Coleman met with the *Virginian-Pilot*'s editorial board six days later, he was at his best—charming and facile in his command of issues. While there were holes in some of his arguments, including the no-tax pledge, Coleman's knowledge of state government was clearly superior to Trible's. After Coleman left, Wood polled his staff about their preferences. Five people voted, and the count was unanimous for Coleman. Coleman's one-two punch in Tidewater—the newspaper endorsement and the ad challenging Trible's military credentials—would soon have a dramatic impact on the race.

In some ways, Coleman was winning an equally significant victory in the Third District. Both Trible and Parris partisans had been pressuring the conservative editorial board of the *Richmond Times-Dispatch* for an endorsement. Coleman seemed the least likely to win that nod. But the newspaper opted for neutrality, and when the editorial board summed up the race a week later, there were kind words for each of the three, including Coleman.

When Judy Peachee walked into Trible headquarters in a suburban Richmond shopping center Monday morning, her first stop was to check numbers from the weekend phone banks. Since mid-April, the campaign polling staff had been tracking the opinions of voters each weekday. But on weekends the only gauge of shifts in the electorate was the less scientifically framed reports from banks of telephone callers who were soliciting support for Trible around the state. The weekend results surveyed by Peachee indicated a slight movement in the Second District toward Coleman, but nothing dramatic.

Peachee made a mental note to keep tabs on the district and turned to more critical matters. Prime among them was a new television ad that the Parris campaign was unveiling to the media at Republican Party of Virginia headquarters. David Hill's tracking for the last week had suggested that Parris had moved into second place in the race, and the Trible campaign was primed to counter his rise. Besides being worried about the content of the ad, Peachee was enraged that party officials were allowing competing campaigns to use party headquarters for press conferences that violated the spirit of the Eleventh Commandment pledge. In an angry telephone call to Huffman, she vented that ire.

The new Parris ad blasted Trible's record as a federal prosecutor in the early 1970s, charging that he "consistently ducked tough cases, cutting deals, plea bargaining, or dismissing charges entirely, . . . over 82 percent of the time." Meanwhile, out of sight of the press, a letter to Republican voters was drumming home the theme in even harsher language. The combination dispelled any notion that Parris intended to ride out his nice-guy strategy to primary day. His natural political instincts were back in charge.

Overnight the Trible campaign produced a television response calling the Parris prosecutor ad a distortion and concluding with the strongest language used by Trible on television during the campaign. "That's why the *Washington Post* calls the Parris campaign for governor 'a depressing thought,' " said the tag line. By Tuesday evening, the ad was airing in markets around the state.

JUNE 7, 1989

The Trible campaign had dealt with one problem, but a more serious one was looming elsewhere. Trible staffers woke Wednesday to the most disturbing news of the campaign thus far. A poll published in the morning editions of the *Washington Post* gave the first independent evidence that Trible's commanding lead had evaporated and the race was a dead heat. Trible and Coleman were tied at 31 points each; Parris trailed with 24 percentage points, the newspaper said. The Coleman campaign was ecstatic, while Trible and Parris rushed to discredit the numbers.

Judy Peachee could look at her own tracking and see the erosion, however. By Wednesday morning, there was no doubt. The weekend trickle of conversions to Coleman in the Second District had become a stream. The undecideds were breaking heavily in his direction. Coleman was also surging in the southwestern Ninth District. Peachee tracked down Trible at a campaign stop in Roanoke and delivered the bad news. Together they hammered out a statement about his strong congressional support for the military, and the candidate began delivering the hawkish message at every stop. That night, Peachee ordered the tracking sample doubled and upped the number of phone bank calls into the Second District.

JUNE 8, 1989

By Thursday morning, momentum clearly was with Coleman. The Trible campaign staff, however, was still diverted by what they regarded as an outright distortion by Parris of Trible's record as a prosecutor. Taking a cue from the opposition, Trible had scheduled a press conference at Virginia Republican party headquarters in Richmond. It did not escape notice at the state office that Trible's press secretary had to call ahead for directions on how to get there. Accompanying the candidate were

Brian Gettings, the federal prosecutor whom Trible once served as an assistant, and Wyatt Durrette, the GOP nominee for governor in 1985. The Parris charges, the trio said, were outrageous and utterly distorted. They produced numbers to back up their claim. Trible fielded a few questions and sped away to a Danville luncheon.

Amazingly, none of the three had said a word about the man who had become Trible's greatest threat. Not only was Coleman surging, but the label of "nastiest campaigner" had just been transferred from Coleman to Parris.

As soon as he could escape the Danville event, Trible canceled the day's agenda and boarded a private plane to Northern Virginia, stopping just long enough in Richmond to pick up Peachee and Weed. By midafternoon, the three, together with media consultant Ian Weinschel, were gathered around the Tribles' kitchen table, feverishly concocting ads that might recapture their evaporating lead. At the airport Peachee had jotted down a radio spot aimed at stabilizing Trible's vote in the Ninth District. Now they sketched out another radio ad accusing Parris and Coleman of resorting to "outright lies," and began planning a final television spot that might make or break their floundering campaign.

As the group pondered opening lines, someone suggested that Trible begin by reviewing his accomplishments in Washington. As Judy Peachee remembered it, Trible replied, "It doesn't feel right. I can't do it." Trible preferred to confront the mudslinging. Later, some critics said the lines he chose only underscored the attacks against him. "You've seen and heard a lot of charges in this hard-fought primary. I've been called a quitter. My patriotism and love of country have been challenged," he said. "One untruthful attack after another. It's time to stop and think."

But think about what? "What is it we're trying to say?" Trible interrupted repeatedly as the group struggled for a brief, compelling message. "That they trusted you. They liked you as a senator. They got mad at you, but now you want to bring it back," Peachee prodded.

Finally, the group settled on lines written by Trible: "Six times

you've elected me to public office and together we made a difference in the life of Virginia." Weinschel threw in the closing
reminder, "We must win in order to govern, and every poll shows,
I can defeat Doug Wilder." The ad was finished.

Already emotionally spent, the group adjourned to Trible's
study. As Weinschel filmed, the candidate perched at his desk—a
photo of his children to one side—and began to deliver the newly
written lines. It was almost twenty-one months since Trible
had struck a similar pose to announce that he would not seek a
second term in the U.S. Senate.

Back in Richmond late that night, Peachee got a telephone
call from a supporter, telling her that Trible had just won 45
percent of the vote in a small Charlottesville-area poll. The numbers, she knew, were meaningless, but they were a sorely needed
pick-me-up. She telephoned Trible's motel to convey the news
and the message, "Sleep well." "My overriding feeling," she
recalled, "was that this media message had better work. If not,
we'd be in second place."

JUNE 9, 1989

More significant numbers awaited Trible in Friday morning's
newspapers. According to the latest Mason-Dixon survey, Trible
now had only a one-point edge. He was at 32 percent; Coleman
at 31, and Parris at 27. The *Post* poll had not been an aberration.

JUNE 10, 1989

As Republicans moved at whirlwind pace into the final weekend before the primary, the state was diverted by the spectacle
at the Richmond civic center. There about forty-five hundred
Democrats were gathered to nominate a statewide ticket of
Douglas Wilder for governor, Mary Sue Terry for attorney general, and Donald S. Beyer, Jr., a Northern Virginia Volvo dealer
making his first stab at elective office, for lieutenant governor.
A quip circulating on the convention floor dealt with changing
times: Who'd have thought in 1985, it went, that the weak link

on the Democratic ticket in 1989 would be the white male? Such talk contained more bravado than many delegates felt. More typical was the assessment of Senator Gartlan of Alexandria as he strolled the convention floor. "Mary Sue is the one solid rock in the whole thing," Gartlan said. "Doug, he's going to come out of the blocks running. He can pull it off, but it's going to take an incredible effort."

The signal that two crucial Democrats—Sen. Chuck Robb and Gov. Gerald Baliles—intended to stand with Wilder was for many the weekend highlight. With a one-two punch in nominating and seconding speeches, the pair sought to dispel lingering doubts about their relationship with Wilder. Baliles used humor; Robb addressed his differences with Wilder more directly.

Baliles went first. "Do I like Doug Wilder? Yes, I do. Do I admire Doug Wilder? Yes, I do." There was a carefully timed pause. "Do I think Doug Wilder is independent? Yes, I do." As the chuckles subsided, Baliles continued. "When I think of Doug I think of a poem written more than a hundred years ago. It says: 'Voyager upon life's sea, To yourself be true, And whate'er your lot may be, Paddle your own canoe.'

"Well, I've looked out the window of the governor's office on more than one occasion and, sure enough, there was Doug paddling by. . . . But he was nice about it. He always waved."

Moments later, Robb talked more soberly about his disagreements with Wilder. As a hush settled on the convention, he began: "Well, Doug and I have had our differences and I did eventually release a couple of tough letters. . . . But our differences and those letters represent only one year in a relationship that has spanned fourteen years." Robb went on to give Wilder partial credit for his election as lieutenant governor in 1977 and as governor in 1981, and to add, "Don't anybody make any mistake about this race. I'm back in Doug's corner in 1989."

Wilder replied by claiming redemption both for himself and the state that was the cornerstone of the Confederacy. "In my lifetime," he said, "I have seen Virginia learn and grow, and in my lifetime, I have learned and I have grown. I believe we are all the better for it." His acceptance speech was low-key, downplaying the obvious emotions of the day. But Wilder touched on the audacity of his own aspirations. "I have learned that big deeds are born of big dreams, and that big dreams become realities only when the brow is willing to sweat and only when the principled commitment runs deep," he said.

Returning Baliles's and Robb's goodwill, Wilder sided with the governor in the only controversy of the weekend. Rumors were rampant that United Mine Workers, on strike since April against the Pittston Coal Group Companies, Virginia's largest mining operation, were planning to walk out of the convention during Baliles's keynote speech. The miners—many of them Democrats—were furious with Baliles for his decision to send several hundred state troopers to the coalfields to keep the peace. But Wilder said he would stand beside Baliles if a disruption occurred, and he urged the AFL-CIO not to diminish the aura of his nomination weekend. In the end, about three hundred miners and sympathizers stood with their backs turned to Baliles as he spoke. But there was no walkout. After the election, state labor leaders said the rumors about a pending walkout were bogus information planted by nervous party officials. "They led the press to an expectation that didn't exist," insists Danny LeBlanc, secretary-treasurer of the state AFL-CIO.

The convention ended without the customary press conference, featuring the newly formed ticket and top Democrats. Earlier, as Baliles and Robb waited in a holding room for their convention entrance, the governor had turned to the senator. "The press is going to ask us one question, and we have to be prepared," Baliles said. "They're going to ask, 'Do you trust him?' and I'm simply going to say 'Yes.'" There was an expectant pause, as if Baliles was waiting for a similar commitment from Robb. But the statement was left dangling, without response. The decision not to hold a press conference eliminated the problem; there was no forum for reporters to ask such insinuating questions.

With the primary balloting less than twenty-four hours away, Trible, Coleman, and Parris combed the state for last-minute converts. In Richmond, Trible worked the Main Street lunchtime crowd, as a political career that was once his lifetime ambition hung in the balance. "Virginians are offended by the negative campaigns waged by Marshall Coleman and Stan Parris," he said for the evening television news. "They've waged campaigns of distortion, deceit, and falsehood."

Parris and Coleman were unrepentant as ever in reply. "If you can't talk about a guy's performance and his voting record, then what message is it that you're supposed to carry?" asked Parris, looking relaxed and good-natured for the cameras. Coleman dismissed Trible's heat with cool detachment. "It's been a robust, engaging campaign," he said of the charges, "and I certainly believe that I'm better prepared to meet the Democrat than I was when we began this campaign."

Back at Trible headquarters, there was cautious optimism that Trible might yet eke out a victory. The free fall in the Second District had finally stopped, and the Ninth District's slip to Coleman appeared to have been arrested. Yet there were indications that Trible was no longer the front-runner. For weeks Coleman and Parris had been running on borrowed funds, while Trible's campaign was the only solvent one. Now at the eleventh hour, undetected by reporters, Trible was taking out a $400,000 loan, secured by the signatures of several wealthy supporters.

The Parris camp, optimistic after a late-breaking endorsement from the rogue hero of Irangate, former Marine Colonel Ollie North, was still expecting the combination of a huge Northern Virginia turnout and disinterest downstate to put their candidate across the finish line ahead of the competition. On television screens, "Parris the Combatant" was back under wraps. "Parris the Grandfather" was trotted out for the closing media volley. Four-in-a-row political commercials, including a Wilder biographical spot, framed news shows across the Commonwealth on election eve, and Parris won the good-neighbor award. "You may have noticed a big difference between me and my opponents. I'm the only one with grey hair," smiled Parris as he perched on the edge of his desk for a final chat. The rosy portrait was fueling an attack of last-minute paranoia at Coleman headquarters. Throughout the final weekend, Boyd Marcus and others wondered if Parris had not replaced Trible as their principal threat. But John McLaughlin urged the campaign to hold fast. Trible, he said, was still the man.

Unexpectedly and unwittingly, Marshall Coleman's old rival in the 1981 gubernatorial race, Chuck Robb, did him a late-breaking favor by arguing publicly that the hardest man for the Democrats to beat in the fall would be Coleman. Speaking at a lunchtime gathering of a Washington club, in what he may have thought was an off-the-record conversation, Robb expounded on Coleman's virtues as a candidate. The Associated Press rapidly distributed the report across the state. While Wilder would "eat Paul Trible for lunch," said Robb, Coleman "has more raw candidate skills than the other two." It was not a view shared by several key Wilder strategists, including Paul Goldman and Mike Donilon, the poll taker.

As the candidates headed to bed, final forecasts predicted that a low turnout favored Coleman and Parris; a turnout well ahead of the 234,000 GOP vote on Super Tuesday, the date of the 1988 southern presidential primary, was expected to bode well for Trible. The Coleman campaign was leaving little to chance. When an electrical storm put out telephone banks in Roanoke, a Coleman stronghold, campaign volunteers rounded up a generator and batteries, and kept the telephones ringing all evening long with the message—"Vote Coleman."

JUNE 12, 1989

Under laden skies and a threat of thunderstorms, Virginia Republicans flocked to the polls. Although the 404,000 who voted constituted only 15 percent of the state's electorate, the turnout was almost twice the size of the Super Tuesday crowd. But the large vote, rather than dooming Coleman, was cementing his victory.

Less than ninety minutes after the polls closed, Judy Peachee knew that the only miracle comeback of the evening would be Coleman's. There was no single indicator. Across the board, from Chesapeake and Portsmouth, from Chesterfield County and Northern Virginia, the numbers were less than Trible needed. When totals began arriving from Northern Virginia, showing that Parris's vote also was soft, "I said, 'Whoa . . . ,'" Peachee recalled. The end was in sight.

At 9:24 P.M., Trible, his wife, Rosemary, and son Paul entered the ballroom of a Richmond hotel and confirmed the inevitable to a somber crowd. To some who listened, Trible's final hour was also his finest. In his concession speech, there was a degree of graciousness and humanity often missing in Trible's public persona. He pledged loyalty to Coleman, quipped about the misfortune of facing his two toughest opponents simultaneously, and pledged to his family that "we're going to start living and sharing life together."

About fifteen minutes later, Coleman made the triumphant walk from his hotel suite to the victory party. As "The Eye of the Tiger"—a *Rocky* comeback theme—blared, Coleman held aloft the arms of sons Billy and Sean and savored the sweetness of rebirth. Calling Wilder a "worthy opponent" and pledging "some rip-roaring rhetoric before it's over," Coleman stood momentarily as a testament of hope to all political losers. This, after all, was a man who had lost elections, endured ridicule and indifference, had been whispered to be on the verge of becoming the Harold Stassen of Virginia politics, and yet had never veered from his twelve-year course.

When the tally was complete, Coleman had won 147,941 votes (37 percent). Trible had 141,120 (35 percent), and Parris trailed with 112,826 (28 percent). Since there is no runoff provision in Virginia primaries, the plurality made Coleman the winner. He had prevailed in half of the state's cities and almost half of its counties, and he had carried six of ten congressional districts. Most impressive, he had penetrated Trible's Tidewater stronghold by carrying the Second District, and Parris's Northern Virginia backyard by capturing the Tenth District.

Also nominated, without opposition, were state senator

Edwina "Eddy" Dalton of Chesterfield County for lieutenant governor and state senator Joseph Benedetti for attorney general. Dalton, who had represented a suburban Richmond county in the Virginia senate for two years, was the widow of former Republican governor John N. Dalton. Benedetti, an attorney, was a well-regarded legislator from Richmond who, nonetheless, was viewed as unlikely to defeat the highly popular incumbent attorney general, Mary Sue Terry.

Rapidly Democrats signaled that the 1989 gubernatorial election would not be politics as usual. In what Republicans fumed was a singularly ungracious act, Democrats hardly waited for the champagne corks to land before unpopping a missile of their own. In time for the 11:00 P.M. news, state Democratic chairman Larry Framme charged that Coleman had won the GOP primary through "a malicious campaign based on half-truths and distortions." Anxious to begin insulating Wilder against similar attack, Framme claimed that the negative campaigning was "a sad testament to their embrace of the mean-spirited and vicious campaign tactics advocated by Republican national chairman Lee Atwater." Politically, it was a masterly thrust, but Coleman responded to the attack with a cool, swift rejoinder. Framme's statement, he said, was "the press release of a distraught young man."

Back at Trible headquarters, Kenny Klinge and Randy Hinaman, Parris's political director, showed up for a night of commiseration and drinking. Some at Coleman's celebration were humming "Ding, Dong, the Witch is Dead" in honor of Judy Peachee, but Klinge had been through too many wars at her side to let his old friend toast in a new day alone. "Darn you guys," Peachee shouted out to the Parris backers as they walked through the door, "if you'd run a good campaign, I'd have won."

Peachee was not the only one surprised by Parris's disintegration. Bob Goodman, whose entire staff had ridden the train down from Baltimore for the Coleman victory celebration, said the shock of the night for him was Trible's second place finish. Parris carried 58 percent of the vote in his home district, the Eighth, second only among congressional districts to Trible's 61 percent in the First. But Coleman's narrow win next door to Parris in the Tenth constituted a repudiation of the congressman by people who knew him well. Activists speculated that Parris's flirtation with racial innuendo and his eleventh-hour endorsement by Oliver North, who was more controversial in Northern Virginia than downstate, might have hastened the move to Coleman.

In the end, the district-by-district percentages that the Trible campaign had counted on for a victory broke down in two places. One was South Hampton Roads, where Trible got 34 percent of the vote in Norfolk and Virginia Beach; he had counted on 45 percent. In every other district, he was almost on target. The second gap was Parris's failure to sweep Northern Virginia. Trible could have withstood a third place finish there, his campaign believed, so long as Parris held Coleman to a distant second. Tidewater and Northern Virginia voters had turned the election.

In the next day's blurry-eyed aftermath, pundits and politicians assessed the damage. The Republican primary had cost almost $11 million, over half of it for a media campaign that was as negative as any in Virginia history. Coleman was over $900,000 in debt, almost half of it to himself. Trible, the man who only a few years before had been a bright light in a flickering state Republican party, had been leveled; a man who six months before had topped the Democrats' "most beatable" list had won.

And yet, for Republicans there was an oddly exultant sense that the process had worked. It had winnowed out a candidate whose credentials seemed strongest on paper, and it had elevated a man who in many ways appeared the perfect match for Doug Wilder. If Wilder was charming and witty and bright, so was Coleman. If Wilder knew how to exploit an issue or avoid a political quagmire, so did Coleman. If Wilder was a tough, pragmatic campaigner, willing to do and say what the trail required, he was no more so than Coleman. Moreover, down by 40 points in the polls when the race began, Coleman had pulled himself up by his bootstraps. He was Lazarus back from the political dead.

Nor was there the sense of agony in Trible's defeat that some had expected. Within a few days of the voting, a story from Trible's election-night farewell in Newport News was making the political rounds, easing disappointment. Leaving Richmond, the Tribles had driven southeast to Tidewater, back to the site of their earlier victories for solace. As longtime friends and supporters hovered near at a late-night party, so the story went, Trible turned to his wife and whispered, "Free at last."

Marshall Coleman's nomination as Republican candidate meant that history already had been made in the 1989 governor's race. For the first time in the century, the state faced a gubernatorial contest in which neither candidate was a favorite of the conservative, monied establishment that once ran old Virginny.

6

A STATE TRANSFORMED

As the heat of the GOP primary battle subsided and both Republicans and Democrats prepared for the general election, there was at least one thing upon which all candidates of both parties, as well as the voters they would soon be courting, could agree: racially, politically, the Commonwealth of Virginia was a state transformed.

In 1776 as the American colonists were beginning their revolutionary struggle, John Adams of Massachusetts wrote Patrick Henry of Virginia a line for the ages. "We all look to Virginia for examples," he said. That was true enough for a while. Four of the nation's first five presidents were from Virginia. The bold spirit of the John Smiths and John Rolfes who planted a New World outpost at James Towne in the early seventeenth century had by revolutionary times developed a generation of leaders equal to the formidable task of forging a nation. There was Patrick Henry, crying out for liberty; George Washington, marshalling a ragtag band of farmers and shopkeepers into a fighting force; George Mason, crafting a declaration of rights; Thomas Jefferson, calling for independence; and James Madison, framing their ideals in a constitution.

But the offspring of those founding fathers often were less visionary, or at times spun visions in conflict with the larger forces of history. Robert E. Lee, Virginia's most revered figure of the mid-nineteenth century, was a model of personal nobility. But his role for posterity is as commander-in-chief of a defeated army in a failed civil war, one whose scars a century could not erase. Harry F. Byrd, Sr., whose name was synonymous with Virginia politics for four decades in the mid-twentieth century, also misread the winds of change. A former governor and vigorous champion of states' rights as a U.S. senator from 1933 to 1965, Byrd failed to make the leap from concern for the rights of states to insistence that they be fully responsible to their citizens. He was wedded to a limited, pay-as-you-go philosophy of government, and state services—from roads to welfare to public health—languished in the last years of his domain. One early 1950s study showed that, in a South already at the hind end of the nation's educational system, only Kentucky spent less on public education than Virginia. As late as 1963 a lower percentage of Virginia's eligible population was in high schools or universities than in any state in the union. Teachers' salaries were thirty-sixth in the nation, and the legislature was still refusing to adopt a state sales tax.

Twenty-five years later, the Virginia in which Doug Wilder launched his gubernatorial bid stood transformed. Politically, the state had cast off the shroud of V. O. Key's famous 1949 characterization. "Of all the American states," Key wrote in his landmark study, *Southern Politics in State and Nation*, "Virginia can lay claim to the most thorough control by an oligarchy. Political power has been closely held by a small group of leaders who, themselves and their predecessors, have subverted democratic institutions. . . . It is a political museum piece."

Touches of the "cavalier, aristocratic, eighteenth-century tone" cited by Key remained in Virginia state government, as did a general warmth toward large corporations and a distrust of labor unions. But there was a dramatic softening of the rigid mold that defined politics earlier in the century. One-party rule by yellow-dog Democrats (as in, "he'd vote for a yella dawg if it was a Democrat") had given way to two-party politics. From Reconstruction to 1948, Virginians had voted once for a Republican presidential nominee, defecting only because of Democrat Al Smith's Catholicism and anti-Prohibitionist views in 1928. In 1952 they voted for victorious Republican Dwight Eisenhower and thereafter they voted only once for a Democrat, Southerner Lyndon Johnson in 1964. In 1989, Virginia's twelve-member congressional delegation was half Democrat, half Republican. And while Democrats still dominated the General Assembly, the little Republican band had increased from a half dozen in 1952 to almost one-third of the membership in 1989. Three Republicans and two Democrats had been elected governor in the previous two decades.

Gone too was the conservative Byrd Organization's heyday when state politics was the fiefdom of a handful of whites, and blacks—like labor unionists—served the electoral process principally as whipping boys at election time. Andrew Buni in *The Negro in Virginia Politics* noted that the average participation in Democratic gubernatorial primaries between 1925 and 1945, which were tantamount to election, ranged between 5 and 7 percent of the adult population. Key put the figure only slightly higher, at 11.5 percent. In contrast, Key observed, even Mississippi was a hotbed of democracy. Forty-four years later, almost 60 percent of eligible adult Virginians were registered, according to estimates. Of those, 66.5 percent were to cast ballots in the 1989 gubernatorial election, a state record. Contributing to the demise of the Byrd Organization and the expanded electorate were both laws opening up the electoral process to blacks and the U.S. Supreme Court's one-man, one-vote decision. That ruling forced the remapping of legislative districts that had given rural voters influence far beyond that awarded city dwellers. A vote in rural Surry County, for instance, might be worth ten votes in Richmond because there were so many fewer residents of the rural legislative district than of the urban one.

Economically, the Virginia of 1989 was more vibrant than at any point in her history. Driven by the booming federal presence in Washington's Virginia suburbs, and by Hampton Roads' complex of ports, shipyards, and military bases, per capita income for six million residents had risen to ninth highest in the nation. An unemployment rate of 3 percent, announced a few weeks before the election, was the lowest in the continental United States. Culture and heritage might link the Old Dominion to the South, but in many ways the Commonwealth had entered a sphere of progress apart from most regional neighbors. The Washington-based Corporation for Enterprise Development early in 1989 ranked Virginia, along with California, Connecticut, Maryland, Massachusetts, New Jersey, and Vermont, as the states with the most dynamic economies—although the report also chided Virginia for lagging in minority and female business ownership and in rural job growth. In 1980, Virginia was corporate home to two Fortune 500 companies. By 1987, the list had grown to fourteen. Prosperity was supported by a diversified economy combining traditional industries—agriculture, mining, forestry, fisheries, tobacco, and textiles—with an exploding service sector. Uncle Sam helped too. Home to the Pentagon, the world's largest naval complex in Norfolk, and one of the world's biggest shipyards in Newport News, the state was host to more federal dollars per resident than any state in the union.

Yet not everything was roses in Virginia. For all her wealth, state government still bore the imprint of Harry Byrd. Virginia continued to lag in its commitment of resources to state concerns. While the individual tax burden grew substantially in the 1980s, Virginia was near the bottom nationally when state spending was measured as a percentage of personal income. Despite a major influx of funds in the 1980s, teacher salaries hovered no higher than the national midpoint. The state now was a leader in the South in per capita spending for elementary and secondary education, but on a national chart it fared only middling well.

Moreover, economically and culturally, an invisible line separated the "haves" of the urban Golden Crescent, stretching down the state's populous eastern corridor, from more rural and less vibrant areas to the west and south of Richmond. A 1988 University of Virginia study put the situation in perspective: "The Northern Virginia . . . area is almost entirely responsible for Virginia's higher-than-average per capita income," the report said. If Northern Virginia were excluded, overall state income would fall to 92 percent of the U.S. average, a figure more in keeping with other Southern states. Per capita income in Northern Virginia ($23,744) was more than double that in the far southwest ($11,231). Simply put, says Gordon V. Smith, a Northern Virginia developer and heavy contributor to Coleman's GOP primary campaign: "If you cut off Northern Virginia . . . , the rest of the state would look like Arkansas."

Virginia is also among the nation's fastest growing states, and that population surge further highlighted the east-west gap. Almost 90 percent of the recent growth had occurred in the eastern third of the state, prompting speculation by University of Virginia planners that 73 percent of all Virginians would live in urban areas by the year 2000. In 1960, the figure had been 56 percent.

The widening split between the crowded, high-tech eastern corridor and the rest of the state produced substantial policy questions for the gubernatorial candidates. While eastern Virginia grappled with choked highways, muddled land-use plans, split-seam classrooms, and sporadic water shortages, portions of western Virginia were preoccupied with a more basic agenda —jobs, inadequate health care, and ill-equipped schools. The east-west division produced a warning from a University of Virginia research analyst in an April 1988 report. "A pattern as extreme as this usually means that the two areas have widely differing needs and attitudes that can be difficult to reconcile," she said. As if validating her words, votes to adopt a state lottery in 1987 and pari-mutuel betting in 1988 mirrored the geographic schism, with the west almost unanimous in its opposition to those proposals, and eastern Virginia equally unified in its support.

For politicians, a tantalizing feature of Virginia's growth was the addition of thousands of newcomers to the body politic. The state's population grew by more than half a million between 1980 and 1987, and half of the increase was due to arrivals from outside. As an upshot, the 1989 electorate was expected to include 100,000 or more voters who four years earlier had not even been living in the state. Predicting their preferences was a favorite parlor game of political activists. A survey for the *Richmond Times-Dispatch* in late 1987 found the typical newcomer to be younger, better educated, more affluent, and more predisposed to suburban life than native Virginians. If the newcomers were moderately conservative in their fiscal views, the survey also found them to be more liberal than old-timers on several matters. Among them were environmental protection, homosexual rights, and race relations.

Their claims to be running a color-blind campaign to the contrary, Democrats were on the lookout in 1989 for every racially moderate voter they could find. The abiding fear, even in a state sometimes praised for racial moderation, was that the pool was too small to win a race for governor. With a few exceptions, most notably the state's disastrous plunge into massive resistance to school integration in the late 1950s, race relations in Virginia have been a point of pride, to white natives at least. The consensus is that there is better-than-average racial accord for a Southern state. That view, faint praise to some, is a cause for celebration to others. The prevailing sentiment was voiced by V. O. Key when he wrote of Virginia in 1949: "Its race relations are perhaps the most harmonious in the South." The race-baiting vitriol that spurred a Theodore Bilbo in Mississippi or a George Wallace in Alabama was generally missing among Virginia politicians.

As with other aspects of political life, however, a degree of civility and fairness masked deep-seated divisions and passions. Byrd, whose opposition to *Brown v. Board of Education* rallied the General Assembly into adopting school-closing legislation, had also been the architect in the late 1920s of a tough anti-lynching law. Open violence and name-calling might be too crass to be condoned, but that did not prevent those in power from systematically denying blacks educational, political, and economic equality.

The starting point for black-white relations in the Old Dominion is 1619, the year a ship controlled by the Earl of Warwick deposited about twenty black indentured servants in the New World. Those early arrivals were soon followed by thousands of blacks who arrived in chains, and did not have the similar good fortune to earn their freedom. By the early nineteenth century, slave markets thrived in Richmond, Norfolk, Petersburg, Williamsburg, Fredericksburg, and other eastern Virginia sites. For a time, Richmond was the country's largest slave market after New Orleans, and several slave traders were among the city's most prominent businessmen.

While some historians maintain that Virginia slaves were generally better treated than their brothers and sisters to the south, any such advances were relative. Two notorious slave revolts put to rest any notion that blacks were a happy, banjo-strumming lot. In 1800, a Henrico County slave named Gabriel Prosser organized a massive slave uprising intended to result in the capture of Richmond and the wholesale massacre of whites. Plans for the revolt apparently involved hundreds—perhaps thousands—of slaves in an area stretching as far as Charlottesville. At the last moment, slaves on a plantation outside Richmond told their master what was afoot. He notified the governor, and with the assistance of unexpected thunderstorms, the intended uprising was quelled.

Thirty-one years later, a modestly educated Southampton County slave named Nat Turner led a bloody, two-day insurrection that sent shock waves across the Commonwealth. Later depicted in a William Styron novel, Turner and his fellow slaves murdered sixty whites before they were stopped. Turner, who was called "the Prophet" by fellow slaves, hid for two months in swampy terrain near the North Carolina border, but was eventually captured and hanged. One casualty of the uprising was what had been a growing movement by enlightened whites to slough off slavery in Virginia. When the rebellion occurred there was a recoil. Even despite that, Thomas Jefferson Randolph came within a few votes of getting a bill through the 1831 Assembly that would have set in motion the liquidation of slavery in the state.

By the time of the Civil War, an estimated 490,000 slaves were living in Virginia. Even freed blacks, with a sizeable population in cities like Richmond, suffered continual indignities. The Richmond city council, for example, in 1859 adopted an ordinance that forbade blacks to walk in Capitol Square unless accompanied by a white, to smoke publicly, or to congregate on street corners in groups of more than five.

Virginius Dabney, in his 1971 history of the state, argued that relations between blacks and whites at the close of the war were generally amicable. "Despite the near-chaos in the first months, . . . there was surprisingly little violence," he wrote. The Ku

Klux Klan was never so virulent as in some Southern states, although sheet-draped men hoping to intimidate blacks did ride across portions of south-central and southeastern Virginia. And yet, as Michael Chesson reminds in *Richmond After the War,* "Jim Crow's career in Richmond began on the day that slavery ended." Hospitals, cemeteries, and even the doors passed through on the way to vote, were segregated by race. The Richmond Railway Company policy restricting blacks to outside platforms on streetcars produced two riots in 1867. Finally the company agreed to integrate four of its six cars. The two lily-white cars were designated by white balls on the roof.

Among the Commonwealth's first black officeholders were 27 members of the 180-person General Assembly elected on July 6, 1869. Six senators and twenty-one house members were black. After the 1869 peak, black representation in the legislature eroded steadily, and by 1885, only one black senator and one black delegate remained. More than a century later in 1989, there were three black senators and seven black delegates in the 140-member legislature.

Prior to Wilder, the high point for black elected officials in Virginia was the brief tenure of John Mercer Langston as congressman from Virginia's Fourth District. Langston, the illegitimate son of a Louisa County planter and a freed slave, was educated at Oberlin College and later became both U.S. minister to Haiti and dean of Howard University Law School. He was ruled to have finished second in a three-way congressional race in 1888, and after a lengthy investigation of election corruption, was declared the winner by the U.S. House of Representatives. The investigation was so prolonged, however, that he served only a few months, and was defeated by a white candidate at the next election.

Any doubts about the attitude of many prominent Virginians toward the newly enfranchised black citizenry were erased by the state constitutional convention of 1902. Trading on techniques newly in vogue across the South, white lawmakers managed to effectively eliminate blacks as a voting force for a half century. Their intent, laid out by Carter Glass of Lynchburg, was explicit. "Discrimination! Why that is exactly what we propose," railed Glass. "That exactly is why this Convention was elected—to discriminate to the very extremity of permissible action under the limitations of the federal Constitution with the view to the elimination of every Negro who can be gotten rid of, legally, without materially impairing the strength of the white electorate."

A combination of literacy tests, blank paper registration forms, poll taxes, and all-white primaries achieved the desired result. Lauding the changes that went into effect on July 10, 1902, the *Richmond Times* proclaimed: "At the hour of noon today the dark cloud will be lifted, and peace and sunshine will come to regenerated Anglo-Saxon people as a result of the organic law made with its own hands." Andrew Buni estimates that of 147,000 Negroes of voting age, all but 21,000 were stripped from the voting rolls by October 1902, and the *Times* reported that half of those remaining were eliminated when the poll tax took effect in 1905.

Meanwhile, local councils and the state legislature were ensuring racial separation through laws and ordinances. By a one-vote margin in 1900, the General Assembly decreed that blacks and whites must travel on separate train coaches. Streetcars were added in 1905, and in 1925 the separation requirements were extended to theatres, opera houses, and "other places of public assemblage."

Onerous as life could be for Virginia blacks, historians insist that it was less frightful than elsewhere. During one bloody phase from 1917 to 1921, there were more than 170 lynchings nationally, most of them in the South. Only three occurred in Virginia during the period. J. Harvie Wilkinson, who chronicled the Byrd Organization, noted that in subsequent decades as well, "violence between the races was not condoned. Virginia's Southside, of all rural black belts in the South, offered the Negro the most genuine protection and paternalism."

What Virginia did not offer its black residents, however, was a voice in the political life of the state. Emboldened by racial gains during World War I, a group of blacks broke from the Republican party in 1921 and nominated their own "lily-black" slate for six state offices. John Mitchell, Jr., editor of the *Richmond*

Planet, led the ticket. But Mitchell failed to unite even blacks behind his gubernatorial bid. His journalistic rival, P. B. Young of Norfolk's *Journal and Guide*, argued that Mitchell's candidacy was racist. Mitchell won 5,046 votes of about 210,000 cast. A year earlier, Joseph R. Pollard, a leader of black Republicans in Richmond, had fared slightly better, winning 17,576 out of 202,000 cast in a U.S. Senate contest.

Those losses ended for several decades significant attempts by blacks to inject themselves into Virginia politics. Not until the 1940s did expectations stir again. Aroused by successes in the courts and by improved wartime treatment in the military, blacks from Norfolk to Roanoke began to run for local office in record numbers. The first major breakthrough came in 1948 when Oliver Hill, a Richmond civil rights lawyer, won one of nine seats on the city council, partially on the basis of an estimated three thousand white votes. Two years later, however, he was defeated when blacks opted to support an entire biracial slate rather than to cast single-shot ballots for Hill.

Throughout the 1950s, there were numerous black candidacies, but only occasional victories. Racially the tone for the decade was set when Virginia's political leadership decided to greet the U.S. Supreme Court's school desegregation order with opposition. Gov. Thomas B. Stanley had received the May 17, 1954, order calmly. But within days, as the call for resistance swept through Byrd Organization ranks, his mood switched from conciliation to confrontation. "I shall use every legal means at my command to continue segregated schools in Virginia," Stanley pledged to a listening South.

The next several years were a time of countless committee meetings and legislative votes as the Assembly, with Byrd's blessing, hammered out a policy of resistance. At times, Confederate flags flew in the balconies at the statehouse as lawmakers railed about the evils of race mixing. By the fall of 1958 when Warren County schools in western Virginia were ordered to desegregate, plans were in place. State law required the governor to close any school under court order to integrate. A school which tried to reopen would be denied state funds. On September 12, 1958, the plan clicked into action, and the doors at Warren County High School in Front Royal were shut. A week later, a high school and an elementary school were closed in Charlottesville. On September 29, 1958, ten thousand children were shut out from six secondary schools in Norfolk, and Virginians were reeling from the devastating consequences of a once-popular policy.

Harry Byrd, who a year earlier had told *Time Magazine,* "we face the gravest crisis since the War Between the States," watched approvingly from his Washington command post. But he could not sidestep the force of law. On January 19, 1959, the Virginia Supreme Court ruled the closings illegal. That same day, a three-judge federal panel in Norfolk declared that statutes authorizing the closings violated the Fourteenth Amendment. Two weeks later, under heavy police protection, twenty-one black children enrolled in previously all-white schools in Norfolk and Arlington. The final hurrah of the Byrd Organization had passed, but a bitter residue remained. In Prince Edward County, deep in the Southside, the local board of supervisors in May 1959 decided to abandon public education rather than integrate. White children were shipped to a private academy. For four years there were no local schools for black boys and girls.

The 1960s brought revolutionary progress for Virginia blacks, as legal and political barriers crumbled nationwide. Black voter registration in the state tripled from about 31,000 in 1941 to more than 100,000 in 1960. By October 1964, the number had surged to 173,832, and blacks—a cohesive political force for the first time since Reconstruction—claimed credit for President Johnson's Virginia victory. A year later, they once again were credited with turning an election, as Lt. Gov. Mills E. Godwin, Jr., defeated two rivals for governor. Ironically, Godwin had been one of the architects of massive resistance. Two decades later, he would be accused of injecting race into the campaign against Wilder for lieutenant governor.

Crosses might burn and throngs march across an embattled Deep South, but Virginians generally greeted the civil rights era with touches of their customary restraint. There were racial incidents, particularly in the Southside, but none approached the crescendo of passion in a Selma or a Birmingham. Activity peaked in the summers of 1963 and 1965. As the August 23, 1963, march on Washington approached, civil rights protesters demonstrated in Danville, Farmville, and elsewhere. Several hundred were jailed, and Martin Luther King, Jr., appearing at Danville's High Street Baptist Church, warned that the city could "easily become another Birmingham." It did not. Nor was there more than a smattering of violence in the summer and fall of 1965 as the Voting Rights Act took effect, and more than thirty rallies were held in tense Black Belt communities.

Once in motion, the wheels of black political progress could not be stopped. The decade saw black school board members appointed in Portsmouth, Hampton, Norfolk, and elsewhere. The first black member since Reconstruction entered the General Assembly. Three blacks won spots on the Richmond City Council, and a trickle of others were elected to councils across the state. As the 1960s closed, the Joint Center for Political Studies—a think tank on black issues—reported that thirty-four black men and women held political office in Virginia.

By 1989, the Joint Center's latest count put the number of black officials in Virginia at 123, 4 percent of the total in a state that was about 19 percent black. More blacks held office in Alabama, Georgia, Louisiana, Mississippi, North Carolina, and South Carolina, but those states also had more black residents. No state with a smaller black population than Virginia had a higher percentage of black officials.

One of the greatest indicators of racial progress came in those elections, including Wilder's 1985 race, in which white voting majorities elected black candidates. While the reverse—blacks voting for whites—was still the norm, state senator Robert C. Scott served a majority white district in Newport News, and blacks had been elected mayors of more than a half-dozen predominantly white Virginia cities, including Fredericksburg, South Boston, Roanoke, Danville, Martinsville, and Newport News.

Change in many communities was still not occurring spontaneously, however. Since 1982, the American Civil Liberties Union (ACLU) had filed Voting Rights Act lawsuits in almost two dozen Virginia localities. The ACLU claimed that election rules unfairly penalized blacks and the organization sought a switch from at-large to district voting. Several similar lawsuits were filed or threatened by the National Association for the Advancement of Colored People and the Lawyers' Committee for Civil Rights Under Law. The court cases were almost uniformly successful, and almost invariably led to increased black representation. Decisions in two controversial cases were handed down in the final months of the 1989 elections as judges ordered shifts to ward voting in Norfolk and Brunswick County. In Brunswick, a majority-black rural Southside county, blacks already held two of five supervisors' seats, but there had never been a black majority on a single board or commission appointed by the council. In Norfolk, where the population was more than one-third black, minorities gained their second council seat only after the voting discrimination lawsuit was filed.

Figures from an ACLU court case challenging appointed school boards suggest the ongoing difficulty of blacks in winning elective office. According to the data, in 1987 only three of Virginia's nine majority-black cities or counties had majority-black governing boards. In twelve localities where the black population ranged between 40 and 50 percent, six had no black council members or supervisors. Two others had one. In the twenty localities with a 30 to 40 percent black population, nine had no black members on the governing board. Six others had one.

Across the state, much like the nation, there were mixed signals indicating racial progress and stagnation. As elsewhere, state percentages of blacks enrolled in colleges and universities had entered a perplexing decline as the decade ended. Yet the National School Boards Association reported in 1989 that the state had bucked a regional trend, and was moving ahead in public school integration. The percentage of black students attending schools where the student body was mostly white had grown from 27 percent in 1968 to 42 percent in 1980 to 51 percent in 1986, according to the report.

Generally, black officeholders from Arlington to Roanoke echoed the words of William A. Kent, a black mortician and mayor of the small, majority-white city of South Boston. "Things have been changing since 1965. It gets better all the time," he said.

And yet, a few hundred miles away in Portsmouth, where blacks and whites lived in roughly equal numbers, such optimism had been overshadowed by several years of racial strain. A bizarre episode, in which the city's first black mayor was found to have secretly sent racial hate mail to other black council members, resulted in a recall vote that heightened tension. Other disagreements involving board appointments, public school policies, and political campaigns had left civic leaders there anguished over how to recapture an aura of good will.

On the housing front, "the feeling is good," said Kent Willis, director of the Virginia ACLU and a state leader in fighting housing discrimination. "When you talk to people who control the market, you sense that things are more open than they used to be." And yet, he added, statistics showed relatively little progress in eliminating segregated living patterns since the Fair Housing Act was passed two decades earlier. One example of ongoing intolerance occurred in the Southside town of Emporia in 1988 when a group of white neighbors—including some of the town's leading citizens—banded together to block a college-educated black couple with white-collar jobs from buying a house in a segregated area. The case resulted in an out-of-court settlement.

In many ways, Virginia's racial climate mirrored the racial climate elsewhere in the nation. National polls indicated a gradual improvement in racial attitudes, but also showed widely varying views between blacks and whites on the degree of discrimination remaining in society. Meanwhile, few were optimistic that severe economic and educational gaps between blacks and whites reflected in the 1980 census would be markedly improved in the 1990 count. In Virginia, those decade-old numbers showed that 8 percent of black adults had completed four years of college, compared with 21 percent of whites. Six percent of whites and 23 percent of blacks lived below the poverty line. Black unemployment was running better than two to one ahead of the white jobless rate. A 1986 report by the Virginia Employment Commission showed the same two-to-one split.

As was true nationally, Virginia blacks were lamenting recent U.S. Supreme Court actions, including an order dismantling a Richmond policy requiring black contractors to be awarded a portion of city business. Many of the affected contractors claimed the policy had been the origin and the mainstay of their success. Yet even as some doors closed, others opened. One telling example of the incremental yet relentless pace of change could be found in Prince Edward County. There, where whites left the school system and public officials abandoned a generation of black school children in 1959, segregationist cries of "Never!" had long faded. By 1989, the former white haven, Prince Edward Academy, was actively recruiting black applicants. And —in a number that grew slightly every year—more than a third of the students in the once-ostracized public schools were white.

Many of Doug Wilder's supporters, if not the candidate himself, were quietly weighing those and other racial indices as the GOP primary ended and the governor's race began in earnest.

What the concern came down to was this. Had Virginia voters become color-blind enough to elect a black man to their highest office if they agreed with his policies, or to reject him, without racial bias, if they did not? Or did racial questions still outweigh all others?

For a century or more, the unwillingness of whites to vote for blacks—whether or not they shared the same political philosophy—had kept any black person from being elected governor of an American state. If Wilder were elected, it would signify that in the state of Virginia at least, the old racial equation had changed. Such evidence of a color-blind electorate would make a profound statement about the diminishing importance of race in Virginia, the South, and the country.

7

STRATEGIES

Some of Douglas Wilder's strategists, watching from afar, joined the celebration over Coleman's primary victory. Although Chuck Robb and much of the press had come to see the former attorney general as the Democratic nominee's toughest possible opponent, several of those charting Wilder's campaign believed otherwise. First, they reasoned, Coleman was the only one of the Republican hopefuls without a solid geographic base. He had support in the western part of the state, where he first held office, and in Northern Virginia, where he moved after losing the 1981 race for governor. But in neither case would his backing approach that of Trible in Tidewater's First District, or Parris in Northern Virginia's Eighth. Either Parris or Trible might deprive Wilder of one of the regions considered essential to a Democratic victory. Traditionally, Virginia Democrats have won state office with a three-cornered strategy, carrying Tidewater, Northern Virginia, and the far Southwest. Even before the 1989 race began, Trible or Parris would have laid claim to large blocks of voters in at least one of those regions.

Second, Wilder and Paul Goldman hoped to frame the election as a referendum on the new Virginia versus the old Virginia. The choice they intended to pose was between looking forward and looking to the past. Both Goldman and Mike Donilon, the pollster, thought Coleman fit more naturally into the future-past equation. Unlike Trible and Parris, Coleman had not held office during the 1980s. He also was the man who lost to Chuck Robb in 1981 at the juncture that set the state on its current course. Wilder voiced the theme that would become the campaign's rallying cry in his nomination speech. "We have come too far together in the last eight years to turn back now," he said. Soon, the message had been abbreviated to an even more powerful line: "We've come too far to turn back now." Later, in commercials and speeches he would add, "Don't let Marshall Coleman take us back." Wilder and Goldman argued that key features of the new Virginia were the economic, educational, and other advances of the Robb-Baliles years. Unemployment had been cut in half; per capita income had risen from twenty-sixth in the nation to tenth; and teachers' salaries had advanced to the midpoint nationally. But many attuned to Virginia's segregationist past believed an even more potent, subliminal message in Wilder's theme was racial—don't take us back to the days of inequality. "You were saying it, but you weren't saying it," says Jay Shropshire, a longtime Wilder ally who was senate clerk during the campaign.

Third, Wilder strategists thought Coleman was vulnerable because of longstanding animosities toward him in the downstate business community, dating to his victorious 1977 race against former Democratic delegate Edward Lane. The old guard was furious when Coleman, in running for attorney general as a moderate, forward-thinking Republican, had dredged up Lane's twenty-year-old segregationist past. Coleman's handling of his 1981 campaign debt had also soured some prominent GOP donors. Lawrence Lewis, a Richmond investor who helped raise money for Parris in 1989, complained that Coleman never repaid a $250,000 loan made by Lewis in 1981. "He has never so much as written me a note to say thanks," Lewis said of Coleman during the primary campaign. Several creditors from the earlier race were also unhappy with the terms of their financial settlements.

Wilder's inner circle approached the matchup with cautious optimism. Polling and focus groups conducted in January had encouraged them enormously about the potential for Wilder's election. Focus groups, a relatively new campaign tool, consist of a dozen or so voters who are asked to react to information about a candidate, including potential campaign ads. Consultants analyze their responses for clues about how to frame a campaign. What Wilder's consultants found was that voters already assumed competence, intelligence, trustworthiness, and several other hard-to-earn intangibles on Wilder's part. They were less sure if they liked him. But when details of Wilder's life were supplied—his struggle to achieve, his heroism in Korea —focus-group participants responded immediately and warmly. "I've never seen a lieutenant governor who had the kind of profile he had before the race began," says Mike Donilon, the pollster.

Usually, notes David Doak, the media consultant who participated in the early polling sessions, voters have a generally favorable impression of aspiring officeholders, but have to be convinced of vital traits. "Voters had done the opposite with Doug," he says. They still did not know much personally about him, but "they assumed that to be where he'd gotten, he had to be tough, capable, and all these other things."

The Wilder campaign was giving them the information they lacked, as well as insulating the candidate from the possibility of an immediate postprimary attack, when it spent several hundred thousand dollars in June and July on a biographical television spot that began by describing Virginia as the "birthplace of the American dream." As photographs of Wilder and his family flickered across the screen, an announcer told the candidate's version of the dream story: "Born in poverty, he created his own opportunities, working his way through school, earning a law degree. Never one to run from a fight, on a lonely hilltop in Korea outnumbered by communist forces, he earned the bronze star for valor and bravery. He returned to raise a family and dedicate himself to public service . . . "

In their early analyses of the race both the Coleman and Wilder camps put Coleman slightly ahead, due partially to a boost in the polls from his primary victory. Each side also analyzed the race in terms of attracting white voters. Almost every black voter was assigned automatically to the Wilder camp. Democrats believed they needed 42 percent of the white vote to win. Republicans, who were figuring on a slightly higher black turnout, thought they had to capture 60 to 62 percent of whites.

The Democratic analysis of the upcoming contest identified several problems for Wilder. About 60 percent of Virginia residents thought the state was going in the right direction, a plus, but an increasing number of those happy voters also identified themselves as Republicans. According to Donilon's assessment, 44 percent of Virginians now saw themselves as Republicans, as compared with 38 percent who thought of themselves as Democrats. (Republicans contend the split is more even.) The problem was particularly acute in the prosperous Washington suburbs. Hitherto considered an essential ingredient of Democratic success, that area was turning Republican at an even faster rate than the rest of the state as affluent young professionals aligned themselves with the economic policies of Republican administrations in Washington.

To capture some GOP-leaning voters, Democrats believed, their first challenge was to attract younger white women. Numerous party surveys have shown the subset known as "white women under the age of forty" to be more open than other categories of voters to a Democrat's message. Next most approachable were white males under forty. "By the time you get to white men over fifty," said one Wilder strategist, "it takes dynamite to move them."

Wilder's inner circle was hopeful that a changed dynamic on abortion, resulting from a long-anticipated U.S. Supreme Court decision, might provide a vehicle for winning young white women to their cause. No one knew what the court's verdict would be, but polls suggested that any weakening of abortion rights would stir a powerful negative response among affected women. Wilder credits Paul Goldman with being the first to recognize the potential power of the issue.

The campaign was also worried about taxes. If services had improved in the Robb-Baliles years, the costs had skyrocketed as well. Internal polls indicated that Wilder was vulnerable on that point, even though he had tried to protect himself by breaking with the governor on the transportation tax plan. Three days after Coleman's nomination, Wilder delivered a tax speech in Williamsburg in which he claimed credit for several tax cuts, including the recent one for private pensioners, and accused Coleman of "campaigning in a uniform he never wore as attorney general—that of a proven tax cutter."

The impact of a negative assault was another concern. There was no doubt that the attack was coming. In 1985 Republicans had identified problem areas for Wilder, among them the controversial rowhouse, the Supreme Court reprimand for failure to properly represent a client, and the late tax payments. Repeatedly, including in the primary just past, Coleman had shown his willingness to go for the jugular in political campaigns. There was considerable worry that Doug Wilder's jugular might be all too exposed.

How to respond to negative campaigning was a major topic in strategy sessions leading up to the general election. In 1985 Wilder had adopted the silent approach, never going on the attack against his Republican opponent for lieutenant governor. Robb, among others, had advised him that it was too risky a strategy for a black candidate to do otherwise. In 1989 there would be no such constraints. "This time we said we're going to come out of the box and take Coleman on from the beginning," says a senior Wilder strategist. The presidential election just past had indicated the hazards of doing otherwise. Many observers argued that Michael Dukakis, the Democratic nominee, lost the election when he failed for weeks to respond to a series of ads questioning his patriotism and toughness on crime.

In their first meeting Wilder and Frank Greer, the media consultant who replaced Doak, focused on how to deal with negative campaigning. "He was very concerned about what happened to Mike Dukakis," recalls Greer. The consultant was fresh from helping Gaston Caperton win the governorship in West Virginia, and they had devised a strategy there that might work in Virginia as well. The idea was both to answer every attack immediately, and also to turn negative campaigning itself into an issue. The notion dovetailed with what Wilder already had in mind.

Stating his position in mid-July in Roanoke, Wilder asserted: "I am committed to waging a clean campaign. . . . At the same time, let me state unequivocally: I will not hesitate to respond to mud or to distortions of my record. I will not, however, respond by stooping to similar tactics. Rather, I will make every effort to set the record and facts straight. . . . Likewise, I will diligently probe my opponent's record and his positions on the issues, questioning him on inconsistencies and on the soundness of his stances." Within that final statement, Republicans later insisted, lay all the room Wilder needed for mounting his own negative assault.

Finally, there was the matter of race. Republicans believe Wilder made subtle racial appeals during the campaign, when he spoke about equality and when he urged, "We've come too far to turn back now." Democrats who asked voters to "Make history" by electing Wilder were also stressing a racial theme, the Republicans say. But members of Wilder's inner circle insist that their strategy as the contest began was no more focused on race than were Wilder's racially antiseptic public statements on the subject. If others wanted to read a racial message into the campaign slogans, so be it. But, "Doug Wilder was always very up front," says Greer. "We're not going to make it an issue."

Even after the campaign, most staffers followed Wilder's cue by refusing to speculate on the role of race in the outcome. One worker quoted Goldman as telling others, "We're not going to worry about something we can't do anything about." But Marian Tucker, house majority leader Tom Moss's political aide and a Goldman admirer, recalls that privately "Paul Goldman said, it's going to come down to race and abortion, and all through the race, he never lost sight of that. We were all in la-la land thinking Virginia was ready to elect a black governor."

Protests to the contrary, there is little doubt that Wilder's brain trust took race into their calculations. Doak recalls polling data indicating that younger voters, and—surprisingly to the campaign—blue-collar voters, were more open to a black candidate than were older or white-collar voters. Even if Wilder did succeed in building up a lead in polls, his backers knew, it might evaporate during the final week of campaigning, because traditionally, voters undecided at the last minute in black-white contests break overwhelmingly for the white candidate.

To a degree, however, the campaign's racial strategy was simply to hope that the Coleman campaign might make the mistake of sounding racist. "We were hoping one of his cronies would say it," says Shropshire. In two previous gubernatorial elections, Virginians had reacted strongly when a former governor and one-time segregationist, Mills E. Godwin, Jr., made speeches viewed as having racial overtones. Virginians might still have racial biases, but they clearly did not want to be confronted with them.

If Wilder's strategy was in place as the general election got under way, some Democrats were worried that other essential ingredients of a campaign were missing. As late as July 1, Wilder had no research team and only one formal position paper—a two-page statement on drugs hammered out by Goldman and press secretary Laura Dillard in a couple of afternoons. Meanwhile, longtime Democratic workers were griping about being left out of the campaign. "That phone never rings from anyone down there (at Wilder headquarters)," complained Gordon Morse, Gerald Baliles's speechwriter, who was astounded that no one from the campaign contacted him about what the governor was going to say at the nominating convention. Even those who did have access to the campaign leaders often appeared unsettled about what they saw. "There was a sense that with each passing day, we kept missing opportunities. We sat in meeting after meeting where it was incredibly difficult to communicate things we needed to do now to make other things happen in October," recalls Scott Reynolds, communications director for the state AFL-CIO. Pauline Fox Huffman, regional director for the union's political action arm, particularly remembers a June 30 meeting in which Wilder aides chastised her and other labor leaders for tensions during the nominating convention. "I was livid," she says. "We were there to get going, and they felt we needed to have our hands slapped one more time."

Other Democrats later recalled a sense of paralysis in trying to start a joint campaign operation that would work through the state party on behalf of the full ticket—Wilder for governor, Mary Sue Terry for attorney general, and Donald Beyer, Jr., for lieutenant governor. "It was extraordinarily difficult originally putting the joint campaign together," says one top party official. "It was difficult getting firm decisions. There was a month and a half where the desire was there, but it just wasn't catching." A member of Mary Sue Terry's political staff echoes those remarks: "We sat in meeting after meeting and nothing came out of it. . . . I think Doug thought he could run the show the way he did in 1985."

One longtime party activist says anger was stirred by the rumor that Laura Dillard had said she was worried that old-guard Democrats "would want to have our piece of Doug." The Wilder staff "wanted it to be their campaign, and it was silly," the party worker adds. Another party stalwart, Moo Murray, says her concern through the spring and summer was that "not enough people felt ownership of the campaign. . . . It did create sniping from folks, saying, 'Nobody called me. He doesn't know what he's doing.'"

In fact, the staff Wilder had put together was much broader than in 1985. But few of those selected had longstanding ties to the state Democratic party. Many were young, and followed Wilder's lead in keeping information about the campaign close to the vest. And, it eventually emerged, there were problems at the top.

The nine foremost players in the Wilder campaign in mid-June were Paul Goldman, who had the title of consultant; Frank Greer, media adviser; Mike Donilon, pollster; Laura Dillard, press secretary; Joel Harris, who had left the lieutenant governor's office and whose specific role as consultant was largely undefined; Joe McLean, campaign manager; Michael Brown, deputy campaign manager; Rob Shinn, finance director; and Jay Shropshire, who had no formal role in the campaign, but was a key adviser.

Paul Goldman was one of the most intriguing figures on the state political scene. A tousled vegetarian fabled for munching raw potatoes and bags full of seeds and dried fruits, for driving a car loaded with dirty laundry and old newspapers, for jogging miles a day, and for treating the telephone as an umbilical cord to life, Goldman is a fount of wisdom and minutiae on earlier political campaigns dating to the previous century. Like a lightning bug, he has flittered through Virginia politics for more than a decade, illuminating one campaign or another before disappearing from sight, only to reappear months later. He grew up in Queens, New York, and once worked in the New Jersey attorney general's office, but little is known about his past—or, for that matter, his present. "He's one of those people who was never born, had no childhood, and lives nowhere," says another Democratic operative.

Goldman's Virginia debut came in 1977 when he directed what was, prior to Wilder's 1985 victory, the biggest upset of recent decades—Henry Howell's ouster of then-attorney general Andrew P. Miller for the Democratic nomination for governor. Miller was the moderate shoo-in; Howell was the liberal iconoclast making his third bid for governor. But after a low-key campaign in which Howell toned down and Miller partisans took the nomination for granted, Howell won. Briefly Goldman was the political man of the hour. Then two weeks later, he was demoted by Howell, who wanted a more conventional manager for the general election, and left the campaign.

Over the next few years, Goldman worked for a variety of Democratic candidates on his forays into the state. He was usually welcomed because his brain was a seedbed of political creativity. But he was often kept in the background because his demeanor seemed so unorthodox in staid Virginia. "My metaphor for Paul was that we kind of kept him locked in a little room and slid food under the door and he slid memos out," says a woman who worked with him in Chuck Robb's gubernatorial race.

Wilder's 1985 victory fixed Goldman's place in the galaxy of Virginia political consultants. But Goldman's attack on Robb for allegedly taking too much credit for Wilder's 1985 victory left the consultant as something of a liability as 1989 approached, even though Wilder had tacitly approved the remarks. The solution to the problem was vintage Goldman—and Wilder. Throughout the winter and spring, Wilder dodged questions about Goldman's campaign role, avoiding commitment even on whether his former consultant would be a player. Behind-the-scenes, however, Goldman was involved in strategy sessions, and was viewed by many Democrats as the person who most reflected Wilder's views. When he finally went on the campaign payroll, there was no press release, although every other employee of similar stature merited an announcement. Nor could his presence easily be detected on campaign spending forms. Through the spring, there were payments to the United States Consulting Group and the National Consulting Group. It was late June before the campaign confirmed that both "groups" were actually Goldman.

Frank Greer, who handled media consulting, liked to refer to himself as "a good ol' boy from Tuscaloosa, Alabama," the son of schoolteachers, the grandson of sharecroppers. But in 1986 he established himself as one of the most skillful media advisers in Washington. That year he helped Wyche Fowler of Georgia, Kent Conrad of North Dakota, and Brock Adams of Washington defeat incumbent Republican senators. The annual account billings of his firm, Greer, Margolis, Mitchell and Associates, are estimated to be $10 million. His specialty is selling candidates perceived as liberal to electorates that are not.

Greer, whose office decorations include pictures of Thomas Jefferson and Mother Jones, the legendary labor organizer, is described as easygoing. He wears jeans to the office, listens to country music, and likes hunting and barbecue. But he becomes passionate when speaking about issues and ideas he is committed to—including the Jeffersonian ideal of equality, and freedom of choice on abortion. His involvement with the latter predated his arrival at the Wilder campaign, and proved a fortuitous benefit of his hiring. Greer's firm designed the Statue of Liberty logo of the National Abortion Rights Action League (NARAL) and handles their national media campaign. Greer has worked for the Public Media Center, which handles advertising for Planned Parenthood. His wife, Stephanie Solien, is a former director of the Women's Campaign Fund, which promotes women candidates. Greer viewed working for the Wilder campaign as a chance to secure his place in the top echelon of the consulting world.

Mike Donilon, the pollster, also committed his services to Wilder with hopes of establishing himself professionally. A protégé of Pat Caddell, former president Jimmy Carter's pollster, Donilon and colleague David Petts established a polling firm in 1987 after Caddell quit the consulting business. They viewed the Wilder race as a potential breakthrough contest for their fledgling firm, and devoted countless hours to the effort. Despite his age, thirty, Donilon has seen major national races, including several featuring prominent black politicians. Through the Caddell firm, in 1983 he worked for Chicago mayor Harold Washington and Philadelphia mayor Wilson Goode. Both experiences provided clues about what to expect from the electorate in black-white matchups.

Chubby-faced, with glasses and sandy hair, Donilon also brought another unexpected quality to the campaign—he liked to talk, particularly on the telephone, almost as much as Goldman did. The pair conversed almost daily, frequently for hours at a time. When campaign workers wanted to talk to one or the other, they often would have to interrupt a telephone conversation between the two. At times the same worker would return a few hours later to find Donilon and Goldman still deep in conversation.

Seldom has one so untested been handed so much reponsibility as when Wilder named Laura Dillard his press secretary for a campaign that would command international attention. Dillard, twenty-three years old at her hiring, was a 1987 Phi Beta Kappa graduate and former debating society president at William and Mary. She worked briefly in Wilder's state office before entering graduate school in theology at Yale University in the fall of 1988. There her focus was nineteenth-century Germany. Her interest was more historical than spiritual. When Wilder and another press secretary, Constance Ober, parted company over a salary dispute early in 1989, the lieutenant governor contacted Dillard, and she agreed to return. Before the campaign ended she would emerge as a player in Wilder's inner circle. None was more loyal—or idealistic. Wilder chose her, she once said, because he trusted her ability, liked her dry wit, and knew that "I'm clearly not somebody who wants to make a career on his coattails.

"He's a person who plays everything close to the vest, and I'm willing to live within those parameters," she said. "I don't pry. I know far less than most press secretaries about his personal life. . . . I like to learn from him, and he likes to teach. It's important to him that he feels he can trust people. He said to me, 'You listen.'"

Joel Harris, whose role as consultant was never defined, even to many of those in the campaign, was another who appeared to command Wilder's trust. But he was also one of Wilder's most controversial advisers, partly because he was once a Republican and had switched parties, partly because he had raised eyebrows by making a great deal of money in real estate and business investments in a short period of time, and partly because he had acquired some influential enemies along the way, including Jay Shropshire. A moderate who left the GOP in a fallout with the party's right wing, Harris showed up in 1985 as a Democrat doing opposition research for the Baliles gubernatorial campaign. By the end of the election, he was also working for Wilder, including helping to construct a last-minute negative ad that was never used. When the campaign ended, he wound up as the overseer of Wilder's state office.

Wilder and Harris shared an appreciation for a first-class lifestyle, an every-hair-in-place perfection in personal appearance, and an interest in making money. Harris introduced Wilder to some business opportunies, and devoted himself to promoting Wilder's political interests. But several of Wilder's other associates—including Jay Shropshire, Laura Dillard, and longtime aide Judy Anderson—were not admirers of Harris. Harris was an owner of the townhouse in which the campaign was headquartered, and he came and went in the early months, helping with fund-raising and various projects. For a while, according to campaign finance reports, he appeared to be the highest paid member of the staff. But though he indisputably had Wilder's ear, several staffers say he was never intimately involved in operations.

Joe McLean had only recently been hired as director of the state Democratic party when Wilder tapped him to manage his historic campaign. A native Tennesseean in his early thirties, McLean had managed one congressional race in Tennessee. Few Virginia Democrats outside the party hierarchy knew him. But he was likeable, willing, and—most important—available. "There was a long effort going back at least twelve months, asking, who's going to manage the campaign? There's not a person around who didn't give serious thought to it," says Bill Wiley, Wilder's treasurer. The trouble was that there was no obvious person for the job. None of the three individuals considered closest to Wilder politically—Goldman, Harris, and Shropshire—was right. Goldman's strengths were as a strategist, not a manager. Harris was viewed too skeptically by many within the Democratic party. And Shropshire already held a more significant post as senate clerk. Finally, with time evaporating, Wilder settled on McLean.

As deputy campaign manager, Wilder named Michael Brown, a former political director of the state NAACP and the individual sometimes credited with bringing a semblance of structure to Wilder's day-to-day operations in his 1985 campaign for lieutenant governor. Brown, who is Wilder's nephew, was the only black member of the inner circle surrounding Wilder, although Richard Taylor, a Richmond attorney who for several years headed an ACLU voting rights project, was later named policy director. The scheduling director, the volunteer coordinator, and a few other members of the roughly thirty-member staff were also black. Brown's role, in addition to backing up McLean, was to work with Democratic constituent groups—minorities, labor, teachers, and others.

Rob Shinn was another of the youthful participants who earned the Wilder organization the nickname of the "Children's Crusade." The man who would head a financial operation that netted almost $7 million—far more than any other Democratic campaign in Virginia history—was in his midtwenties. The primary political credit of Shinn, who grew up in Bethesda, Maryland, was as the southern financial director for Richard Gephardt's abortive presidential campaign in 1988. Doak, who had worked with Shinn on that effort, introduced him to Wilder. If Shinn was young, he was also quick to learn. Buford Scott, who was committed to helping with fund-raising, recalls when the new finance director showed up in his office for a chat. "He came in, sat down, and called me Buford. I said, 'If you're going to get on in Richmond and Virginia, you'd better not call anyone by their first name until they ask you to do so.' Right away, he said, 'Yes sir, Mr. Scott.' He showed himself to be bright and responsive immediately."

The final member of Wilder's brain trust was Jay Shropshire, clerk of the senate since 1976. A Southsider who grew up in segregated surroundings, he also identifies personally with those who have risen to power from modest means. When Wilder arrived in the senate in 1970, Shropshire, then an assistant clerk, was one of the first to make him welcome. Their relationship, although it occasionally ran warm rather than hot, grew with the years. Few frequenters of Capitol Hill in Richmond love political intrigue more than Shropshire, or are better at manipulating the levers of power. It is illustrative that Shropshire's closest political allies include both Wilder and house speaker A. L. Philpott, considered by many to be the essence of an old Virginia politician. Shropshire engineered the 1985 breakfast, hosted by Philpott, that Wilder credits with being the turning point of that campaign. No other action better symbolized the erosion of racial barriers to his campaign, the candidate believed, than Philpott's decision to publicly support him. Shropshire would become chief of staff in Wilder's administration.

The majority of the other members of Wilder's staff were in their twenties, dedicated to the lofty ideal of electing a black man governor in a Southern state. Typical of them was Bob Blue, a twenty-two-year-old University of Virginia graduate who deferred Yale Law School for a year to work on the policy staff. When he joined the campaign, Blue's father, a Charlottesville engineer who supported Wilder, "kept making a lot of jokes about my rearranging the deck chairs on the Titanic," Blue recalls. "I thought we had a chance all along."

Across town at Marshall Coleman's headquarters, the Republican nominee's staff entered the general election on a high from their candidate's primary upset. Some felt that Coleman had already passed his chief hurdle in being elected governor, though no one believed that Wilder would be a pushover. The first order of business was handling two internal problems: eliminating the debt run up by the primary, and extending an olive branch to the defeated candidates and their staffs. At a press conference the morning after his victory, Coleman served notice that he intended to attack Wilder on both taxes and his past personal

problems. "Either the lieutenant governor has not been working very hard for tax relief, or he has been very ineffective at it,"
Coleman declared. He also declined to rule out the use of negative ads. "It's going to be a very spirited campaign," he promised.

Assessing the matchup with Wilder, Coleman strategists
believed they had no alternative other than to attack Wilder
aggressively. The state of Virginia, despite Coleman's plucky
attempts to find fault, was in good shape. While American voters are often attracted by the notion of change, making a case
for shifting directions would not be easy. Second, as they saw it,
Wilder had a rare political advantage. He could run both as the
candidate of continuity, the logical heir to the Robb-Baliles years,
and as the candidate of change, for what greater change could
there be than to elect a black man governor? "We recognized
early on that if we just emphasized the positives, the history-
making aspect of the Wilder campaign, coupled with the Robb-
Baliles years, made him the sure winner," says Frank Atkinson,
deputy campaign manager for Coleman. The candidate's two
strongest weapons, his staff believed, were Wilder's votes on
criminal justice, and various personal problems the campaign
lumped together as "character issues."

The Coleman forces were highly sensitive to the racial aspects of the upcoming contest. In the twenty-five-page "Agenda
for the 90s" released by the candidate the previous December,
he already had pledged that color would not insulate Wilder
from attack. Taking note of the charge made in 1985 that the
use of the word "liberal" was a code word for "black," Coleman
advised: "Throughout my public career, I have steadfastly
supported the principle of equal opportunity. . . . That support
reflects a deep, personal and lifelong commitment on my part
to racial fairness. There is no room for racial politics of any
kind in the public life of Virginia, and I will not tolerate it in my
campaign.

"I intend to see that the substantive differences between the
candidates for governor are aired fully during the coming campaign," he continued. "And I will not be intimidated or deterred
by groundless charges that my discussion of Mr. Wilder's record
and views is racially inspired."

Despite that ultimatum, "we were constantly aware of the racial backdrop of the campaign. Everybody was," says Frank Atkinson. Decisions were made not to highlight certain issues, such as "workfare" (requiring welfare recipients to perform certain jobs in order to get welfare benefits), because of fear that the remarks would be interpreted racially. Even though Coleman intended to emphasize crime, his backers also determined that there would be no Willie Horton–type ad. George Bush had been charged with playing racial politics in 1988 when he ran a television ad featuring Horton, a black murderer who went on a crime rampage while out of jail on a prison release program.

Atkinson argues that on balance race was an advantage for Wilder. Bob Goodman, the Coleman campaign's ad man, matter-of-factly suggests otherwise. The Coleman organization believed that racial voting by whites, coupled with the GOP's efficient turnout operation, would be good for at least a 5 percentage point boost at the polls, he says. If the campaign was no more than 5 points down going into election day, he believed Coleman would be the winner.

While Wilder was collecting a staff loaded with youthful devotees, Coleman was assembling an organization heavy with political veterans. Ironically, many had worked more often against him than for him. Coleman's campaign manager, his deputy campaign manager, and his communications director all had been part of the effort to deny him the GOP nomination for lieutenant governor in 1985. What those operatives and others had come to believe was that no other Republican had the intellect and competitive flair needed to defeat a seasoned pro like Wilder. They might not be emotionally devoted to Coleman on a personal basis, but they approached their jobs with a cool professionalism and a determination born of operating from the head, not the heart. The heat of the campaign would fire the forging of emotional bonds.

Their allegiance to the tall, lean candidate who still sported boyish good looks had come from watching him wage the most tenacious quest for the governorship in recent Virginia history. The starting point for that determination, believed many—

among them a brother, a former Sunday School teacher, and several friends—was a childhood marred by the tragedy of his father's death. Bill Coleman, the candidate's father, was already past thirty with a wife and two young sons, when he gave up his job at the Waynesboro DuPont plant in 1950 and set out on a spiritual quest. His goal was the ministry, and he began commuting to the Crozier Theological Seminary in Chester, Pennsylvania. When he arrived, Martin Luther King, Jr., was a member of the third-year class.

On one of those trips, Coleman swerved to miss a child who had run into the road. His car hit a brick wall, and his dreams collapsed with it. Eleven months later, after battling severe head injuries, Coleman committed suicide. The person who found the body was his skinny, mischievous nine-year-old son, Marshall. The boy, who by all accounts idolized his father, had come home from school at lunchtime, as he often did, to spend extra time with his dad. "He was a person I really loved and admired," said Coleman during his campaign for governor. "I knew he would want me to keep striving and make the best out of the situation."

After graduating from the University of Virginia with a Phi Beta Kappa key, volunteering as a Marine during the Vietnam War, and finishing law school, Coleman set up practice in the western Virginia college town of Staunton. The city had a tradition of political moderation, and in the late 1950s its two Democratic delegates to the General Assembly had broken with former senator Harry Byrd, Sr., by opposing massive resistance to the integration of public schools. By the early 1970s, Republicans were in control politically, and their agenda was a progressive one. Coleman rapidly established himself as chairman of the local Republican party, and when a vacancy arose for the House of Delegates in 1972, he was in position to claim it. Democrats did not bother to nominate an opponent. Three years later he maneuvered his way past more senior Republican politicians to become the district party nominee for the state senate, and won handily. At the Assembly, he was conservative on fiscal policies and progressive on social issues. When he ran for attorney general a few years later, Coleman courted black voters by declaring that he had supported all of Sen. Doug Wilder's social legislation. He was also a maverick whose penchant for seeking headlines caused house speaker A. L. Philpott to brand him "untrustworthy." Gambling on a race for attorney general against Democrat Ed Lane in 1977, he became the youngest man and first Republican ever to hold that state office. He promised to serve as "the people's lawyer," and adopted a populist, budget-cutting, openly political approach to the job. One of his first acts was to fire the Democratic attorneys who represented the state at local highway condemnation hearings, and hire Republicans to do the lucrative work.

Four years later, Chuck Robb brought Coleman's meteoric political rise to a halt. During four years as lieutenant governor, Robb had established himself as a prudent politician to whom bankers and corporate executives could relate. His dark good looks and his White House marriage to Lynda Bird Johnson Robb gave him a star quality with voters, and he had adopted enough of former President Johnson's social agenda to appease Virginia liberals. In one obvious political move in the early stages of the 1981 campaign, he reversed his earlier opposition to the Voting Rights Act, which protects the balloting of minorities and is considered sacred legislation by many blacks.

Running against Robb for governor posed a difficult strategic problem for Coleman, who had first won state office by siphoning off liberal Democratic votes. With Robb as his opponent, rather than Ed Lane, he decided to move further to the political right. Donning grey suits and keeping his irreverent wit sheathed, Coleman picked up Main Street support, though not enough to offset Robb's star-studded appeal. With his political career in jeopardy, Coleman acquiesced as former governor Mills Godwin sought to rally conservative voters by listing five reasons to back Coleman. Three of the five had racial implications. A charge was born that Marshall Coleman would do what it took to win.

In 1985 Coleman tried a political comeback by running for lieutenant governor, but a party still bitter about the earlier loss to Robb denied him its nomination. Not long afterwards his second marriage, to Niki Fox Coleman, ended. Neither individual has commented publicly on the reasons for the divorce, although both have suggested that Coleman's devotion to politics was a factor. Coleman and his first wife, Maureen Kelly, a Staunton-area schoolteacher and the mother of Sean and Billy, had separated not long after his election to the state senate in 1975. He and Fox, an artist and writer, were married about a year later.

Coleman's zeal for high office seemed no more tempered by defeat than by victory. After his 1981 loss for governor, he moved his residency to Northern Virginia and was soon back on the political circuit. After the 1985 defeat as well he quickly reappeared. In early 1987, he began paying to make one-minute commentaries on state issues, two to three times a week, on some sixty radio stations around the state. The goal was to court rural voters whose support he had lost in the 1985 convention. The spots continued for a year. Despite a busy schedule as a Washington attorney, he also planned three or four activities a week across the state. Sometimes he was campaigning for GOP candidates or attending party functions. At other times he would simply send out invitations for Republicans in a certain locality to meet him for a discussion of issues and a dutch-treat lunch. He had hired Dennis Peterson, who ran John Chichester's 1985 race against Wilder, as staff, and in August 1987 formally launched a fund-raising effort looking toward a gubernatorial campaign.

Meanwhile, Coleman's financial portfolio was becoming healthier than ever. When Coleman moved to the Northern Virginia suburbs on the heels of his defeat for governor, he was a man of modest means. He had just spent four years in a public office where his top annual salary was $45,000. He and his wife moved into a rented townhouse. Eight years later, he lived in a $1 million home and estimates placed his annual income at $500,000. Much of that wealth stemmed from Coleman's friendship with Dwight Schar, a developer and former high school science teacher who runs the nation's largest homebuilding firm, NVR L.P. Schar, a neighbor of Coleman's, orchestrated his hiring by the blue-chip Washington law firm of Arent, Fox,

Kinter, Plotkin & Kahn in 1985, and tapped him to handle his company's lucrative account. Coleman managed a public stock offering for Schar's former firm, NVHomes, and then assisted its hostile takeover of the Pittsburgh-based Ryan Homes, an industry giant. When the transaction was complete, Coleman emerged as a director of the newly formed company, which in 1988 had revenues of $1.3 billion. Along the way, Schar also built Coleman's 5,000-square-foot brick home in a neighborhood that the candidate himself had once likened to Disney World, and he brokered its $500,000 mortgage. When Schar emerged as a major donor in the Coleman campaign as well, Wilder was handed an issue that offset the focus on his own financial entanglements.

With the primary race just behind him, Coleman already had in place a fully operative staff for the general election contest with Wilder. He made only minor adjustments in what many party members credited with being an unusually well-functioning, division-free staff. Only as the election reached its tension-filled climax did cracks appear in the veneer.

In addition to the outside consultants, Bob Goodman and John McLaughlin, other players in the Coleman campaign included Boyd Marcus, the campaign manager; Frank Atkinson, the deputy director; Dennis Peterson, communications director; Bruce Hildebrand, the press secretary; Betsy Davis, finance director; Anne Kincaid, director of coalitions and a link to the pro-life movement; and Richard Cullen, a Richmond attorney who is one of Coleman's oldest, closest friends.

Boyd Marcus, a former administrative assistant to Rep. Tom Bliley of Richmond, was an unemotional, nuts-and-bolts strategist who hoped to use the Coleman campaign as a national launching pad for his consulting business. Active in state Republican politics since the late 1970s, Marcus entered the contest having never lost a political race that he managed.

His deputy, Frank Atkinson, who at times functioned almost as an equal in the campaign, was a nonpracticing attorney known in Republican circles for a keen intellect and intense devotion to conservative causes. He served two stints in the Reagan administration's Justice Department, one as departmental chief of staff and special counsel to then–attorney general Ed Meese. It was Atkinson who was the prime force behind the "Agenda for the '90s" document, which listed Coleman's positions on numerous issues and was one of the most ambitious position papers ever presented by a gubernatorial candidate in Virginia.

Dennis Peterson, who had managed John Chichester's 1985 bid for lieutenant governor against Doug Wilder, was from 1986 to 1988 the political aide most identified with Coleman. The bond was formed when he told Coleman that he believed the party had made a mistake not to nominate him in 1985, and urged a run for governor in 1989. The rivalry with Boyd Marcus for directorship of the campaign left some lingering tensions. Peterson's visibility decreased further after the primary, when he handed over day-to-day press responsibilities to Bruce Hildebrand, and began managing special projects, including visits by President Bush. Hildebrand, who handled press operations for Parris during the primary, then became spokesman for the general campaign.

Betsy Davis, a soft-spoken veteran of several GOP campaigns, headed fund-raising operations, a job that proved to be a staggering task; ultimately Coleman raised more than $11 million, including loans, for the primary and general elections. At times, Marcus said, the candidate had to be so involved in fund-raising that he could maintain only the shell of a public schedule.

Anne Kincaid, who directed television evangelist Pat Robertson's 1988 presidential campaign in Virginia, was liaison to a variety of constituent groups, including those opposed to abortion. Kincaid's access to Coleman lessened as the general election progressed, but she found ways to ensure that her voice would be heard. Her chief staff ally in promoting the pro-life cause was Mike Thomas, a former executive director of the Virginia Society for Human Life, who oversaw the campaign's get-out-the-vote effort.

Richard Cullen was not a paid staff member, but his longtime friendship with Coleman made him an integral part of the campaign organization. Early in their careers, when both were living in Staunton, Coleman helped Cullen get his first political job, as an aide to former representative Caldwell Butler of Roanoke. During Coleman's subsequent campaigns Cullen remained a faithful booster and strategist, and was widely expected to be chief of staff if Coleman won.

As June 1989 passed, the Wilder and Coleman staffs began implementing campaign strategies that were months in the making. Within days, however, they would have cause to be reminded of Wilder's version of a favorite quotation from Ralph Waldo Emerson. "Events are in the saddle," Wilder often said, "and they ride mankind."

8

THE ABORTION DECISION

One hundred miles north of Richmond, across the Potomac, eight men and one woman cloistered behind marble pillars detonated a political bomb that sent shock waves reverberating throughout the nation. Shortly after 10:00 A.M. runners bearing the news dashed through the corridors of the U.S. Supreme Court building and thrust copies of the opinion, *Webster v. Reproductive Health Services*, into the hands of network reporters. Within moments, a decision that affected the lives of American women as intimately as any in the previous sixteen years was being revealed to an expectant nation. By a five to four vote, the high court held that states could restrict abortions beyond limits set in 1973.

The view of abortion as a fundamental privacy right, established that year in the landmark case of *Roe v. Wade*, was now in jeopardy. "We are smiling," said Dr. John Willke, president of the National Right to Life Committee. "They have begun to dismantle *Roe v. Wade*. We intend to take our fight to the people," responded Molly Yard, president of the National Organization for Women (NOW).

The 1973 decision, which thereafter prompted intense debate, gave women an unrestricted right to abortion in the first three months of pregnancy, and said that states also could regulate abortion in the second trimester to protect the health of the mother. Only in the final three months of pregnancy, when many fetuses could survive outside the womb, were legislatures allowed to pass laws protecting fetal life.

Few if any issues so galvanized conservatives during the remainder of the 1970s and the 1980s as opposition to that ruling. Republicans profited from the zeal of the growing right-to-life movement, while paying little price for opposition to abortion, because those who favored abortion rights did not vote as a political bloc.

The pro-life movement, as the antiabortion forces came to be called, concentrated much of its energy on electing officials who would appoint jurists opposed to abortion. Their greatest victories lay in the elections of presidents Ronald Reagan and George Bush, both of whom urged the U.S. Supreme Court to overturn *Roe v. Wade*. Of the five justices who prevailed in *Webster v. Reproductive Health Services*, three were Reagan appointees. The July 3 ruling upheld a Missouri law that banned the use of public hospitals for abortion, and required doctors to determine whether a fetus twenty weeks or older could survive outside the womb before performing an abortion. It did not, however, overturn *Roe*, as the pro-life movement had urged.

In Virginia, the abortion decision was the first—and most significant—of several spontaneous events that would take the gubernatorial election out of the hands of campaign managers for a time and propel it in unpredictable directions. Marshall Coleman, who had traded away any maneuvering room on abortion in return for fundamentalist support in the primary, was true to his most recent pledge. Eight years earlier, when he campaigned for governor, Coleman had supported freedom of choice on abortion. But, mirroring the conversion of George Bush, he said now that he had changed his mind, and was dismayed by the escalating acceptance of abortion as a birth control alternative. He had come to believe, Coleman said, that a child was born the moment a sperm and an egg united. Unlike Bush, however, Coleman made no allowance for pregnancies resulting from rape and incest. Abortion is murder, he said, and should be banned—through a constitutional amendment, if necessary.

Now Coleman, in words that would soon stir panic among some of his advisers, hailed the new Supreme Court action: "Those who believe the right to life is paramount and who favor adoption over abortion, as I do, will be heartened by this important ruling. I welcome the opportunity to work to restore that inalienable right to Virginia's pre-born children."

Wilder, who had hedged his bets in the weeks leading up to the Supreme Court ruling, replied with a statement attacking Coleman's position, while leaving his own views largely undefined. In a press release, he pointed out major differences between himself and his opponent. Coleman favored a constitutional ban on abortion; he did not. Coleman would allow abortions only when the life of the mother was in jeopardy. Wilder believed government should not interfere with abortions in cases of rape, incest, or gross fetal abnormality: "In all these tragic cases, this most personal of decisions ought to be made by a woman in consultation with her loved ones, her religious advisers, and her doctors—without governmental coercion," he declared. "And yet," he added, "a need exists for appropriate limitations on abortions."

For instance, Wilder said, parental notification and consent should be required before women under the age of eighteen could get an abortion. In 1978 he had voted against such legislation, but in 1985—the year he ran for lieutenant governor—Wilder had supported a parental consent bill. The switch, he said, was due to the experience of watching his own daughters grow toward womanhood. Wilder concluded his abortion statement by noting: "After studying the decision of the court, I will offer further comment." The day passed without Wilder's addressing the matter of the overwhelming majority of abortions, involving adult women whose fetuses are healthy and whose pregnancies have nothing to do with rape or incest.

Nor had Wilder been forthcoming about his opinion on such abortions in the weeks leading up to the Supreme Court decision. His former colleagues in the senate widely considered him to be a supporter of abortion rights. Following one debate on abortion funding, Sen. Joseph Gartlan, a Northern Virginia Catholic who led antiabortion forces in the Senate, received a playful note from Wilder asking: "Why can't Supreme Court decisions just be left as they are?" Gartlan, recalling the 1896 case that established the separate-but-equal doctrine of segregated public facilities for blacks and whites, fired back: "Should that also apply to *Plessy v. Ferguson*?" But throughout 1989 Wilder had left himself leeway on the issue.

In an April interview with a *Richmond News Leader* reporter, Wilder paused when asked if he were pro-choice on abortion. "I don't think when you reach certain instances that your personal beliefs have any play at all in something. . . . If I were the governor, I would enforce the law of the land," he said. A month later, he was equally unenlightening in an interview with reporters for the *Virginian-Pilot/Ledger-Star*, based in Norfolk. "You run into, 'Where do you stand?'" he said. "What difference does it make? The question is, what does the law say? . . . I support the law of the land."

The closest Wilder came to a pro-choice endorsement in that May 1989, interview was an acknowledgement that in the early 1970s, when he was part of a legislative committee drafting an abortion law for the state, "I supported the right of a person to have an abortion under certain circumstances. So you could not classify me as a foe of abortion, and yet I have my own personal feelings." Precisely what those feelings might be remained a secret between Wilder and his campaign manager.

Two days after the Supreme Court ruling, however, Wilder offered a clue on where he stood, with off-the-cuff remarks to several reporters suggesting that he would favor limits on abortion beyond parental consent. "I don't think that abortion for purposes of birth control should be available," he said. "My God, none of us would be here." Informed of his comments by the Associated Press, Molly Yard of the National Organization for Women labeled them "wimpy" and suggested that, if Wilder expected to win, "he's got to be much stronger on the issue of women's reproductive rights."

Within hours, he was. In his third statement of the week, with his press secretary admitting the confusion about Wilder's position, the candidate said flatly that he was pro-choice and would favor only a single alteration in the law—parental consent for those under eighteen.

The political sagacity of the position was confirmed rapidly in news accounts and national polls. ABC News rated Virginia as one of eleven states with a pro-abortion legislature. A host of state lawmakers predicted that the General Assembly would be unwilling to adopt a statute similar to the Missouri law upheld by the Supreme Court in *Webster v. Reproductive Health Services*. As Wilder strategists reviewed polls showing that a solid majority of Americans generally favored abortion rights—and even more of them advocated its use in cases of rape and incest—there was growing awareness that Wilder had been handed a dynamic emotional issue that might work for him in much the way that race threatened to hamper his cause.

After the election, Wilder aides insisted that his initial statement on abortion did not reflect any confusion about his position. Rather, they said, it was a calculated move to focus the debate on rape and incest. "We decided, strategically, don't call yourself pro-choice to begin with. We wanted rape and incest to be the fault line," says Paul Goldman.

JULY 10, 1989

The Coleman campaign's first major post-*Webster* strategy huddle was slated for Monday in the candidate's law office in McLean. Media consultant Bob Goodman, who drove down from Baltimore, had been on semi-vacation for the last week, and was eager to discuss the ramifications of the decision. His own view was that, since Coleman's position paralleled President Bush's, it was probably manageable. Not until the discussion got under way did he begin to realize how wrong he had been: Coleman did not occupy Bush's position at all. The president had drawn the line at rape and incest; Coleman had not. His reaction, says Goodman, was "shock, utter dismay. My first thing was, 'Marshall, I think that's an untenable position.'" In the discussion that ensued, Goodman was alone in arguing that the candidate needed to abandon his stand on rape and incest, even if it prompted charges of flip-flopping. His view, the ad consultant recalls, was that "*Webster* sent a chill up the back of every woman in America. It sent a chill up my back too, because I'm a pro-choice person myself."

During the weeks that followed, the Coleman campaign was

beset—at times, almost paralyzed—by an ongoing debate about how to deal with abortion. At the poles of the argument were Goodman and Anne Kincaid. Goodman's view was that Coleman needed to get as far away from banning abortion for rape and incest as he could. Kincaid, who says the July 10 meeting was the first major strategy session to which she was not invited, argued that the candidate should make Wilder out to be the extremist. That could be achieved by aggressively talking about controversial abortions, such as those in the third trimester or for birth control and sex selection, she believed.

In the middle on the issue were Boyd Marcus and Frank Atkinson, whose primary goal was to get the focus off abortion and onto other matters. But they too believed something needed to be done about Coleman's rape and incest stand. The consensus at the Monday meeting was that Coleman should soften his position by saying he would never propose limitations on abortion in cases of rape and incest, and that the legislature would never approve such restrictions. Over the next week, pro-life Republicans, including Richmond mayor Geline Williams, Sen. Mark Earley of Chesapeake and Del. Philip Hamilton of Newport News, concurred. The risks of retreating were substantial, given Coleman's earlier switch from a pro-choice stance, but the risks of intransigency, they believed, were greater.

Throughout the months of debate that followed, Goodman and Kincaid shared at least one belief. Neither of them thought that banning abortions was a burning issue with the candidate. Rhetoric to the contrary, "I don't think that this was an issue that prior to *Webster* Marshall was deeply concerned about," says Goodman. "I don't think he ever saw the governorship as having anything to do with an issue like that."

"I knew Marshall was not where he totally felt the conviction yet," admits Anne Kincaid. "But the subject was not one he shied from," and his position was right, Kincaid felt. Indeed, when all three of the GOP primary candidates were asked about abortion at one of their final debates, their responses "sounded like a national right-to-life convention." She had urged pro-life people to support Coleman rather than Trible, Kincaid says, because "my total conviction was that [Trible] didn't have the fire in the belly" to defeat Wilder.

JULY 15, 1989

The first debate of the 1989 gubernatorial race was scheduled out-of-state, in West Virginia. The Virginia Bar Association was holding its annual meeting in White Sulphur Springs at the Greenbrier, a palatial resort that spurs the local economy, though not enough to stamp out nearby scenes of Appalachian poverty. Against a backdrop of manicured lawns and elegant lounges frequented through the years by presidents and cabinet officers, Coleman and Wilder confidently agreed to a genuine debate format such as was rarely seen in either state or federal elections. Two veteran debaters, skilled at extemporaneous jousting, agreed to question each other directly before responding to queries from a panel.

The major issue involving the debate format—direct confrontation—was resolved easily enough, but an assortment of details kept campaign aides negotiating up to the moment the candidates walked on stage. The Wilder campaign wanted to change the dark green tablecloths set up by the Greenbrier staff for white cloths, arguing that the brighter color would look better on television. Bar association staff rounded up new tablecloths, but decided that switching them was too much trouble. The Coleman people wanted the candidates to enter from the back of the stage, but there were no doors to do so. Each side insisted that the other candidate not arrive in the room first. Finally they agreed to appear simultaneously and to walk toward the stage from opposite sides of the room.

As the two candidates met at center stage to begin the first debate, exchanging smiles and a handshake, Coleman whispered: "The next time we shake hands, you'll be congratulating me." After opening statements and a tax-related question from the moderator, the direct exchange began. Wilder went first, setting the pace and tone for the next ninety minutes with a broadside on abortion. "It's clear that your position on abortion is out of step with Virginia values and law," Wilder began. "How can you justify saying to a woman who's a victim of rape and incest that she cannot have an abortion? . . . How can you say what's best for her?"

Coleman was ready. The decision had been made to unveil his slightly altered position on rape and incest at the Greenbrier, and he was primed for a careful, intellectual response. "Abortion is one of the great moral issues of our time," Coleman began, his voice taking on the studied, dispassionate quality that often marked his public statements. "It's an issue that has divided our county and our state. I think we ought to protect the lives of the pre-born," he said. Acknowledging wide disagreement on the point, Coleman said "medical evidence and my own conscience bring me to believe that this is a human life." The policy of the state ought to be to discourage abortion, he said, cautioning against "a rhetorical and demagogic approach. People of good will will have different views." Tweaking Wilder, he concluded, "last week alone, you had three different views on abortion."

"I never had but one view," Wilder shot back. "That government should not interfere." Without pausing, Wilder again pressed Coleman at his most vulnerable point. "How can you say to a woman who's a victim of rape and incest that you can say what's best for her? How can your judgment supersede hers?"

Then, as if in passing, Coleman revealed his carefully crafted retreat. "I'm not going to propose legislation outlawing abortion in cases of rape and incest during my term," he pledged. Later, during questioning by a panelist, Coleman elaborated. "In consultation with pro-life members of the General Assembly," he had concluded that "some exceptions, even if *Roe v. Wade* is overruled, are going to remain on the law books in Virginia." Prime among them, he said, were rape and incest.

Still, the issue did not die. Moments later, panelist A. C. Epps, a wealthy Richmond lawyer with patrician bearing and Democratic leanings, again raised the matter of abortion, asking Wilder if he were concerned about its use as a birth control tool. There was a brief exchange between the two candidates, and then Wilder delivered one of several highly personal and effective responses that resulted in his being widely declared the winner of the first debate.

"What you have to do," Wilder lectured Coleman, "is put yourself in the place of the woman affected. I guess I can more readily identify with that because I have two daughters. I can't imagine any situation where they would be victimized by crime, by rape, and that government would say to them, or to me as their father, that they could not or should not be in some degree of destiny as to what happens to their future." Coleman's argument that rape and incest accounted for only 1 percent of abortions was bogus, he said. "If it's in one instance, it's still a question of character, still a matter of principle."

The audience, dominated by white males and generally regarded as moderate to conservative in political leanings, applauded, as they did several times for Wilder that day.

In the aftermath, even Republicans in the audience conceded that Wilder had appeared warmer, more relaxed, less programmed, and generally sharper than Coleman. Not unlike George Bush and Michael Dukakis in presidential debates a year earlier, Wilder seemed more human, Coleman more remote. Even Wilder's wandering sentences and occasional breaches of syntax seemed more natural, while Coleman's carefully crafted, grammatically perfect responses appeared artificial. After months of watching Coleman romp around his primary opponents during debates, reporters and audience alike at first seemed surprised, then amused, and finally captivated by the interplay. Just as at the capitol correspondents dinner weeks earlier, Coleman was good, but Wilder was better.

JULY 22, 1989

Friday, July 21, had been one of those rare dream days during a political campaign when the press of crowds and staff is left behind and a candidate finds momentary peace. Wilder and Frank Greer filmed television commercials southwest of Roanoke on the farm of state senator Madison Marye, a retired army officer whose gregariousness was a guaranteed tonic for campaign fatigue. Flying back to Richmond that afternoon, Wilder and Greer joked about the campaign and practiced a few questions for the campaign's second debate the next day in Virginia Beach. The real grilling had taken place twenty-four hours earlier when campaign staff staged a mock debate under Greer's direction in a suite at the Commonwealth Park Hotel. Back in Richmond, Wilder hurried off to get a haircut and Greer huddled with Laura Dillard over an opening statement for the debate. With most of the staff already en route to the beach, Greer by early evening found himself in a back office at the Commonwealth Park, pecking out the words on a borrowed typewriter.

Dwight Holton, Wilder's director of advance, interrupted the flow. "We've got a problem," he reported.

Dwight Holton was the younger son of former governor Linwood Holton. It was Linwood Holton who, as the first Republican to be elected to the state's highest office in the twentieth century, was credited with having opened the door to improved race relations in Virginia during his 1970–1974 term. Governor Holton used his inaugural address to vow to make Virginia "a model in race relations" for the nation. Quoting Abraham Lincoln, the first Republican president, he urged: "Let us, as Lincoln said, insist upon an open society 'with malice toward none; charity for all.'"

The senior Holton's first executive order as governor called for an end to discrimination in hiring state employees, and the most enduring image of his administration was the photograph carried by newspapers across the country on the day he escorted his daughter, Tayloe, into Richmond's John F. Kennedy High School, which was 92 percent black. The Richmond School Board had told the Holtons that, because the governor's mansion is on state property, they could send their children to any public school they pleased. But instead of choosing a public school with few black students or a private school, the Holtons chose the public schools to which their children would have been assigned if their parents had been ordinary citizens. Agitation over busing of children was at its height when the Holtons made their decision, and the image of the governor walking his daughter into an integrated school was a courageous signal to the nation that Virginia was shedding her racist past.

Now, almost twenty years later, young Dwight Holton was a Democrat, working for Doug Wilder, and calling from the Cavalier Hotel in Virginia Beach, the site of the next day's scheduled debate before the Virginia Press Association. "Bob Goodman's here, and he's setting up cameras," said Holton.

Greer, who helped negotiate the presidential debates for Democrats Mondale in 1984 and Dukakis in 1988, was incredulous. "It's got to be a mistake," he said. "No mistake," replied Holton. Bob Goodman, Coleman's media expert, was arranging two top-quality broadcast cameras for his own use, as well as lighting—a clear signal that he was interested in more than home movies. One camera was set to film Coleman with an American flag draped behind him. Lights were trained on the area. The second camera was focused on the more dimly lit spot where Wilder would stand.

Before the Greenbrier debate, when Wilder staffers huddled over ground rules, they agreed to insist that footage from the debate not appear in any commercials. The objection—standard to many political campaigns—was that debate film too easily can be edited to show a candidate off guard. The Coleman campaign had apparently had the same concern; when actual negotiations began, they were the first to raise the idea of banning rebroadcast. As the two candidates prepared to walk on stage at the Greenbrier, Frank Atkinson reminded Wilder staffers, "And no rebroadcast, right?" Holton quipped, "Without permission from major league baseball."

If the ground rules were clear at the Greenbrier, they were muddled a week later. Laura Dillard's recollection of a predebate meeting with Frank Atkinson and Dennis Peterson of the Coleman staff, and Louise Seals of the *Richmond Times-Dispatch*, coordinator for the debate, was that both participants agreed to retain the same rebroadcast restrictions as at the Greenbrier. The Coleman staff insisted otherwise. In fact, Atkinson was keenly aware of any rebroadcast discussion, he says, because the campaign had already decided that it would like to make commercials at Virginia Beach. Stung by the *Webster* ruling and the Greenbrier debate, Republican strategists believed it was critical for Coleman to recapture the offensive. The decision had been made to unleash a negative assault on Wilder in Virginia Beach that would shift the focus off abortion and back to Coleman's agenda, and to film the results for use in commercials. "Without abortion, we would have raised the same issues, but not in the same time frame," says Boyd Marcus. "We wouldn't have shot out that early, but we had to get the focus back on Doug Wilder." When Atkinson returned to Coleman headquarters from the debate negotiations and reported that nothing had been agreed to about filming, Marcus was elated. "We were taking advantage of the rules, but we weren't pulling a fast one," he insists.

Both campaigns would later argue that what happened next was a deliberate plot to scuttle the Virginia Beach debate. Democrats had gotten wind of the tough personal grilling that Coleman intended to give Wilder, and retreated in fear, Republicans said. Republicans were still smarting from Wilder's manhandling of Coleman a week earlier and were hoping to recoup through a bold roll of the dice, Democrats said. If Wilder balked at the filming, the GOP would claim victory; if not, they would soon be airing television ads with debate footage cut to show Wilder at his worst. Goodman, who brought lights, cameras, and a crew of seven or eight to the debate, acknowledges that he had arranged for editing facilities, and was prepared to have a spot on the air the next day. But he argues that any distortion of Wilder's performance would have been out of the question, given the audience of reporters and editors. "We didn't know whether they were going to try and screw us or not," replies Holton. "But it certainly was an option."

After speaking with Greer Friday night, Holton placed a telephone conference call to Wilder and Paul Goldman. Wilder's reaction to news of the camera setup was calm and unequivocal. "There will be no filming of commercials tomorrow," he said. The Democratic candidate's view was that an agreement between the campaigns not to use debate film in commercials was being violated.

By Saturday morning, as reporters began arriving at the Cavalier, the situation was stalemated. Coleman's staff refused to dismantle the cameras. Wilder said he would not go on unless they did. As the staffs huddled in corridors and hotel rooms, and press association organizers scrambled for a solution, the moments ticked past. Dillard began typing out a statement by Wilder saying, "I regret to inform the members of the Virginia Press Association, members of the audience, and the people of Virginia that there will be no debate today. Frankly, I am disappointed." In a final huddle in their hotel suite, Goldman and Greer warned Wilder that reporters would likely be angered by the cancellation, and would direct their wrath at him. Wilder was unimpressed. The debate was off, he said.

As the 1:00 P.M. starting time passed, Frank Greer went downstairs to confirm the obvious. As he entered the room, he saw Coleman being led toward the stage by Dennis Peterson. Greer's worst fear—that cameras would record Coleman standing next to Wilder's empty chair—was about to be realized. Holton watched the scenario unfolding, too. He saw Greer waving his arms in the background, noticed that the lights and sound equipment were too far away for him to pull any plugs. "There are situations where you do what you have to do," says Holton. In an instant, he bounded onto the stage, blocking Coleman's path. At six feet, five inches, his frame was an imposing barrier. "Marshall and I stood about six inches apart," recalls Holton. "I was sure he was muttering something about my father under his breath. But he said he didn't want to violate any rules, and he left."

Amidst the mayhem, Coleman staffers began distributing copies of four embarrassing questions their candidate had intended to ask from the stage. The first dealt with Wilder's scuttling of Owen Pickett's 1982 race for the Senate, a particularly potent issue there in Pickett's hometown. Another raised the Robb letters, and their inferences about Wilder's truthfulness, loyalty, and competence as a manager. In a twist on the old "when did you stop beating your wife" theme, Coleman intended to ask: "Which thing Chuck Robb said about you is untrue?"

Two final questions cut even more deeply to the core of Wilder's integrity. The first focused on a bill he had introduced twelve years earlier calling for the state to pay fifty thousand dollars to a former client who had lost that sum in a numbers raid. The client, Maggie Allen, had been cleared of charges, largely through a technicality, and the money was never returned to her. Coleman argued—and Wilder later denied—that he introduced the bill because she threatened him with a malpractice lawsuit. "How do you justify that use of your public office to benefit yourself personally?" he planned to ask.

The last question reintroduced a controversy that had plagued Wilder in his 1985 race. Among several pieces of property he then owned in the city was a deteriorating, vacant rowhouse. Located in a rapidly gentrifying area of the city, the house had spawned repeated complaints from neighbors and several charges by city officials of building-code violations. Some neighbors claimed the building was open to vagrants and a fire hazard for adjoining properties. At one point, a special grand jury was even convened to determine if the house qualified as a public nuisance. The charges were always dropped when Wilder began improvements on the property or promised to do so. But some neighbors said work stopped once the heat was off. Wilder responded that the charges were politically motivated. He offered as proof the fact that owners of numerous nearby houses in similar condition had never been taken to court.

On balance, Wilder seemed to have operated within the confines of the law. No fines or penalties were ever levied against him because of the house, and by 1989 it had been sold. But even friends remained perplexed about why he had allowed the politically damaging controversy to stretch out over years, and why he—a millionaire—was not more sensitive to complaints of individuals who were not only neighbors, but constituents. Coleman planned to take advantage of lingering concern. His last question was the most explosive: "What do you say to those Virginians who say that it would not set a good example for our young people to have a governor who was worth a million dollars and drove around in expensive cars, but did not care enough about the health and safety of citizens to fix up his property for over three years?"

At a packed press conference following the debate cancellation, Wilder first agreed to answer Coleman's questions. But when angry reporters began peppering him for details of the Maggie Allen case, he reneged, leaving the room. Republicans had achieved what they wanted. The curtain had been raised on what would prove to be the worst month of the campaign for Wilder.

9

A STRIKE, INVESTIGATIONS, AND PROBLEMS

One of the fortunate happenstances of the campaign, Wilder says, is that he was not in Richmond very often during late July and August. Instead, he was traveling the state, replaying the three-thousand-mile trip to every county and city that helped elect him in 1985. "If I'd been in Richmond during the course of the bad month, it could have affected me," he says. "That's why I was very pleased not to be here."

Almost as soon as the candidates left Virginia Beach, the drumbeat began. Coleman was determined to get abortion out of the headlines, and character in. He was hitting hard on the Robb letters, the relief bill introduced by Wilder for Maggie Allen, and the rowhouse. Reporters were supplied with thick packets of information about those difficulties and others. As soon as a newspaper article about a problem appeared, delegate Frank Hargrove of Hanover County, vice-chairman of the GOP caucus, was poised to issue a press release demanding further investigation.

Before August was past, Attorney General Terry would twice rule on the legal propriety of financial actions involving her running mate. Wilder's former aide, Joel Harris, would quit the campaign amid a swirl of controversy about his business dealings. Wilder would move his financial operation out of a house owned by another supporter whose company had recently been convicted of defrauding the federal government. He would bring in new campaign management, tacitly acknowledging the concerns about the operation. And the state's most explosive racial incident of the post–civil rights era would erupt in Virginia Beach. If all that was not enough, Wilder was having to dodge verbal bullets in the very spot that warmly propelled him on his way in 1985—the Southwest.

JULY 29, 1989

Outside a souvenir shop perched on a mountain ledge a few hundred yards from the point where Virginia, Kentucky, and Tennessee converge, Wilder shouted to be heard above the din of tractor trailers making the steep grade. "Coming back here invigorates me, energizes me. . . . We're here to finish the job," he told a dozen Democrats, gathered to help launch the reenactment of his 1985 statewide trek. Moments later, Wilder and the caravan were rolling down Route 58, out of the mountains and into the span of green valley that slices Virginia's westernmost county. The first stop was Monte Vista, an aging, white-columned mansion refurbished by a retired coal baron once active in Kentucky politics. About two hundred people sampled sausage, gravy, and some of the six hundred biscuits baked by Evelyn Bacon, and listened as her husband, Edgar, Lee County's "Mr. Democrat," predicted a November victory.

The focus of the next day's news accounts was not so upbeat, however. As he left his motel that morning, Wilder had held an impromptu press conference. The topic on everyone's minds was the sixteen-week coal strike that had idled hundreds of miners in neighboring counties. At issue in the strike by the United Mine Workers (UMW) against the Pittston Coal Group Companies, Virginia's largest mining operation, was the company's decision to pull out of an industry-wide agreement that had governed retirement, health, and other benefits for miners since 1950. Pittston argued that the Bituminous Coal Operators' Association agreement, established under the guidance of legendary union leader John L. Lewis, was outdated and unresponsive to market fluctuations. About two dozen companies had quit the pact between 1984 and 1988, due either to the failure of their businesses or the belief that they could negotiate a better deal by bargaining separately with the union. The UMW saw the unraveling of the industry-wide coal agreement as a potentially fatal blow, jeopardizing hard-earned benefits. The union also believed Pittston was trying to break the union by transferring major assets to the nonunion side of the company.

Since the strike began April 5, 1989, there had been several thousand arrests of local miners and their supporters, due largely to their illegally congregating and blocking the roads outside Pittston plants. Although there were also numerous instances of rock-throwing and punctured tires, the level of violence did not approach that in past strikes, and the UMW was gaining publicity through its emphasis on methods of civil disobedience associated with Mahatma Gandhi and Dr. Martin Luther King, Jr. The authorities, however, seemed unimpressed by the tactical shift. State and federal judges had imposed millions of dollars in fines against the union, and Governor Baliles had dispatched several hundred state troopers to the area to police the strike. The governor's action had infuriated miners who had backed Baliles en masse in his 1985 election. Why should they support the Democratic party, some were asking, if the party was no more loyal to them?

Questioned about Baliles's handling of the matter as he headed toward coal country on July 29, Wilder seemed to be distancing himself once again from the governor. "I think a lot of people thought it exacerbated the situation," the candidate replied when asked about the presence of the troopers. "The question is whether that ounce of prevention was worth the pound of cure." Pressed about whether he disagreed with the governor's handling of the strike, he concluded: "To be honest with you, in terms of what did take place, honest men could differ." Within hours, Laura Dillard was on the phone to Chris Bridge, the governor's press secretary, trying to smooth over the words. By the next day, Wilder was saying that the remarks had been taken out of context and that he stood "four-square behind Baliles." The wider impression was either that the two were squabbling once again, or that Wilder had failed to get his message straight.

The candidate arrived in the coalfields a day later, and the hours he spent there were among the most revealing of the campaign. Paul Goldman argues that elections are not won by five-month ad campaigns, but by real candidates reacting to real events. Certainly Wilder had no prepared script as he drove into Dickinson and Russell counties, about to encounter a depth of frustration and hostility that would surprise even him. Almost every job in the two isolated, mountainous counties is linked to coal, and few residents were neutral on the strike.

The first indication of the emotion came when Wilder stopped at an automobile dealership soon after entering Russell County, the site of several Pittston operations, and was greeted by J. C. Justice. The eighty-eight-year-old retired railroad worker wanted to talk about one subject: Governor Baliles. "Baliles got all these counties the last time he ran," Justice complained. Now, he said, there was hardly a person who would vote for the man for dog catcher. "If you're for the union, I'm for you. If you're agin' it, I'm agin' you," he concluded. Wilder gamely protested that Baliles was only trying to do his job, and moved on.

Dodging thunderstorms, Wilder proceeded through small towns and down narrow, winding roads to arrive at United Mine Workers' headquarters in Castlewood. The candidate was whisked into a private meeting with about fifty union officials and workers. Emerging ninety minutes later with his tie loosened, Wilder insisted that his private message had been no different than his public one: "I said the same thing I've said all along—that I'm committed to fairness and equity and justice."

Standing at Wilder's side, Cecil Roberts, UMW national vice-president, said Baliles's actions had been "unfair," while Wilder offered fairness. But neither he nor the candidate could say specifically where the differences lay. "We thought we could ask him questions and he could be open with us, but he couldn't do that," Robert Bailey, a South Clinchfield miner, complained as he left the room. As the meeting disbanded, an unidentified miner came up to Wilder and Dillard, produced a tape he had made of the private meeting, and proceeded to shred it. But there had been at least five tape recorders in the room, the miner warned. Anything Wilder had said might soon be public knowledge.

As Wilder's second day in mining country began, a banner headline in the morning edition of the *Coalfield Progress* seemed to sum up his previous day's performance: "Wilder Pledges Fairness; Gives No Details." Cresting Red Onion Mountain on his way into Clintwood, the Dickinson County seat, Wilder abruptly halted his seven-car caravan beside a makeshift hut where UMW members stood watch over the entrance to a Pittston Coal Group plant. His attempt at pleasantries left James Collius, the sixty-one-year-old miner who met him, unmoved. Collius wanted to know: "Why do you think we shouldn't have our pensions as well as you people?" "I never said you shouldn't," replied Wilder, quipping that he had come to coal country looking for vote security.

"The way you'll get security is to back us up. If you don't back us up, you'll not get it down here," said an unsmiling Collius, jabbing a calloused finger at Wilder's chest. "What do you think about these state police escorting these [Pittston] trucks down here?"

"I think the state police want to do the right thing," said Wilder, producing a stare from the miner. "That's why I'm here. I came to talk. . . . I can't write the contract. All I can do is pledge fairness and equity."

"He don't sound like he's fair to my way of thinking," grumbled Collius as Wilder drove away. "I don't see nothing to even vote for this time." As for giving Wilder credit for stopping by, "Why should I?"

A few miles away in Clintwood, population 1,300, a half-dozen protesters greeted Wilder with signs and venom outside the library. "They've treated our people like dogs. I'll write in somebody without he convinces us," promised Frankie Perrigan, a disabled miner's wife, who carried a sign reading, "State Troopers—Canine Dogs." Others throughout the day would threaten write-ins for John L. Lewis, George Meany, Mother Jones, and similar labor heroes. Inside the library the mood was tense. "We're good normal people," pleaded a woman, one of about two dozen individuals in camouflage fatigues and UMW armbands who peppered Wilder with questions about his views of the governor and the state police. "Is it fair for the state troopers to follow behind and in front of the coal trucks?" someone wanted to know. "I'll never respect a state trooper again as long as I live," said another. "If he don't do no better than Governor Baliles, we don't need him," shouted Perrigan from the back of the room.

Wilder threaded his way through the questions, deflecting a few with humor, defending the good intentions of Baliles and the troopers, repeating his litany about "fairness and equity." "I'll say it to you as clearly as I can, I'm not going to take sides," he insisted. "But isn't it nice to have someone you can say these things to, someone who will come to you?"

There, and later as the scene was repeated at a senior citizens' center in the tiny mining community of Clinchco, Wilder was at his best. Extemporaneously, with skills honed before juries in dozens of courtrooms, he came across as a man speaking person-to-person to neighbors in pain, seeking to diffuse anger with reason. "I know the emotions that grip you. I know the strife that occurs when brother is against brother. That's not good, not good for any of us. I don't want to see this continued," he said. "When the rights of the poor working people were involved in Virginia, I've been there. I'll be there in January like I've been before," he pledged. "I've not turned my back on you. You can't point to one single instance where I have in twenty years. . . . I'll be fair, equitable, and just."

Some three hundred miles away in Richmond, workers at Coleman headquarters distributed a press release saying Wilder's performance in the coalfields proved he was "unsteady, uncertain, and unreliable" when it came to defending the state's right-to-work law. Sacred to Southern conservatives, such laws protect the right of workers not to join a union, even in a unionized plant. Wilder dismissed the charge, saying he had been unequivocal in his defense of the right-to-work law. He moved on to other counties the next day, hoping that his presence, if not his neutral message on the strike, had won votes in the coalfields. In 1985 the trip to the Southwest had been a springboard. In 1989 it was an exercise in damage control.

Back in Richmond, major news organizations were investigating the business dealings of Joel Harris, Wilder's former state aide and a consultant to his political campaign. There had been speculation dating back almost a decade about Harris's role in a business known as the Virginia Gold and Silver Trading Company. Not long after Harris bought the company, the former owner was accused of fraud, and was eventually convicted. Harris, the new keeper of the books, testified for the government at the trial. When some Republicans intimated in campaign literature that Harris was involved in the transaction, he had won a public apology and an out-of-court settlement as a result of such charges. More recently, there had been questions about a retail wine and beer business in which both Harris and Wilder's son, Larry Wilder, were involved. The Alcoholic Beverage Control Commission had taken minor disciplinary action against the company, and the problems appeared to have been resolved.

Still, questions persisted, fueled partially by an assortment of political enemies acquired by Harris in his switch from the Republican to the Democratic party several years earlier. Some campaign workers expressed concern that he had become a political liability for Wilder.

Both Harris and Wilder apparently agreed with them. At about 2:30 P.M. on August 4, Paul Goldman called Jay Shropshire with the news that Harris was out of the campign. The formal announcement that Wilder's consultant was leaving politics to pursue private business interests came about two hours later. "Everybody was relieved," says Shropshire, whose distaste for Harris is undisguised. "Everybody was telling Doug Wilder he had to go. When that boy left, you began to create a cohesive campaign staff."

For his part, Harris waited until after the election, when Shropshire was named Wilder's chief-of-staff, to return the swipe. "The governor-elect is a man of enormous talent, but it is my personal opinion that he has not chosen the best person for the job," said Harris soon after the mid-December appointment. "Jay places his personal interest above everyone's, including Doug Wilder's." The proof, said Harris, was Shropshire's willingness to criticize him during the campaign. "People who have Doug's best interests at heart do not create political problems for him." Harris attributed Shropshire's dislike to a perception that he was a rival for the job of chief-of-staff.

Shropshire, who refused even to visit Wilder's headquarters during the campaign because the building was owned by Harris, declined to comment on the statement. Earlier, he said his dislike stems partially from an incident in which someone on Wilder's staff tried to check Shropshire's grades when he was completing an M.B.A. degree at William and Mary a few years before. Shropshire attributed the episode to Harris, but Laura Dillard says she was responsible for what boiled down to a misunderstanding with an overly zealous intern. The worker was only supposed to pick up a college catalogue, not check Shropshire's grades, she says.

Harris insists that his departure from the Wilder campaign was voluntary, and no one in authority disputes that interpretation. "I did it purely for business reasons," he says, pointing to efforts to launch a company that will dispose of infectious medical waste. But Republicans saw the moment as yet another opportunity to plant doubts about Wilder's personal and business involvements. "We know the press has been actively investigating him," Marcus told the *Washington Post*. "It will be extremely interesting to see what is really behind this move."

AUGUST 7, 1989

As Harris was leaving, Mark Warner was arriving. Much of the staff first met Wilder's tall and rangy Northern Virginia coordinator on the weekend of the nondebate in Virginia Beach. Warner, who at thirty-four had already made a multimillion dollar fortune in the cellular telephone business, was donating time to the campaign, partially because he had a personal interest in running for public office some day. He had only met Wilder in the spring and the two had probably spent no more than a dozen hours together. But at Virginia Beach Wilder called him aside, voiced some concerns about the direction of the campaign, and urged Warner to consider commuting to Richmond one or two days a week to help get operations in shape.

Warner was newly married. His wife was pregnant, and he had just spent two months in the hospital after nearly dying from complications involving a burst appendix. He had undergone thirty-two transfusions during the hospital stay. But politics was the reason he had relocated from Connecticut to Northern Virginia, and he was being offered a chance to play a vital role in the campaign of a man who might be the next governor. He agreed to come.

Warner says he found a campaign structure that only "needed kind of a kick start" to get it rolling. "The systems were there. They just weren't fully operating." There are some Democrats, Wilder among them, who agree with that assessment. There are others who say it was the arrival of Warner that salvaged the campaign organization. Clearly, the job of campaign coordinator quickly evolved from a one-to-two-day-a-week task to full-time work. Within days of his arrival, the staff realized that coordinator actually meant boss. "After a week to two weeks, you knew Mark was really in charge," says Michael Brown, the deputy manager. Joe McLean continued to be involved in special projects and some day-to-day operations. And, according to finance reports, his salary was not cut. But by the final week of the campaign he was not even at work in the state headquarters. Instead, he had been dispatched to Tidewater to help set up a get-out-the-vote effort.

"It was a question in my judgment of bringing in additional support rather than replacing," says Wilder. "Joe was never fired or terminated. He was given additional responsibilities which he was more comfortable in."

Brown is among those who argue that "there was more in place than people realize" when Warner arrived. But Frank Greer and others give Warner credit well beyond administering a "kick start." "He came in at a moment of disarray and no one knowing who to trust, and pulled everything together. He's the untold hero of this campaign," says Greer. "I think Doug knew it was going to hell," adds Danny LeBlanc, secretary-treasurer of the state AFL-CIO. After Warner arrived, "it was like a new campaign."

Warner had a good sense of organization, could make quick decisions, and projected a sound, calming influence. The son of a middle-management insurance executive, Warner entered politics in Ella Grasso's first campaign for governor of Connecticut in 1974. After holding several low-level political jobs on Capitol Hill, he graduated from Harvard Law School, worked in finances for the Democratic National Committee, and in 1982 started a company that deals in cellular telephone franchises. By 1989, his worth was easily in excess of $10 million. He had also become active in Northern Virginia politics, helping to raise money for several Democratic candidates. In the spring, when Wilder's regional coordinator, Toddy Puller, decided to run for the state legislature, Warner was tapped to fill her place. It is a testament to his strengths that Wilder, a man who does not place trust lightly, rapidly took Warner into his confidence. His price tag was also right for the candidate's frugal tastes: both as regional and state coordinator, Warner volunteered his services.

Part of what Warner accomplished was no more difficult than raising the comfort level of key Democrats, some of whom were feeling excluded. "He told them, 'Come on down to headquarters. Now, look. Here's a press secretary. Here's a pollster. Here's a fundraiser.' Once he did that, people realized things were a hell of a lot better off than they thought," recalls Bill Wiley. "I don't think there was so much chaos as a perception of chaos."

Not long after his arrival, Warner invited critical members of the Robb-Baliles coalition to an afternoon session at his weekend getaway house on the Rappahannock River in King George County. The guests included Chris Bridge, Baliles's press secretary; secretary of the Commonwealth Sandy Bowen; delegate Al Smith, a fundraiser; Curry Roberts, Baliles's secretary of economic development; Ben Dendy, a former special assistant to Robb; and Stewart Gamage, who formerly headed the Virginia liaison office in Washington. Against the backdrop of a striking art deco house built for an actress named Jan Brown in the 1930s, Warner let the group vent their complaints about disorganization, and then asked, how do we fix this? Next, Frank Greer, Mike Donilon, and Paul Goldman outlined what was happening with campaign strategy. It was the first intimate glimpse many of the guests had had of the campaign, and they left impressed.

Warner scheduled similar show-and-tell sessions with key businessmen, and he visited labor leaders, reporters, and others. "He came to my office and sat down for two hours and wanted to know what was going on," says Danny LeBlanc of the state AFL-CIO. Adds his colleague Scott Reynolds, "Mark arrived as a national Democrat, feeling that labor was going to be a part of the campaign."

Not everything Warner accomplished was symbolic, however. For example, state party officials had been meeting since the June convention with staff from each of the three statewide Democratic campaigns. The party's goal was to run a joint operation for such overlapping functions as voter registration, phone banks, direct mail, and election day get-out-the-vote efforts. An elaborate plan had been devised, but nothing was happening with funding. At one point in the summer, the Democratic National Committee (DNC) indicated willingness to make a substantial dollar contribution to the effort. But, during a mid-July meeting, DNC chairman Ron Brown wanted a firm indication that the Wilder, Terry, and Beyer campaigns were supporting the idea of a joint campaign. In short, he wanted to see money up front, and particularly from Wilder as the head of the ticket. No cash arrived.

"We were getting assurances money would come, but nothing was happening," recalls one of those involved with the joint campaign effort. Finally, as August arrived, party leaders began to consider scaling back to a token effort. "It was reaching the point where we would have to start committing money we didn't have," the strategist says. Within days of Warner's arrival, there was a substantial contribution from the Wilder campaign, and the joint effort was under way. By the end of the campaign, Al Smith—a leading fundraiser for Robb and Baliles, and the delegate who once blocked Wilder from entering the Commonwealth Club—was telling anyone who asked that Wilder's campaign was the best-organized one with which he'd been associated.

AUGUST 8, 1989

Coleman researchers investigating Wilder's background noted a curious fact. A financial disclosure filed in June had listed among the candidate's holdings rental property in Richmond and open land in Powhatan County, and had noted that both parcels were recorded in the name of HLS Associates Trust.

Four years earlier, on the eve of being sworn in as lieutenant governor, Wilder had been cited for building code violations at the controversial rowhouse on Church Hill. At a hotel meeting with reporters hours before the swearing in, Wilder dismissed the charges, saying "the deed has passed." The investment property had been sold, Harris said. Reporters duly recorded that land records showed the new owner was HLS Associates Trust, administered by H. Louis Salomonsky, an architect and friend of Wilder's. The matter was forgotten.

Now, based on his own report, it seemed that Wilder must have some financial link to the trust. "It now appears that the transfer may have been a sham and that Mr. Wilder may have retained and attempted to conceal his continuing control of the property," Coleman said in a statement. "These highly unusual business arrangements have at least the appearance of impropriety and deception." He called on Wilder to "step forward and answer the many questions that have been raised by his irresponsible conduct in this matter over a period extending at least seven years." Wilder, hoping to get the debate schedule back on track, challenged Coleman to air the question at a scheduled joint appearance before the Fairfax Chamber of Commerce ten days later.

Wilder had more to worry about than the chamber debate, which had evolved into back-to-back appearances, when he awoke Friday morning. Stripped across the bottom of the Metro section of the *Washington Post* was a headline announcing, "Vacant Row House Comes Back to Haunt Wilder." The story, by Thomas Heath and Don Baker, reported that the rowhouse had remained in Wilder's possession for more than a year after he claimed to have sold it. The sole beneficiary of HLS Trust was L. Douglas Wilder.

In an interview, Wilder denied ever using the word *sold* in connection with the HLS Trust transaction, and said he did not reveal his role in the trust because nobody asked. He contended also, as he did repeatedly throughout the campaign, that the charges involving the house were trumped-up political complaints. Over the years, Wilder faced two summonses and a special grand jury investigation involving the house, which was sold by the trust in 1987. The first complaint was dropped after Wilder promised to fix up the house. The second was dismissed after the deed was transferred to the trust. The grand jury found no cause for action. "This is the only house in the history of the world that has been cleared by a grand jury," Wilder would say, his voice rising in high-pitched exasperation, during the campaign.

But now, there was a new twist. Did his belief that the complaints were politically inspired give Wilder the right to mislead the public? Coleman hammered the theme as he addressed the Fairfax Chamber of Commerce, and in Richmond, Del. Frank Hargrove called on Mary Sue Terry to appoint an independent prosecutor to rule on whether Wilder had violated the state conflict-of-interest law. Should he have reported the holding even before a 1987 change in the law required lawmakers to list their trust assets?

What saved the charges from dominating the next day's headlines were the theatrics of Wilder at the Chamber of Commerce meeting. Seated in the audience as Coleman took his turn before a panel of journalists, Wilder jumped to his feet when

Coleman called for two statewide televised debates. Why not begin by debating immediately? Wilder asked, as he bounded onto the stage. After several moments of confusion, University of Virginia political scientist Larry Sabato, who was moderator for the event, observed that it would be inappropriate to change the rules on the spot. Wilder returned to his seat. Coverage in state newspapers the next day began with the debate controversy. Most readers had to look inside their papers to find details of the house flap.

AUGUST 21, 1989

Despite the widespread perception that Coleman was dominating the campaign in August, the Republican candidate's advisers were worried about midmonth polling results. John McLaughlin surveyed in two different ways. Some polls sampled the entire electorate. Others, acknowledging the reality that Coleman would have miniscule black support, looked only at the attitudes of white voters. The latest numbers showed that Coleman was leading among whites by 46 percent to 36 percent. Using a complicated formula, Coleman's associates believed the figures meant that, in a worst-case scenario, Wilder might actually be ahead among all voters by as much as 46 percent to 39 percent. "We were not happy with that," recalls Boyd Marcus. "There wasn't a lot happening, but what was happening was more favorable to us. It didn't make us feel terrible, but we were a little bit surprised."

Coleman began running a television ad designed to boost his favorable image before Labor Day. "When they ask you who Marshall Coleman is, tell them this," it began. "He is a father who loves his sons more than life itself. He is a Marine who loves his country. He is a citizen who has had the honor of serving you as attorney general."

Wilder was also getting ready for the negative assault to come. Two ads were designed to shore up his image. In one, Chuck Robb spoke to the camera: "On the really important issues, we've always agreed—like educating our children, and building

a better life for Virginia families." In the second, five individuals
—a state senator, a businessman, a teacher, a local supervisor,
and a retiree—endorsed the candidate. One cited "confidence"
in Wilder; two mentioned "trust."

AUGUST 25, 1989

There was more bad news for Wilder in the Metro section of the
Washington Post. Heath and Baker reported that Wilder had
omitted from his financial disclosure two items whose worth
appeared to exceed the state's $10,000 reporting threshold. One
was twenty-seven acres of Louisa County land that were deeded
to Wilder when he defended Curtis Poindexter in a sensational
1976 murder trial. The other was 2,500 shares of stock in Virginia First Savings Bank. A day earlier, the newspaper said, Wilder had filed an amended disclosure form listing the assets, both
of which were held by his trust. The revision followed newspaper inquiries. Willful violation of reporting requirements is a
misdemeanor punishable by up to twelve months in prison and
a $1000 fine. No Virginia official has ever been convicted of
intentionally violating the law.

Lou Salomonsky, the trust's administrator, took responsibility. Salomonsky's newly revealed relationship with Wilder did
not sit well with some of the candidate's supporters, and the
bad publicity heightened their concern. Salomonsky said any
reporting mistake was his, and stemmed from unfamiliarity with
the law. But he also insisted that the value of each of the two
holdings was not much, if at all above $10,000. The stock was
worth about $10,000 when he bought it, and the value had
peaked at about $11,875 the previous January, he said. According to the newspaper, the land was assessed at $32,000 by Louisa County officials. But Salomonsky questioned that figure. A
few days later he produced an independent assessor's report
saying the plot was landlocked, and actually worth no more
than $10,000.

This time, Wilder beat Hargrove to the punch. He called on
Attorney General Terry to investigate the charges. "As you know,

my opponent and his party have been making political charges against me for several weeks," he said in a letter to his running mate. "Today I am requesting that your office look into these charges so that once and for all, we can clear up the air." Coleman chimed in by urging Mary Sue Terry to conduct "a thorough investigation and aggressive prosecution of Mr. Wilder for ethical abuse."

Terry was already working double-time keeping up with the charges and countercharges. Earlier in the day, she had turned down Frank Hargrove's August 18 request for a special investigation. Wilder had not violated the conflict law by failing to report ownership of the rowhouse in 1986 and 1987, she said, because the legislature did not then require reporting trust holdings. Perhaps Terry was in conflict by ruling on the ethics of her ticketmate, responded state senator Joseph Benedetti, her GOP opponent.

An event that might well have emotional repercussions among Virginia voters also made headlines that day. From outside the state, newspapers brought a chilling tale of the murder of a black youth in the predominantly white Brooklyn, New York, neighborhood of Bensonhurst. The young man was killed after he and three companions were chased by about thirty whites who were apparently seeking revenge over a failed romance. The episode would lodge quickly in the national consciousness, renewing troubling questions about race relations in the nation at the close of the decade.

SEPTEMBER 1, 1989

With the traditional Labor Day campaign kickoff only hours away, Atty. Gen. Mary Sue Terry was pushing to wind up the investigation requested by Wilder. She had appointed two senior deputies to the case, including the resident office Republican, deputy Atty. Gen. Stephen Rosenthal. Rosenthal had once been a protege of former GOP governor John Dalton. Democrats wanted the report out of the way before voters began focusing more intently on the contest in the post–Labor Day period. They could only pray that more disclosures were not coming.

Late Friday afternoon, Terry released the findings. Not unexpectedly, she concluded that there had been no willful violation of reporting requirements. "Two of the most respected and most trusted senior attorneys in my office have studied the facts in the case, and have concluded that no such basis exists," she said. "No further action is warranted and none will be taken." Approaching the stock and the land separately, the lawyers concluded that the sales commission on any sale of the stock would reduce its value to below $10,000, and that Wilder had no motive for hiding his ownership. Determining the value of the land was more problematic. The assessment had apparently been based on the face value, plus interest, on two notes surrendered by Wilder when he accepted the land as payment by the family of Curtis Poindexter, the man who murdered a judge in a courtroom melee. In 1981 the same land had been conveyed for $2,500. The attorneys said they could not say with certainty whether the value of the acreage was more than $10,000, and they argued once again that Wilder had no reason to hide ownership. Noting the Republican claim that Wilder wanted to avoid bringing up the Poindexter case because of the heinous nature of the crime, they wrote: "Given that this representation is a matter of public record and was widely reported, we find such a suggested motive to be highly speculative."

Republican partisans protested that the report was a whitewash, and Coleman warned: "The willingness of the Wilder-Terry team to thumb their noses at our state ethics laws will not go unnoticed by the Commonwealth's voters, who long have demanded the highest integrity from their elected officials."

As August ended, Wilder supporters had begun to sound like fair-goers who had taken one thrill ride too many. "It's a good day for us. We didn't get a single headline," Shropshire quipped one morning late in the month as he walked across Capitol Square. "All I want for Labor Day is to never hear the words *row house* again," sighed Warner as the holiday approached. And across the state, Democratic workers began to think seriously about the prospect of eight years of party control in state government coming to a close. "I was concerned about my continued employment security, to be honest," recalls Moo Murray. "During August and part of September, I was thinking, God, this could be goodbye."

10

SPARRING IN SEPTEMBER

SEPTEMBER 3, 1989

In the predawn hours of Sunday morning, a wave of racial violence swept the ocean front at Virginia Beach, destroying the complacency that had seemed to characterize black-white relations in the Old Dominion. For the next forty-eight hours the state was transfixed by stories and television coverage of young black men and women in confrontation with police officers and National Guard troops, most of them white. Before the Labor Day weekend ended, more than one hundred oceanfront shops and restaurants had been damaged or destroyed by rioting. Some seventy individuals were treated for injuries, miraculously few of them serious. Dozens were arrested. And watchers worldwide were gaping at photographs of baton-wielding policemen and cowering students, reminiscent of the 1960s.

Speeding to the beach from his Northern Virginia home, "a hundred different thoughts were running through my head," says Jack Gravely, state president of the NAACP. One of them, he acknowledges, was whether Doug Wilder's campaign could withstand the state's worst racial episode in recent times.

The forces that converged at Virginia Beach had been set on a collision course for months. Through the 1980s, the Labor Day weekend event known as Greekfest had grown from a party frequented by a few hundred of Virginia's black college students to an annual happening that attracted thousands of students—and, increasingly, nonstudents—from up and down the East Coast. By 1988 the crowd had essentially outgrown the facilities and entertainment offered by promoters, and several ugly incidents had soured elements of the business community on repeating the event.

The city sent numerous signals, among them, petitions, letters, and public announcements, indicating its clear hope that there would be no Greekfest in 1989. The unfriendliness only cemented the determination of young blacks to repeat the party. As the weekend approached, some city officials changed tactics and began to search for ways to accommodate the visitors. But a stronger message came from Virginia Beach police chief Charles Walls, who announced in late August that the National Guard would be readily available during the weekend, if needed.

Arriving on Friday and Saturday, throngs of young people combed the beachfront, turning sidewalks and parking lots into packed masses of humanity. Everywhere, the heavy sound of rap music filled the air, and groups of dancing youths picked up the chant: " . . . Fight the power. We've got to fight the powers that be." There were numerous small confrontations between police and the visitors, and a sense of rising tension as midnight passed. Then, about 2:00 A.M. Sunday morning, like water bursting through a dam, thousands of people flowed into the streets, and some began a rampage of looting. The rioting continued, at times unabated, for a couple of hours. Slowly, as a wedge of police officers moved down the main thoroughfare, an uneasy calm was restored. By morning, about a hundred National Guard troops were on the street. For the next two days and nights, clashes continued. At times, police were targets for bottles, eggs, and debris. At others, bystanders who happened to be black—a newspaper photographer, an NAACP official, a hotel employee among them—were rudely arrested and treated as vandals. At last the long weekend ended. The nightmare was over. The crowds went home, leaving a city in shock.

To many, the worst aspect of the weekend was not the immediate events, but the inescapable reminder of a persisting racial gulf. In the days that followed, Virginia state senator Sonny Stallings heard both sides. There were whites who told him, "Now you see how those people are." And there were blacks who said that for the first time, they felt racial hostility at their offices, or were the object of racial epithets as they walked into a convenience store or drove down a street. "It's going to take a long healing process," said Stallings. As for damaging Wilder's prospects, "in this part of the state, I think it has."

Suddenly state political analysts were besieged by out-of-state reporters wanting to know what impact the events in Virginia Beach were going to have on the election for governor. One conclusion was certain—they would not help Doug Wilder.

SEPTEMBER 4, 1989

Far away from Virginia Beach, Wilder chose to celebrate the unofficial start of the campaign season—Labor Day—in the shadow of the Blue Ridge Mountains. Honoring a Democratic tradition, he left big-city voters behind, and joined parades in Buena Vista and Covington, small industrial communities not far from the heartland of the fertile, apple-growing region that spawned Harry Byrd. Marshall Coleman and his ticket-mates took a more practical approach to the holiday, foregoing the same customary parades in the Shenandoah Valley in favor of speechmaking in the crowded Northern Virginia suburbs.

For much of the previous week, Paul Goldman had been working with Wilder and others on the Labor Day speech. It was, all believed, the point at which the theme for the fall campaign should be set. The idea of casting the election as a choice between moving Virginia forward or backward had long been established. But Goldman and the others were still struggling for the right words to capsulize the message.

By Sunday night the consultant was working on his third draft of the speech. Laura Dillard joined him and for the next few hours they haggled over the words and message. The exchange was typical of many throughout the campaign. There were no major ruptures in the Wilder organization, but there were a host of people with strong personalities. Debates among Goldman, Frank Greer, Mike Donilon, and Dillard were often long and heated until Wilder stepped in and settled the matter with a decision.

The speech Goldman was planning was not for the mild-mannered. There were references to extremism on Coleman's part, to "blind ambition," and to "the self-righteous, holier-than-thou" wing of the Republican party, as represented by television evangelists Jerry Falwell and Pat Robertson. Dillard thought some of the language went too far, and she and Goldman argued the points as the night wore on. Finally, just hours before the speech would be delivered at a breakfast in Buena Vista, she carried the finished product to Larry Framme, who took it to Wilder.

Repeatedly throughout Labor Day, Wilder delivered the lines that would be the focus of the final months of his campaign:

> The force I represent is Virginia's New Mainstream. . . . Virginia's New Mainstream looks forwards, not backwards. It tries to unify people, not divide them. It realizes that the greatest responsibility of government is to protect our individual freedoms, not allow self-appointed censors to use state government for the purpose of imposing their personal views on the rest of us.
>
> "The opposing force, the one represented by my opponent, is Virginia's New Extremism. This force advocates a self-righteous, moral majority approach to public policy and will impose for the first time in modern Virginia politics a litmus test for employment in state government. They believe government should dictate the most personal of personal decisions.

He accused Coleman of wanting to dismantle sex education mandates, and of planning to appoint to key positions "only those people who want to ban abortion and who agree with his other extreme views."

Coleman later described both claims, which became a staple of Wilder's campaign rhetoric, as distortions. The source was brochures from the GOP primary in which Coleman pledged to appoint persons "who share the pro-life commitment to direct agencies with responsibility over abortion-related matters," and people who "share the traditional values and family authority principles" to the state Board of Education. Coleman had also urged rescinding a newly adopted statewide mandate for "family life education" programs, including sex education.

In Northern Virginia, Coleman took a less thematic approach to Labor Day. Throughout the day, he highlighted his antidrug agenda, criticized Attorney General Terry's ruling on Wilder's financial disclosure statement, and spoke of the GOP ticket as leaders Virginians could trust. Proposing that the election be "a referendum on whether Virginia should become a leader in the war on drugs," he criticized Wilder's drug plan and promised that his own program would dovetail with a major package to be unveiled by the president the following night.

The GOP campaign also quickly tried to diffuse Wilder's New Mainstream initiative. The slogan was fitting, said a press aide, because "the only way Doug Wilder can place himself anywhere near the mainstream is by redefining what the mainstream is." But some of Coleman's staff grudgingly applauded Goldman's lines. When Don Harrison, who helped run computer operations for the GOP campaign, heard the terms, his reaction was a complimentary, "Oh, damn."

SEPTEMBER 6, 1989

As the FBI launched a probe into the Greekfest riots, both Wilder and Coleman were reacting gingerly to the events. Passing through Tidewater, Wilder said curtly that violence would not be tolerated, that he supported Governor Baliles's decision to call out the National Guard, and that he was conducting his own private investigation of what had occurred. Coleman also took a strong law-and-order stand.

Privately, however, both sides were experiencing conflicting tugs. Some Republicans were urging Coleman to use Virginia Beach as a backdrop for issuing a position paper on crime. Others wanted him to make a television commercial that showed segments of the rioting in Virginia Beach and questioned Wilder's willingness to respond forcefully to such events. Boyd Marcus and Coleman weighed the alternatives and opted for caution. "My instincts were to totally stay away from it," says

Marcus. "I felt it could blow up in our face if we tried to exploit it. There was a risk of going down there and doing something high profile and then having a shopkeeper say something racist. The risk was too great."

For Wilder, there was a danger of angering an important constituency, no matter what position he took on the weekend. A poll conducted by a Virginia Beach firm, Issues and Answers Network Inc., underscored the racial division in perceptions of the events. Seventy-four percent of the city's residents polled said they felt the local police had showed restraint in dealing with the rioters. But only 37 percent of the blacks sampled agreed. Seventy-six percent of merchants and 71 percent of residents said racism had not been a factor in the city's response to the weekend. But among blacks, who make up about 9 percent of the Virginia Beach population, almost half—47 percent—said there were racial motivations in the actions of police and city officials. Meanwhile state and city NAACP leaders were talking of a possible class-action suit against the city on behalf of some of those injured and arrested.

A week later, as he prepared to speak at a housing conference in Norfolk, Wilder gathered reporters to issue his carefully planned response. After talking with city officials, students, the governor, and others, Wilder said, he had concluded that "it was a handful of people who caused the problems," and that most of them were not students. He also believed that the city should appoint a fact-finding commission to explore the causes of the riot, and pledged that as governor "what happened this Labor Day will not happen again. . . . Violence of this type—of any type—will not be condoned or tolerated while Doug Wilder is governor."

The NAACP's Gravely, who was informed in advance of what Wilder intended to say, was not pleased. He had hoped that Wilder would either be more critical of the city's handling of the events, or would say nothing at all. Across the political spectrum, the editorial-page staff of the *Richmond Times-Dispatch* was also unhappy with the comments. Noting that Wilder had not instigated the riot, had said "all the reassuringly right words" in its aftermath, and was probably being unfairly linked to the events purely because of color, writer Robert G. Holland in a midmonth piece proceeded to chastise Wilder for not saying more.

"If Wilder wanted to target specific outside agitators, he could start with Spike Lee, the radical-chic black film maker from New York City, whose hate-filled media creations played no small role in inflaming emotions at Virginia Beach," wrote Holland. The candidate might also point out the differences between the rioters in Virginia Beach and the civil rights activists of the 1950s and 1960s, he said, raising a series of negative racial images. "The civil rights protesters did not drip with heavy gold chains, or drive fancy cars. They were not out to raise Cain and pillage jewelry stores."

In Washington, conservative columnist Pat Buchanan, appearing on "The McLaughlin Group," a syndicated television show, pronounced the Wilder campaign dead. "The Democrats have got a pretty good candidate, a black candidate, in Doug Wilder in Virginia, who could have been elected, and was doing fairly well," Buchanan said. "I think this racial violence in Virginia Beach and the fact that it's been nationalized by the TV media are really going to finish him off in Virginia, and Coleman will be the next governor."

SEPTEMBER 8, 1989

While the editorial page of the *Times-Dispatch* was censuring Douglas Wilder, the news staff was taking a critical look at Marshall Coleman's personal finances. A Friday morning article by William Ruberry, stripped across the top of the Metro section, pointed out that a company affiliated with Dwight Schar had issued about $8.4 million in loans through a state housing agency, the Virginia Housing and Development Authority (VHDA), during the past year. The company had earned about $84,000 on those loans. The amount was relatively minor, but it was of interest because Coleman had said earlier that his benefactor did no state business. By the next day, with media attention growing, officials of VHDA confirmed that the Schar-related company also handled authority loans worth $149 million for ten other lenders. Earnings from the VHDA, which provides low-interest loans for qualified buyers, were actually about $600,000 in the previous year. Schar said the work done through the housing authority was "insignificant" in his total financial picture, and insisted that he had no interest in active involvement in state government if Coleman was elected.

Two days earlier the *Times-Dispatch* had also reported a few minor discrepancies in Coleman's financial disclosure form. He incorrectly listed the address of a partnership as Fairfax, Virginia, rather than Auburn, California, and he had described the arrangement as a limited, rather than a general partnership. Another financial deal made headlines two weeks later when the *Washington Post* reported that Coleman had made quick and hefty profits in the past year buying and selling two investment houses purchased from Schar's company, NVR L.P. The houses were bought and sold under the name John M. Coleman.

There was nothing illegal in either of the Schar-related transactions, and Coleman's disclosure problems could easily have been a minor oversight. But the stories underscored the depth of Coleman's financial links to Schar. They also appeared to cancel out much of the negative impact of the earlier articles about Wilder's financial disclosures. There was wide disagreement between the two campaigns about who had committed the more serious offenses. Republicans charged Wilder with deliberately misleading the public about controversial holdings; Democrats said it was dangerous for Coleman to be so financially tied to one person. However, there was little dispute that the various reporting errors and financial arrangements had been reduced to a jumble in the minds of many voters.

SEPTEMBER 12, 1989

The battle of the airwaves began in earnest Tuesday afternoon as Coleman unveiled the first negative commercials of the campaign. The subject was crime, specifically Wilder's 1977 vote against adding the killing of a police officer to the list of offenses punishable by death. As the camera focused on a Richmond memorial to slain policemen and then scrolled the names of those killed in action, the announcer recalled: "When the Virginia legislature added the killing of policemen to those crimes subject to the death penalty, most Virginians applauded. But one senator—only one—voted against it. His name, Douglas Wilder. Don't our police deserve better? Doesn't Virginia?" A second ad again mentioned the death penalty vote and contrasted Coleman's and Wilder's positions on several antidrug proposals.

In launching the crime ads, the Coleman campaign had several goals. They wanted to keep the focus off abortion as much as possible. Polls showed that most Virginians backed the death penalty, and strategists believed that doubts about Wilder's conversion during the 1980s from foe to supporter could be exploited. Privately, they also thought the ads could help Coleman capture the state Fraternal Order of Police (FOP) endorsement that Wilder had won in 1985. That year FOP support had helped Wilder dispel the stereotypical notion that, as a black politician, he would be liberal on crime issues. If crime was to be a centerpiece of the Coleman campaign against Wilder, stripping him of that protection was probably essential.

The Wilder campaign had several immediate complaints about the ads. First, the death penalty vote cited by Coleman was made twelve years earlier in 1977. Second, technically, Wilder was not the only senator to vote against the bill. Moments after the first tally, a Republican senator from western Virginia had asked for another count, noting that he had intended to vote nay. And third, they said, what mattered was not a 1977 bill, but the fact that in 1983 Wilder had supported the death penalty for killing a police officer.

The discussion that followed over the 1983 vote was typical of several that left voters in a quandary about who was telling the truth. The bill cited by Wilder was not a straight up-or-down death penalty vote. Instead, the legislation pointed those looking for the legal definition of police officer to a new section of the state code. The section of definitions cited in the statute that established the death penalty for killers of policemen had since been abolished. According to the Wilder campaign, the entire statute could have been voided by a court because there was no formal definition of a police officer. According to the Coleman campaign, the change in the law was a technicality, and Wilder was misleading the public to say he had voted to give police slayers the death penalty.

Such arguments aside, what the Wilder campaign also saw in the ads was the opening they wanted to start making Coleman's negative tactics an issue in the campaign. The hope was that future Coleman messages would be blunted by viewer disgust with mudslinging. Their own negative attacks would be justified as a response to Coleman's. "We reached Doug that day and said, 'This is what we've been waiting for,'" recalls Greer.

The Coleman campaign unveiled its commercials in early afternoon. By 6:00 P.M., Greer says, the Democratic response ad was ready. He decided to wait a day to start airing it, for fear that viewers would see the answer before they saw the Coleman commercial. Leaving comments on the death penalty until last, the ad began: "Marshall Coleman has launched another vicious negative ad campaign of distortion and false attacks—the same tactics he used against Paul Trible. But this time, we won't let him get away with it. The fact is, Doug Wilder supports the death penalty for the killing of a police officer, supports mandatory sentences for drug dealers, and wants to make them pay for the war on drugs.

"Now you know the facts about Doug Wilder—and Marshall Coleman. And the fact is, we just can't trust Marshall Coleman," the ad concluded.

Two days later, Coleman extended the series with a third spot, reacting to Wilder's response. "Douglas Wilder doesn't like it when people talk about his record," said the announcer. "But he can't hide the facts. . . . When he tells you he voted for the death penalty for killers of policemen, tell him he's wrong. When the law passed, Mr. Wilder was the only one to vote against it. Virginia, it's a matter of trust. And Doug Wilder's got a problem." It did not escape notice by those speculating on the Coleman strategy that the announcer's voice, heavy with sarcasm, was a woman's.

SEPTEMBER 19, 1989

Through the late summer, the major tactical question in the Wilder organization was about when to begin airing television ads on abortion. Ironically, Wilder and several key aides say, the individual who was most worried about a possible backlash was the expert on national abortion politics, Frank Greer. "I hammered on Greer to get our commercials out," Wilder recalls. "He wanted to hold them."

In hindsight, the hesitation seems misplaced. Both political polls and several polls commissioned for news organizations were indicating that a solid majority of Virginians generally supported abortion rights, even though many also thought abortion was morally wrong. The percentage who favored allowing abortion in cases of rape and incest was overwhelming. But it was also true that the Wilder camp was charting new ground. No candidate for statewide office anywhere had ever made abortion rights the centerpiece of a campaign. And for the last decade, no issue had been more identified with a liberal agenda than support for abortion. In Washington media circles, much of the talk about the Virginia race focused on the evolving abortion strategy. A popular view was that highlighting the issue was too risky. "The media community put a lot of pressure on Frank," recalls one member of Wilder's inner circle.

Nor were groups like the National Abortion Rights Action League (NARAL) especially supportive of Wilder's adopting the abortion theme wholesale. Early on, they had been displeased with his decision to support parental notification for eighteen-year-olds, and there had been subtle suggestions that they intended to concentrate their focus on the New Jersey gubernatorial race. The events of August made it appear that Wilder was losing, and national abortion activists did not want to carry the blame for his defeat. By mid-September, they were reevaluating Wilder's prospects, but there was a new concern about timing an abortion attack. The fear was that the issue would not have enough staying power with voters to affect the election if Wilder began emphasizing it too soon.

Another practical concern was money. The Wilder strategists agreed that abortion, once it reached the airwaves, must remain in the spotlight until the election. Particularly in Northern Virginia, that would be a costly proposition. And finally, Greer was concerned that the debut of the abortion ad would cause Coleman to unleash a fusillade of character attacks on Wilder. The counterview, voiced by Goldman, Mike Donilon, and others, was that the attacks were coming regardless of what was said about abortion.

Of all the strategists, none was more insistent than Donilon that Wilder needed to hammer on abortion as early, as long, and as often as possible. In July he had assessed various demographic groups and had come up with a reading under which Wilder would win about 51 percent of the vote. The approach was unique. Instead of planning a geography-based strategy, in which the candidate concentrated on certain regions of the state, Donilon was looking at age and sex groupings. His conclusion was that, along with black voters, Wilder needed to carry 60 percent of white women in the eighteen-to-thirty-nine age category, and 55 percent of white men. If that happened, Coleman could carry older voters by two to one, and Wilder could still win narrowly, he believed. No other issue came close to abortion as a rallying point for the under-forty age group. "I didn't see any other way to win," Donilon says bluntly. "I was a Johnny-one-note on it."

Those who argued for an early airing also had another concern. They were worried that Coleman might drop his opposition to abortion in cases of rape and incest, and that the switch would deprive them of a major weapon. Particularly in rural areas of the state, abortion was viewed skeptically by many voters. But in cases of rape and incest even they took a more liberal view. Democrats outside the campaign were urging Wilder to attack Coleman on abortion by accusing him of waffling on the issue after the primary. But the candidate and his staff much preferred to keep Coleman in place on the far right of the issue.

At first Wilder considered beginning the abortion ad campaign immediately after Labor Day. However, the cost of sustaining the commercials was a problem, and Greer argued that the decision might undercut the strategy of portraying Coleman as the negative campaigner. "I didn't want Doug to be perceived as running the first negative ad," Greer recalls.

The campaign focused next on September 14, a Thursday, as a day to start showing the abortion ads but two days earlier, Coleman began running his slain-police-officer ad. In the strategy huddle that followed, Greer argued that the abortion ad should be postponed in favor of a response on crime. Donilon countered that abortion could be sidetracked indefinitely if the campaign set its agenda by Coleman's timetable. Wilder resolved the dispute. The police officer response would begin on September 14 and run until the following Tuesday, he said. At that point, regardless of what ads Coleman was running, the abortion commercial would air.

As the nineteenth approached, several Wilder strategists recall that Greer still had misgivings. At a dinner meeting, the media specialist urged Wilder to test reaction to his ad in a focus group before airing it. "I remember Doug saying, 'I don't care what happens to the focus groups. You're running the ad,'" recalls one of those also at the table. Throughout the decision process, says Donilon, "Doug really had a lot of guts on it. He was taking hell from every side, both the abortion opponents and the abortion rights advocates." (After the election some Wilder strategists, including Goldman, were irritated by the belief that Greer was receiving national credit for decisions that Wilder had made.)

If there were disagreements about when to air the abortion commercial, there is no dispute in the Wilder camp that the ad prepared by Greer was a masterpiece. Wilder says he vetoed an earlier proposal because it did not sufficiently contrast his position and Coleman's. The final product presented the abortion debate in libertarian terms consistent with Virginia conservative political traditions. It asked, in effect, not whether abortion is right or wrong, but who makes that decision? The woman, or the government?

The commercial began with a shot of a fluttering American flag, superimposed on a view of Monticello. The scene faded quickly into another, featuring a statue of Thomas Jefferson, as the announcer spoke: "In Virginia we have a strong tradition of freedom and individual liberty—rights that are now in danger in the race for governor.

"On the issue of abortion, Marshall Coleman wants to take away your right to choose and give it to the politicians. He wants to go back to outlawing abortion, even in cases of rape and incest," the ad continued, as a shot of Coleman filled the screen. The next visual showed Wilder listening to a woman, while the narrative said: "Doug Wilder believes the government shouldn't interfere in your right to choose. He wants to keep the politicians out of your personal life."

The concluding messages were accompanied by alternating shots of Coleman and Wilder: "Don't let Marshall Coleman take us back. To keep Virginia moving forward, Doug Wilder is the clear choice."

As the campaign awaited reaction, a poll released by Mason-Dixon Opinion Research bolstered confidence. According to the survey, Coleman was leading Wilder by 44 percentage points to 38. Despite Greekfest and the difficulties of August, Wilder had lost only one point and Coleman gained only one since the research firm polled in midsummer. Perhaps even more significantly, when respondents were told of the candidates' positions on abortion Wilder took a 46 to 42 percentage-point lead.

Two days later, in a joint appearance before the Richmond Bar Association, Coleman took the tack he would follow for the next several weeks. Ignoring the heightened focus on abortion, he spoke of drugs, and argued that middle-class users—including lawyers—were a critical element in the nation's drug problem. Moments later, Wilder scoffed at the notion that some in the room used illegal drugs, and turned the focus back to abortion. Pressed by reporters after the event about abortions for sex selection or birth control, Wilder was steadfast. "I trust the women of Virginia to decide," he said.

There was celebration, and no small amount of astonishment, for Wilder supporters across the Commonwealth as Sunday editions of the *Washington Post* reported a narrow lead for the Democrat in the gubernatorial race. The newspaper's first poll of the campaign gave Wilder a fragile 45 to 42 percentage-point lead, with a sampling error of plus or minus 3 percent.

Perhaps more significant, however, was a series of internal measures of how voters perceived the candidates. In ten categories ranging from trustworthiness to strength as a leader, the numbers gave Wilder a solid advantage over Coleman. For instance, 31 percent of those surveyed said the statement, "He has the right qualifications to be governor," described Coleman well or fairly well. Forty-seven percent said it applied to Wilder. Twenty-three percent saw Coleman as a "strong leader"; 43 percent thought the term fit Wilder. On trustworthiness, the gap was 24 to 40 in Wilder's favor; on "high moral character," it was 29 to 44; and on "would keep the state's economy strong," it was 28 to 35. The only measures where Coleman came close were in ability to hold down taxes and toughness on crime and drugs. Even in those two categories, which political polls showed to be among Wilder's most vulnerable points, the *Post* put Wilder slightly ahead. Respondents gave the Democrat a 15 to 17 edge on taxes, and a 42 to 44 advantage on crime. Perhaps least encouraging of all for Republicans, 53 percent of those surveyed said they believed the campaign had been too negative. Forty-three percent blamed Coleman, while only 4 percent held Wilder primarily accountable.

Even Democrats acknowledged privately that they did not believe the internal numbers were correct. Republicans, aghast, quickly pointed to the *Post*'s miscalculation four years earlier, when the newspaper gave Wilder a 24-point lead on the eve of an election he won by 4 percentage points. They also noted the absence of demographic data about those surveyed, making it impossible to determine whether certain groups had been oversampled or undersampled. And they suggested that Wilder's strong black support gave him an advantage in early surveys. While whites who might later support Coleman were still non-committal on the election, Wilder had a solid base of enthusiastic loyalists. Still, there was an indisputable psychological lift for Democrats who only a few weeks earlier had suspected they were pursuing a lost cause.

SEPTEMBER 26, 1989

Coleman, who often seemed strengthened by adversity, countered with his own surprise two days later. During a joint appearance before the Virginia Manufacturers Association, he revealed that the Fraternal Order of Police would soon announce its endorsement of him. Exuberantly Coleman read a statement from George Austin, who had been president of the organization when Wilder won its backing in 1985. "Four years ago, Doug Wilder did not tell us the truth about his weak law enforcement record, about his support for releasing violent criminals early, about his failure to support law enforcement officers when it counted," the statement said. "The issue is trust, and the record shows that Marshall Coleman has earned the trust and the support of police officers." Moments after the debate, Wilder appeared dejected as he told reporters, "It doesn't help me." The statement was one of the few in the entire campaign in which Wilder revealed any glimmer of disappointment or self-doubt.

Coleman's victory followed a hard-fought battle. For weeks, Republicans had courted the estimated 5,900 law enforcement officials that make up the organization. At a point when Wilder had yet to unveil a comprehensive law-and-order platform, Coleman had already issued a twenty-two-page document called "Making 20 Years Mean 20 Years," and in some weeks had distributed almost daily press releases on crime positions. His six latest television ads, leading up to the endorsement, had focused on either crime or drugs. The latest offering, which had been showing for several days, showed a gloved arm holding a revolver, and recalled a 1970s vote by Wilder against making it a felony to point a gun at a police officer. "Thirty-four state senators voted to give our police this important added protection. But Douglas Wilder voted no," the announcer said. "And Virginians will never forget his explanation. He said—now get this—he said it might cause the police to commit murder. Huh?"

Wilder countered that the votes being cited by Coleman were a decade or more old, and that while the Republican talked tough, it was actually he who had put more anticrime legislation on the books. He pointed to his sponsorship of the state's first antidrug paraphernalia bill, legislation doubling the time before convicted capital murderers can be considered for parole, and a bill making escape from jail a felony rather than a misdemeanor. In the aftermath of the endorsement, Democratic sources leaked the word that the Fraternal Order of Police split had been twenty-six to eighteen for Coleman. The FOP chapters, each of which had one vote, broke twenty-one to sixteen for Coleman, while the executive board split five to two in the Republican's favor, they said.

The next day's GOP press release was entitled "Wilder camp reeling from FOP endorsement." Actually, a misstep by Coleman appeared to have saved the Democrats from that fate. Upset by the Austin statement, FOP officials issued a disavowal that blunted the impact of their endorsement. "Although Doug Wilder does not have the endorsement today, we firmly believe in his integrity and sincerity as a political candidate," the executive board said. "We did not feel then [in 1985], nor do we feel now, that Doug Wilder is weak on crime."

Wilder's day began poorly with the FOP endorsement of Coleman, but there was a boost for him that night on an estate outside the university town of Charlottesville. The state's wealthiest residents, billionaire John Kluge, and his wife, Patricia, hosted their second fundraiser for Wilder, and receipts totalling more than $500,000 made the evening the most lucrative of the Democrat's campaign.

Wilder had met Patricia Kluge in the spring at a luncheon hosted by Felicia Warburg Rogan, owner of the Oakencroft vineyards and winery, and a member of Wilder's fund-raising circle.

Impressed by the candidate, Mrs. Kluge invited him home to meet her husband, a German emigrant who built one of the nation's largest fortunes through a broadcasting conglomerate including television and radio stations. A year earlier Kluge had contributed $100,000 to the Republican National Committee for its efforts in the presidential campaign, but in Virginia his limited political involvements had been primarily for Democrats. The attachment had produced some carping from Republicans, particularly after the state lent a $250,000 subsidy to the first Virginia Festival of American Film, a favorite project of Patricia Kluge's. The couple also stirred controversy when game-keepers at their estate were convicted of killing dozens of federally protected hawks and owls. The Kluges voluntarily shut down their game preserve in response.

Apparently attracted by the parallels between his own rags-to-riches rise and Wilder's, John Kluge made his first $100,000 gift to the candidate at a May fundraiser at the couple's forty-five-room mansion. At the September event, he duplicated the present, delighting guests with the claim that his second $100,000 check was prompted by a telephone call from Coleman. As the Kluges told it, Coleman phoned their home with the message that he expected to be elected governor, and thought they should be acquainted. Kluge responded with a check to Wilder.

The combined gifts made the billionaire the largest individual contributor to Wilder's eventual $7 million war chest. The second largest donation came from Bahman Batmanghelidj, the Fairfax developer, who gave $146,000. And the third major donor was entertainer Bill Cosby, who supplied $100,000. Like Wilder, the three donors had all moved from the fringes of American society to its core.

SEPTEMBER 27, 1989

As the end of September approached, leaders of the Coleman campaign gathered for a huddle that would set their strategy for the next several weeks. It was eight days since the Wilder abortion spot had begun running, and the only response had been the counterattack on crime. Robert Goodman and his son, Adam, entered the meeting expecting that the group would agree to start airing a commercial they had prepared scoring Wilder's record on rape legislation. "I was chilled by the rape victim spot," recalls Adam Goodman, political director for the consulting firm. "I thought it was an incredible piece of work. We thought everyone would have the same opinion that it should go up by the end of September." In fact, the ad fell victim to the same lack of consensus that characterized other discussions on abortion. "Never in this campaign was there unanimity of opinion on abortion by anybody," says the younger Goodman.

With Anne Kincaid sidelined, no one at the meeting argued for an aggressive, frontal assault. The notion that Coleman should be speaking out in opposition to the most controversial abortions was not then viewed as a desirable option by those in charge of the campaign. Bob Goodman's original proposal that Coleman discard his opposition to abortion in cases of rape and incest also had long since been abandoned. The two alternatives under active consideration were to continue trying to divert attention from the abortion issue, or to attempt to undermine the notion that Wilder was concerned about women's rights. The rape ad fit the latter category.

In Boyd Marcus's and Frank Atkinson's minds, however, a more pressing problem than abortion was looming. The positive ads in late August and early September, plus the assault on crime issues, had brought Coleman back to even with Wilder, they believed, but numbers reported to them the previous day by McLaughlin showed a discomforting trend. The results reflected a neck-and-neck race, with Coleman at 42 percentage points and Wilder at 44. However, the percentage of voters viewing Coleman unfavorably was also climbing. The number had grown from the low to the midtwentieth percentile, a danger sign to those who knew the overall campaign strategy. From the beginning of the race, Coleman's managers believed they had only to stay even with Wilder until mid-October, when they would unleash a character assault that would devastate the Democrat. Negative campaigning usually creates some backlash, however, and they could not afford to have a large percentage of voters already viewing their candidate negatively at an early stage.

While Marcus and Atkinson were skeptical of the *Washington Post*'s internal numbers from the previous Sunday, the figures still fed their doubts about the candidate's image. There was also pressure from the Republican National Committee (RNC) to avoid appearing too negative. Some of the money being promised by the RNC had strings attached. It could only be used for positive advertising.

"If there was ever a point at which the campaign fell victim to conventional wisdom and moved off strategy," says Atkinson, it was at the September 27 meeting. The group—including RNC chairman Lee Atwater—agreed that the rape ad should be postponed. It was more important to bolster Coleman's image with a dose of positive commercials, they believed. In retrospect, Marcus says the decision to delay responding on abortion "may have been a crucial point in the campaign." Says Bob Goodman, "The first two weeks in October took our lunch."

OCTOBER 4, 1989

As Republicans readied for the second of George Bush's three visits to Virginia on Coleman's behalf, a group of thirty-four business and financial leaders published full-page advertisements in major newspapers welcoming the president to the state. "Like most Virginians, many of us supported you in your efforts last fall," the ads said, "but, in good conscience, we cannot support your choice for governor this fall." The group, describing themselves as "independent voters," said their loyalties were with Douglas Wilder.

Some of those on the list were more independent than others. In fact, several were Democratic stalwarts, distinguished from the average party member only by wealth. Others, however, were genuinely unaligned, and capturing their support was a coup for Wilder. Several of the same names appeared again later in the day as the candidate unveiled a Commission on

Excellence to advise him on gubernatorial appointments. Wilder later acknowledged that he took the unusual step of naming such a committee largely to allay fears that he would make sweeping changes on state boards and commissions. Wilder did not directly attribute the concern to race, but there is little doubt about what fostered the fears to which he alluded.

Among those appearing on one or both lists were such rock-solid corporate citizens as Thomas Capps of Dominion Resources; Hays Watkins of CSX; Warner Dalhouse, chairman and chief executive officer of Dominion Bankshares Corporation; W. Wright Harrison, former chairman of the board of Sovran Bank, and William F. Franck, a Martinsville industrialist and former chairman of the Virginia Manufacturers' Association. If blacks, union members, and other traditional Democrats were vital to Wilder, they may have been no more so than the group of elite Virginians who publicly cast their lot with him. What the endorsements said to moderate and conservative white Virginians was, "You have nothing to fear."

Characteristic of the lot was Dalhouse, chief officer in one of the Commonwealth's leading financial corporations, headquartered in Roanoke. Typically a Republican voter, Dalhouse said that his decision to support Wilder was based on several issues, including abortion, and on his personal reaction to the two candidates. After interviewing each about Roanoke-area projects, his impression was that "Marshall was telling me what he thought I wanted to hear. . . . Doug Wilder was more business-like, more judicious." In addition, "I like the guy. . . . It's not long into a conversation that you're totally unaware he's black. Some of my friends go into apoplexy to hear me say this, but I like him and I trust him."

If Wilder found some loyalists in Virginia's monied circles, however, Coleman appeared to find more. Spending his evening in the company of Bush and of supporters willing to pay $25,000 a couple for dinner, he raised a reported $2 million, the largest take in a single night in Virginia political history.

Earlier in the day at Virginia State University, a predominantly black state school just south of the capital, in Petersburg, Wilder spoke at greater length about race and opportunity than in any other public appearance in the campaign. Like most of the candidate's speeches, the performance was impromptu, surprising even his staff. Wilder insisted afterwards that there was no intention of issuing a rallying call to black voters with his words. Faced with an audience of young blacks, he had simply wanted to impress upon them the possibilities that awaited if they worked hard.

Wilder began by mentioning his own days at Virginia Union University in Richmond almost four decades earlier. "You see the changes that have taken place in that period of time," he said. "It's a good thing when you travel around the country, and you meet people, and you see people like Colin Powell, who's the chief-of-staff of the joint chiefs." Referring to students he once taught in constitutional law and government, he continued,

> How good it is now to see some of those students doing the kinds of things they're doing. You name it, and they're there. They're running governments in localities in Virginia and beyond. They serve as judges. They serve as doctors. They serve as lawyers. You name it, they're there.
>
> And when you consider the greater opportunities, when you consider . . . what used to be, and what did take place, it causes people to say, well, do you think we can win in 1989? And I say, why do you think I'm running in 1989?

He paused as the applause subsided. "And it causes the media sometimes to ask questions," he continued. "Can it really be taking place? Is this really going to happen on November 7? Are they really going to do that there? . . . Isn't this the same place that said education was for some, not for all? Isn't this the same place that said that guy couldn't even go to a law school in his own state? Isn't this the same place that said separate but equal was the law?"

Switching emphasis, Wilder went on,

> This is the same place that had someone write that all men are created equal and that they are endowed by their creator with certain inalienable rights, and that among these are

life, liberty, and the pursuit of happiness. . . . This is the same place that George Mason believed in the rights of man, so much so that the Bill of Rights—the first ten amendments to the United States constitution—were Virginia's contribution. This is the same place that gave rise to those who said give me liberty or give me death.

And so, when I was a young man coming up, that was the Virginia that I believed in. That was what I thought was possible for me. I thought that it wasn't that I was born in Church Hill in Richmond, and that I could not be. Or that I was born in Virginia, and that I could not be. Or that I went to Virginia Union, and could not be. Or that I went to Howard Law School, and could not be. I never thought any of those things, because I believed that the breath of freedom that was infused in this nation started in Virginia, started at Jamestown. It started with people believing that possibility existed for the fullest development of potential.

And that's why it's so important in November, not for purposes of history, but for purposes of progress. Not for purposes of Doug Wilder, but for purposes of people who may have felt like he, who may have looked like he, who may have been born under the same circumstances as he. . . . You and I have the responsibility to make certain that what takes place on November 7 isn't something that can happen once in a lifetime, but something that should be expected.

11

THE ELECTION APPROACHES

A League of Women Voters debate, nationally televised by cable and originating from a crowded Petersburg studio, signaled the start of the campaign's final month.

For Republicans, the exchange came at what was probably the lowest point of the contest. A day earlier, Boyd Marcus had received a grim report from John McLaughlin. Instead of being bolstered by the round of positive ads, Coleman was being undercut. Apparently his failure to respond on abortion was critical. According to the campaign polling expert, in just under two weeks the candidate had fallen from a dead heat with Wilder to 14 points behind. White voters were evenly split between the two candidates. Since the survey was set up to reflect a worst-case scenario, Marcus suspects that Coleman would have been about nine points behind Wilder in an independent survey. The numbers were compatible with those of Mike Donilon, Wilder's pollster, who believed the Democratic candidate took a lead for the first time in the campaign in late September.

Marcus delivered the bad news to Coleman the morning of the day that he and Wilder were set to face off on their first television debate. The Republican candidate was nursing a bad cold, and he was weary from the exhausting campaign rounds. "It was a very intense time for him, trying to raise money, and still doing enough public appearances to make it look good. He was spending almost all his time raising money," recalls Marcus.

As the debate began, even the first glimpse of the candidates hinted that it was not to be Coleman's evening. A local makeup artist had applied heavy rouge to the candidate's cheeks, and the contrast with the rest of his pale face made him look a bit like a cadaver prepared for a funeral.

Disturbed by the latest internal poll, Coleman and his strategists decided to confront the abortion issue directly in his opening statement. He had been recently approached, Coleman began, by a young woman with a "troubled and gentle face." What she wanted to know was whether the Republican intended to outlaw abortions in cases of rape and incest if elected. "Everyone knows there's not going to be a law passed in Virginia on rape and incest," he said, gazing directly at the camera. Wilder had spent hundreds of thousands of dollars spreading fear on the subject, and now the question was, "Will fear rule our lives?" Wilder's campaign chiefs listened intently throughout Coleman's statement. As soon as he mentioned abortion, they felt certain that he intended to alter his position in some way. When he did not, they were amazed. Donilon and others later argued that Coleman only gave new life to an issue of which the public was beginning to tire.

Prior to the debate, Wilder and his staff had prepared six possible questions for the period in which the candidates grilled each other directly. It was Wilder's call as to which he actually used. One of the six dealt with whether Coleman would sign a bill restricting abortions for rape and incest. There had been internal debate over whether the query should be used at all, but after Coleman's opening statement, Wilder made the decision. Three times he asked a version of the question: "What would you do if the bill came on your desk miraculously or in some other way?" Three times, Coleman either avoided answering or chided: "You know there's not a single legislative supporter who would even introduce the bill. It is a false fear."

"I want to give you every opportunity to be clear," Wilder continued several minutes later. "As governor, would you want to see abortion limited in Virginia, yes or no?"

Coleman's response was of the sort Anne Kincaid preferred, but it was framed defensively. "An unborn child is a life that should be loved and cherished," he said. "I don't feel abortion should be used for birth control or sex selection of the child." Again accusing Wilder of "fanning fear," he protested: "I would suggest that it's the only issue you've got."

What Kincaid and some others had expected was that Coleman would aggressively question Wilder about whether he was willing to sign legislation limiting abortions for purposes of birth control or sex selection. Coleman had entered the debate armed with the names of legislators who would introduce such bills, and Kincaid was dismayed when Coleman failed to return Wilder's yes or no question with his own query, she says.

The rest of the debate was equally confrontational. Several times Coleman responded to claims by Wilder with the complaint, "Now I know how Chuck Robb felt when he wrote those letters and suggested you were engaging in distortion and half truths." When Wilder called for an end to negative campaigning (moments after he questioned Coleman's links to Schar), the Republican countered, "Your record is a very, very negative thing," and "no ad could be worse than your plain distortion of my abortion record." Other memorable lines came when Coleman prodded Wilder about his former investment property on Church Hill. Claiming that there were "enough rats to perform scientific experiments," he asked, "Why didn't you just sell one of the Mercedes, buy a Pontiac and fix it up?"

"I really can't believe you're still chewing this rag," replied Wilder, who at times could be heard chuckling in the background during Coleman's responses.

The prevailing view of commentators was that Wilder won what had been a fairly dismal showing by both. "We were embarrassed in front of the nation," fumed the editorial page of the *Virginian-Pilot* two days later. "Not once during the debate—not once in 60 minutes—were Virginia's mammoth challenges in transportation, prisons or Medicaid mentioned. There was only one reference to education. . . . Mr. Wilder had the night's most perceptive comment. That came near the end of the debate: 'We've wasted an hour,' he said . . . Amen."

Wilder's tacticians were highly pleased with the outcome, however. Editorial writers might complain, but the emotional issue most likely to sway voters, they felt, was abortion. And the subject was now back in the headlines.

OCTOBER 11, 1989

For Coleman, the time for caution was past. As Vice-President Dan Quayle arrived in Richmond to campaign for the GOP ticket, Coleman announced that the kid gloves were off. He intended to escalate the attacks. A day later he unveiled two ads designed to appeal directly to the women of Virginia. The first was the one that Bob and Adam Goodman had hoped to begin running in late September. It focused on Wilder's 1972 introduction of a bill allowing teenage rape victims to be questioned about their sexual behavior. The second was upbeat, stressing Coleman's support of day-care tax credits for low-income parents, and similar tax breaks for companies that provide child care assistance for their employees.

The rape-victim video began as an actress veiled by shadows recalled an imaginary courtroom scene. "Don't you have boy-friends?" a voice said. "Isn't it true. . . . Tell us about that. Tell us! We know that . . . " Switching to the announcer, the ad continued: "Remembering . . . after the rape, the ordeal of questioning by the rapist's lawyer. . . . It was Douglas Wilder who introduced a bill to force rape victims age thirteen and younger to be interrogated about their private lives by lawyers for accused rapists. So the next time Mr. Wilder talks about the rights of women, ask him about this law he tried to pass."

For the next week the air war intensified, with each side issuing attacks and counterattacks. Wilder protested that the rape bill, which did not pass, was seventeen years old and had been labeled "by request," an indication that a legislator does not necessarily support a proposal and is introducing it for a constituent. Pursuing the tactic of blaming negative campaigning on Coleman, he released an ad lamenting, "He's at it again. Marshall Coleman has launched another vicious negative ad campaign of false attacks and distortions. The same tactics he used against Chuck Robb and Paul Trible. But we're not going to let him get away with it. The fact is," the commercial continued, "Doug Wilder supported the Virginia law that protects the victims of rape, and he supports a woman's right to choose." Never forgetting the key message, it concluded, "And the fact is, Marshall Coleman wants to outlaw abortions even in the case of rape or incest. Don't let Marshall Coleman take us back. To keep Virginia moving forward, Doug Wilder is the clear choice."

Coleman's rebuttal to the counterattack again mentioned "the bill to force rape victims as young as thirteen years old to endure humiliating questioning by defense lawyers." It added that Wilder "voted for three straight years against a law that would have protected all rape victims from that degrading experience." And it concluded, "The pattern continues, because Wilder's now trying to win an election by exploiting the fears of every woman in Virginia. Is this the kind of man we want for governor?"

Wilder's claim that he voted to protect rape victims, and Coleman's charge that he had not, both referred to sexual assault reform legislation considered by the Virginia General Assembly in the late 1970s and early 1980s. In 1978, 1979, and 1980, Wilder voted against the proposed legislation, which would have limited the rights of defense attorneys to cross-examine rape victims. But in 1981, when the bill finally passed the Assembly, he supported it.

Meanwhile Wilder was trying to divert attention with ads accusing Coleman of "radical proposals" for dismantling the state's new sex education mandates, and requiring "many state employees in education and health to adhere to his extremist antiabortion views." Coleman insisted that he did not oppose sex education programs, but thought individual localities should decide whether and how to teach the subject. He also maintained that his pledge during the primary to appoint pro-life individuals to health department positions dealing with abortion policy would affect only a few jobs, and had nothing to do with the Board of Education.

On October 16, six days after the Coleman rape ad began to be shown, John McLaughlin produced new polling figures showing that the gap beteen Coleman and Wilder had been whittled from about 14 percentage points to 8. Again, the estimates were conservative, and Marcus believed that in an actual election, Coleman would have been only about 4 points behind. So it was time for the personal assault to begin. "Throughout the campaign," says Marcus, "our feeling was, if we can get ourselves relatively close, we've got these character things in the can. They'll break him."

Goodman had prepared six character ads. They focused on the Robb letters, the legislation introduced on behalf of Maggie Allen, the Supreme Court reprimand, the rowhouse, honoraria taken by Wilder from Virginia organizations, and his failure to report the land holdings in Louisa County. The campaign decided to air first the one most difficult to rebut—the ad focusing on the reprimand.

As the camera trailed a set of feet walking across a marble floor, the announcer's voice rose above the hollow echo of the footsteps. "In the entire history of Virginia, only one candidate for governor has ever been reprimanded by our Supreme Court," the man said. A gavel sounded, and separate voices pronounced words taken from the court's opinion: "Conduct . . . unprofessional! Inexcusable! Misleading your own client! This proceeding is to protect the public!" The announcer continued, "Only one candidate for governor ever reprimanded by the Supreme Court. That lawyer's name: Douglas Wilder." There was a two-second pause, followed by the conclusion, "Is that the kind of man we want for governor?"

It was the only attack ad of the campaign to which Wilder did not respond. Essentially, as the lieutenant governor had said throughout the campaign, he offered no defense, only his apology.

OCTOBER 19, 1989

Voters who felt inundated with abortion and crime finally were given a respite as the candidates, stung by the criticism of their earlier debate, discussed a wealth of issues at a second televised encounter.

Republicans had taken special care to ensure that the debate would not be a repeat of the October 9 fiasco. Staff members arrived early at the studio to check out camera angles. Coleman supporters staged a rally at a nearby hotel to boost the candidate's spirits. And Bob Goodman brought his usual makeup artist down to Richmond to prepare the candidate's face. In contrast to appearances at the first debate, the skin tones of the two candidates looked on television to be about the same shade of tan.

There were exchanges over taxes, the environment, smoking bans, and college admission policies during the hour-long session. But the candidates also found time to continue their cross fire over character and ethics, with Coleman concentrating on the reprimand and Maggie Allen, and Wilder pounding his opponent for accepting millions of dollars in contributions from individuals with land development ties. Dr. Martin Luther King, Jr., also made his way into the debate. When Coleman quoted King's admonition that individuals be judged by the "content of their character," Wilder bristled. For Coleman to quote King after he had once opposed a state holiday honoring him is "almost despicable," he said.

The discussion of issues produced a few disagreements, but more similarities. Both men were firm in opposition to raising taxes, imposing affirmative action quotas, and using the governor's office to promote the admission of women to the Virginia Military Institute. (VMI in Lexington stands almost alone nationally as a single-sex school supported with state funds.) Both candidates described themselves as environmentalists. Coleman brought several views in line with Wilder's as he backed off from a previous proposal to limit the enrollment of out-of-state students at Virginia colleges, and his earlier call for elimination of guidance counselors in elementary schools.

The liveliest moments of the debate, even so, remained those when the candidates clashed on each other's character and on their relationships with land developers. Wilder began one memorable exchange by noting, "For the last four years, you've served as the lawyer for Northern Virginia's biggest land developer." The reference was to Schar, who—along with family and business associates—was reported to have contributed more than a half million dollars to Coleman. "How does this experience qualify you to be the governor of Virginia?"

"You've represented criminals, and I'm not going to say that's wrong, and you've spent a lot of time trying to get money from developers," replied Coleman. "I really resent your suggesting to me that there is something wrong when people contribute to my campaign." At his feistiest, he continued, "There has never been a hint of scandal or a question of impropriety during my time in public office, not ever, not once. You can't point to it. . . . I can't see how you can have the arrogance to stand there and question my integrity when you have this pattern that's so troubling."

Wilder replied coolly, "I was not questioning your integrity. I was questioning your experience."

Neutral observers later called the debate a draw, or gave the edge to Coleman. Republicans clearly felt buoyed by the performance. But Democrats, noting that the audience was smaller than for the first debate, appeared unconcerned.

OCTOBER 20, 1989

Mason-Dixon Opinion Research chronicled the October shift to Wilder with new poll results that gave the Democrat a lead of 45 to 43 percentage points. Although the margin was statistically insignificant, Wilder had gained 7 percent since the firm's last survey a month earlier, while Coleman had slipped 1 percent. The numbers mirrored almost exactly those recorded in September, when the firm informed respondents of the candidates' positions on abortion.

Wilder's advantage among women had more than tripled in one month to a lead of 49 to 39 percent. His largest surges had come in Northern Virginia and Hampton Roads, the regions of the state where pro-choice sentiment was greatest. In Northern Virginia, there had been a 14-point swing to Wilder since the previous survey; he had gone from trailing by 10 percentage points to a 46 to 42 lead. However, Brad Coker, president of the polling research firm, noted that Wilder also seemed to have soaked up most of the advantage to be gained on the abortion issue. The positions of the two candidates were widely known.

As if on cue, the Wilder campaign unveiled a new television ad, highlighting what it hoped would be an important ancillary issue: the heavy funding of the Coleman campaign by developers. A graphic showed buildings popping up in a pastoral setting, while an announcer complained that "big Northern Virginia developers" had contributed half of Coleman's $6 million treasury "because they want special treatment."

Once again Wilder's attack was presented as a response to Coleman's negatives. "Marshall Coleman will say and do anything to try and get elected," the ad began. "But this time he's gone too far. His negative ads are insulting and offensive, and even worse, they're just not true. And who's paying for these ads? The big Northern Virginia developers."

Surely those charting the Wilder campaign a year earlier could never have predicted the emergence of two of the issues that were now dominating his rhetoric: abortion and the influence of developers.

OCTOBER 22, 1989

Among the silent heroes of the Wilder campaign effort was the Rev. Paul Matthews, a forty-five-year-old former undercover investigator and education department official in Pennsylvania, who had journeyed south in 1984 to attend Richmond's Union Theological Seminary. Through an unexpected chain of events, within a year the tall, heavy-set Baptist minister, whose energy appeared to match his bulk, wound up as executive secretary of the state NAACP. A friend of Michael Brown and an admirer of Wilder, Matthews agreed in the summer to coordinate the candidate's contacts with black churches across the state. He was offered a salary, but declined.

By Matthews's estimate, the agenda he planned took Wilder to more than sixty-five churches — most of them black — on nine Sundays beginning in early September, while surrogate speakers, including Robb, appeared at others. If radio broadcasts of the services were counted, he believes the audience was as high as fifty thousand people on some days. And he estimates that the collection plates passed along the way hauled in between $300,000 and $400,000. Whatever the precise numbers, there is little doubt that three-quarters or more of the time that Wilder spent courting black voters was on the Sunday marathons coordinated by Matthews.

As Tom Bradley discovered in California and numerous commentators have noted through the years, the tightrope walked by black politicians running in majority-white settings is a perilous one. If the candidate ignores black voters, as Bradley was accused of doing, the dampened minority turnout can cost a politician the election. But if racial rhetoric is too fiery, particularly in a state as reserved as Virginia, the loss of votes among whites can be equally or more damaging. In 1985, for instance, Wilder chose to downplay black appeals, and the percentage of registered blacks who voted that year was lower than in any statewide election since at least the mid-1970s.

As late as mid-September 1989, prominent black leaders across Virginia had been complaining privately, and occasionally in public, that Doug Wilder was being too coy with his black constituency. Black faces almost never appeared in his commercials. Whites were running his campaign for the most part. And the message he was delivering was race-neutral. But by election day, the complaints had been largely silenced. A major reason was that most of those same leaders had seen Wilder at church, or had joined him for one of the closed-to-the-press receptions that accompanied his Sunday visits.

To explain the impact of such meetings, Matthews stresses what politicians and scholars have long emphasized, the continuing social and political importance of the black church, particularly in the South. "The church in the black experience has always been the focal point for all our activity. It's the center not only of spiritual expression, but of community and social activity," he says. "In 1985 there was not an organized effort in the churches; this time we were organized."

Planning for the Sunday excursions was perfected almost to a science as Matthews crafted a system for racing from church to church. Ministers were warned not to give lengthy introductions, and even as Wilder began speaking to one congregation, runners were sent ahead to prepare the next group for his arrival. On one Sunday Wilder made brief appearances before eleven different Richmond congregations, and Delegate Frank Hall visited another six, leading up to an afternoon rally at First Baptist Church in South Richmond.

Matthews was careful to include in the schedule a variety of denominations—Episcopal, AME Zion, United Methodist, Church of God in Christ, Presbyterian, Catholic, and others, as well as the predominant Baptist sects. He also slated visits to synagogues and churches with mostly white memberships, although there were fewer such stops. At times, hundreds of worshippers were in the audiences. But Wilder also visited small churches, including some with congregations of no more than fifty. Either way, says Matthews, "the ripple effect was enormous. People would call friends, call relatives all over the country, and say, 'Guess what? Guess who I saw today!'"

For weeks, word of Wilder's Sunday travels was communicated largely by mouth. Full agendas were not listed on the candidate's campaign schedule, and only in the final weeks of the race did reporters began accompanying Wilder regularly on his pulpit excursions. Even in the worship services, his messages rarely had strong racial overtones. Typically he told anecdotes from the campaign and urged people to vote. But at the private gatherings also scheduled each Sunday, as Matthews and others acknowledge, the candidate talked about more sensitive subjects, such as how many blacks might be appointed to his cabinet, or what specific things he had done to promote black interests through the years.

With the election just over two weeks away, Wilder arrived in Roanoke for a typical Sunday tour. He began at the Hill Street Baptist Church with an 8:00 A.M. service that had been set up especially for him. The choir and the congregation came early that day to meet a political hero. At 9:20 A.M., a community forum, off limits to reporters, was held with a group of black community leaders at a local black restaurant. Next, Wilder squeezed in a radio interview, and hurried to an appearance at Pilgrim Baptist Church, where the Sunday morning service is broadcast to a radio audience. At 11:45 A.M., he was scheduled to be the Men's Day speaker at First Baptist Church. From there, he dashed to appearances at Shiloh Baptist and First Baptist in nearby Salem.

"These things energized him," says Matthews. "Sometimes he'd be grumpy from the night before. But when little old ladies on walkers are saying, 'I'm praying for you,' it energized him for the week to come." Matthews recalls numerous highlights from along the way: the Sunday in Alexandria when Wilder, without any preparation, delivered the Women's Day message at one church, and the Men's Day sermon at the next; the day in Roanoke when Matthews sat beside a three-year-old girl who recognized the candidate from television and family discussions and knew his name; the story told by a Portsmouth minister of a relative who was so inspired by Wilder's victory in 1985 that she ran for local office in South Carolina and won; and the event at a Chesapeake church where the congregation raised $10,000 with such devices as selling a hug from Wilder for $200, and small children contributed dimes to the collection plate. Matthews found himself constantly amazed by the number of people whom Wilder appeared to know personally, and by the candidate's ability to deliver different, spontaneous messages at every stop. "He'd pull out some poem, some Shakespeare piece, something from Thoreau, and I'd sit there amazed.

"This campaign mobilized the black community in politics more than any other in the history of Virginia," says Matthews. "From the black churches' perspective, we were the balance of power that brought him in."

OCTOBER 24, 1989

Boyd Marcus terms the Supreme Court reprimand advertisement "the biggest misfire of the whole campaign." Coleman officials, who had been banking on the character ads to propel their candidate to victory, were stunned when John McLaughlin reported four days after the ad began running that Coleman was once again losing ground. "I couldn't believe it," recalls Bob Goodman, the media consultant. Just as bad, Coleman's negative rating among voters was soaring. The percentage of the electorate that viewed Coleman unfavorably was approaching the high thirties, while Wilder's negative rating was still in the low to midtwenties. "He was running all these ads saying we were doing negative advertising, negative advertising. We were bad, terrible people," says Marcus.

Both Boyd Marcus and Bob Goodman attribute the unexpected reaction to the impact of abortion on the campaign, although each describes what was happening with a slightly different twist. "The press coverage was all focused on abortion, and people had stopped listening to us," complains Marcus. In Goodman's view, "On abortion, we were on the lunatic fringe, and we didn't have the credibility."

Frank Greer and Wilder believe that their decision to lambaste Coleman for negative advertising was also at work. Voters had been sensitized to the issue by the 1988 presidential campaign, in which numerous postelection commentaries stressed the negativism of George Bush's ads and the strategic mistake made by Michael Dukakis in failing to respond. Against that backdrop, the public seemed more inclined to listen to Wilder's complaints about tactics than to charges that Coleman insisted were based on verifiable facts.

Deciding to take one more shot with two weeks left, the Coleman campaign Tuesday unveiled a second character ad, featuring previously unseen shots of the controversial rowhouse. Repeating lines from the first debate, the announcer described the house as "a haven for rats and vagrants," and asked, "Wouldn't you think a millionaire with two Mercedes in his garage could have spent a few dollars to make the property safe for neighborhood children?"

Greer, who was primed to answer a house ad, gleefully responded the next day with yet another counterattack on developers and "Coleman's negative campaign." "Coleman's just trying to hide the fact that for the past four years as a lawyer for the big Northern Virginia developers, he's been threatening neighborhoods, homes and families," the ad claimed. "We were ready to go on that," recalls Greer. "I kept saying, 'Come on. Hit me on the slum property.'"

THE ELECTION APPROACHES **215**

Along with the response to the house ad, Wilder issued a second new commercial appealing to the Republican-leaning women he viewed as critical. Pursuing Donilon's strategy of courting white women under forty, the spot featured a woman who said she was putting aside her normal Republican tendencies to vote for Wilder because of abortion. "In the past, I have voted Republican. But this November I'm voting for Doug Wilder," said Jean Durfee, a resident of Annandale in Northern Virginia. "Marshall Coleman wants to take away the right of a woman to choose—even for poor women who are the victims of rape and incest. Doug Wilder trusts the women of Virginia, and the voters of Virginia trust Doug Wilder."

Republicans complained that if Durfee was a usual Republican voter, she nonetheless had failed to vote in the GOP's presidential primary a year earlier. Still, they could not ignore the pounding on abortion that seemed to face them at every turn. For several days Coleman had been trying to shift the focus onto claims that the state faced a pending financial crisis. Economists were predicting a financial downturn generally in 1990. The state had spent heavily for new programs in the Baliles administration, and millions of dollars would be lost if the courts ordered Virginia to repay the federal pensioners whose incomes the state had been taxing for years. Coleman had unveiled his claims earlier in the week at a Roanoke luncheon, but the news was upstaged in the next day's papers by the unsolicited endorsement he received from the National Right to Life Committee.

On Wednesday Coleman arrived at the Amtrak station in Alexandria, ready to talk about the transportation issues that were a major component of his appeal to Northern Virginians. But he was met by a group of abortion protesters, who again switched the focus to Coleman's least favorite subject. "Public opinion is going to be a factor in what kinds of laws and rules we have in the future," said the exasperated candidate, trying once more to soften his position.

As the weekend approached, the Coleman campaign detected

a slight improvement in their polling numbers. The house ad, and another attacking Wilder for votes involving spouse-abuse bills, seemed to be helping slightly. But the gains were not enough, and the apparent erosion of likely Republican voters was especially dangerous. "We decided the key to the election was the Republicans we were losing," says Marcus. "We had to do something to bring them home." The entire Coleman strategy was turning.

OCTOBER 29, 1989

Sunday morning editions of the *Washington Post* brought the startling news that Wilder was being propelled by women, younger voters, and suburbanites to a 52 to 37 percentage-point lead over Coleman in the governor's race. Both Mike Donilon and John McLaughlin were showing Wilder with comfortable leads, but nothing approaching that landslide. Still, even as Democrats expressed skepticism about the numbers, speculation that Wilder might actually win a historic race by record numbers began to creep into the thinking of some. Few of those who were deeply schooled in politics agreed. What some experts saw was that, assuming a competent campaign by Coleman in the final week, Wilder might well have gone as far as he could go. Many of the undecideds were either Republican-leaning voters still looking for a good reason to back Coleman, or Democrats open to voting Republican in the race for governor. It is a rule of thumb in black-white contests in a heavily white setting that the overwhelming majority of those still undecided as the election closes will vote for the white candidate.

While Wilder was receiving enthusiastic receptions at a round of black churches in Norfolk, Coleman canceled appearances and went into seclusion with campaign advisers at his home in McLean. The critical last week of the campaign was about to begin, and the victory that once seemed almost assured was still eluding them. The group decided that Coleman, after weeks of trying, could no longer ignore abortion.

Coleman emerged from the retreat with plans for three new television ads and a promise—soon broken—to drop his attacks on Wilder's character. From now until election day, "I will not bring those up voluntarily," he said of the charges in an interview with Don Baker of the *Washington Post.*

The first of the new ads featured Mary Vaughan Gibson, president of the Virginia Federation of Republican Women and a pro-choice advocate. It was viewed by many as the most effective appeal offered by Coleman to pro-choice women in the campaign. Speaking directly to the camera, Gibson said: "I'm pro-choice, but I'm not a single-issue voter. And on the things that matter most in my family, Marshall Coleman has the right ideas, like putting a cap on property taxes, improving day care, and keeping drug dealers away from my kids. And frankly, Mr. Wilder's votes against rape victims and against abused spouses turn me off completely. . . . On women's rights, on everybody's rights, it's Marshall Coleman all the way."

The other ads, filmed at Coleman's home, showed only the candidate. In one, Coleman recited a litany of the issues he had stressed in the campaign—crime, drugs, day care, low taxes, roads, and a government of "people we can trust." The other ad included Coleman's first direct mention of abortion in a commercial. "Let's set the record straight," it began. "I'm not going to restrict abortions for rape and incest. But should a teenager seeking abortion get the permission of her parents? I say yes. Should abortions be performed because a parent wants a boy instead of a girl? I say no." Quickly moving on, the ad continued, "Now look at the Wilder record on women's rights. Mr. Wilder voted three times to allow rapists and their attorneys to grill the victim and twice to let wife abusers back into the home. Don't those votes say it all?"

Democrats, delighted that their strategy seemed to be working so well, decided to keep the focus on abortion. Campaigning at the Northern Virginia Women's Center, Wilder released a letter distributed by Coleman to ministers just prior to the June primary. In the June 5 letter, Coleman promised "to work to prohibit all abortions in Virginia, except to protect the life of the mother." Wilder termed it "unprecedented" for Coleman to try to mislead the public by "insisting he had a different position."

In Richmond, the Virginia Organization to Keep Abortion Legal was fueling Wilder's arsenal by releasing a list of fifty pro-choice Republicans who intended to back the Democrat. Most of the group were women, and almost all lived in the population centers of Northern Virginia and Tidewater. "I'm not a feminist at all, but I think if men bore children, abortion would be a sacrament," said one of those women, T. J. Trent, a twenty-nine-year-old former stockbroker whose family moved to Richmond in 1988. Trent was registered as a Republican in their prior state, Indiana, and her husband "has never once pulled the lever for a Democrat 'til now," she said.

OCTOBER 31, 1989

As Coleman's new abortion ads began appearing, Republicans seemed finally to have found evidence that might divert attention from one emotional issue to another. Appearing at a Richmond news conference, Reed Larson, the president of the National Right to Work Committee, produced tape recordings of the closed meeting between Wilder and striking miners in Castlewood on July 31. The words, he alleged, proved the Democrat's support for destruction of the state's right-to-work law.

Unfamiliar to many non-Virginians and newer state residents, the right-to-work law has long been one of the primary political rallying points for conservative Virginians, along with opposition to labor unions. Endangerment of the statute, which protects the right of nonunion members to work in union plants, has been a hot button, pressed in numerous elections over the years. Its impact as an issue has faded somewhat as younger, suburban voters have gained political clout. But in many rural communities and among business leaders, the right-to-work statute is still viewed as sacrosanct. Both Wilder and Coleman pledged their support repeatedly throughout the campaign.

Larson's charge that Wilder had told the public one thing, and striking union members another in secret, not only addressed an emotional issue. It also went to the heart of questions about whether Wilder was actually more liberal, and less trustworthy, than he claimed. The Wilder campaign termed the release of the tape "another act of desperation," and said Larson's interpretation of Wilder's comments was "a blatant distortion." Those who eventually listened to the recording of the eighty-minute session with miners came away with mixed impressions of what Wilder had said. A major reason for the discrepancy was that language was garbled during the key part of the tape, with several people talking simultaneously.

At issue was Larson's claim that Wilder agreed to work to weaken the law by adding a "free rider" clause, allowing contracts that required even nonunion members to pay fees to the union for representing them in contract talks. Asked about the right-to-work law early in the session, Wilder was recorded as saying:

"You know, I told you when I first came in here that I'm not going to make one statement one place and another statement another place, and I'm not. The right-to-work law has as much chance of being done away with as a snowball in hell." Interrupted by a miner, he protested, "Let me finish. Let me finish. There is nothing that is going to do that. All the king's horses and men are not going to do that. Now, if you want to tie my hands behind me to that extent to say, do you pledge as governor to do away with the right-to-work law, you don't have to worry about it, I would never be your governor. Because the money and the forces that would be arrayed against me would be too awesome to contemplate."

Moments later, he was asked directly if he supported the law. "I support the right-to-work law, yes," Wilder replied. "And I said that. I have to do that. . . . If I wasn't going to do that, I would be wasting your time, your effort, or your money." After some continuing discussion, Jackie Stump, the local UMW president, agreed that attacking right-to-work directly was useless.

"You've got to go around the corners of it," Stump said, according to the tape. "And what we have worked on and what we're looking at right now is what we call the free-rider clause. . . . Now you've pledged your support on that?" Wilder is heard saying clearly, "That's correct."

Several seconds of confusion follow in which Wilder appears to reply to a Stump statement advocating indirect tactics, by commenting, "You get the camel's head in the tent." Again, as competing voices are recorded, there is a moment where Wilder seems to say, "We'll pass that. I told you that." The tape becomes clear again with Wilder continuing, "You know, I've been in elective office twenty years. When I first got there, people said we wouldn't see this, we wouldn't see the other. I've seen a lot of things. It's taken a long time to do it."

Responding to Larson's charges, Wilder denied that he supported weakening the right-to-work law with a free-rider clause, and implied that his comments were either being misrepresented or that the tape might have been doctored.

Editorial writers for the *Richmond Times-Dispatch* and the *Roanoke Times & World-News* eventually enunciated the opposite poles of opinion on the episode. The Richmond newspaper, which ran editorials about the tape for four consecutive days, said, "This tape shows exactly who has been lying—and it hasn't been Mr. Larson. . . . In his exchange with UMW leaders, Mr. Wilder makes clear that he has been publicly supporting right-to-work only for reasons of sheer political expediency." The "real tipoff to the deceitful game Doug is playing," the newspaper said, came when he told Stump, "You get the camel's head in the tent."

In contrast, the Roanoke newspaper in a November 3 editorial countered, "We should be grateful to the National Right to Work Committee for letting us hear Lt. Gov. Douglas Wilder standing his ground before a group of riled-up union miners, even when the doors were closed to the media." Describing a radio ad in which Larson played the offending sections of the tape, the editorial continued, "It's hard to say which was more distorted: the sound on the original tape or the spin that Larson imparted to its contents."

For weeks Anne Kincaid, director of coalitions for Coleman, had been trying to be heard above the din of competing voices on abortion policy in the campaign organization. Beginning in late July, she had written more than a half-dozen proposed television spots, and had tried to press them on the candidate. "I'd slip them under doors. I'd fax them to Marshall's house at night. I'd fax them to Goodman," she recalls. One proposal written during the summer accused Wilder of extremism and claimed that he "dances to the tune of radical N.O.W. President Molly Yard." Submitting the idea, Kincaid wrote across the top of the paper, "Urgently need ad for preemptive strike before Greer's ad calls Marshall Big Brother interfering in the most personal of personal decisions . . . !!!" On a proposal sent to Coleman two weeks before the election, she scrawled, "I'm on my knees begging you to cut a spot—Please, people must see you address this issue now!" What Kincaid believed was desperately needed was an ad that highlighted the most controversial aspects of abortion, and that portrayed Wilder as an advocate of abortion on demand.

A former Planned Parenthood worker who once counseled women seeking abortions and who says that feminist singer Helen Reddy was briefly her idol, Kincaid says she became just as intense in her opposition to abortion after experiencing a Christian conversion. Dynamic and determined, she installed a bassinet beside her desk at Coleman headquarters and, until asked to stop, deposited there thousands of rulers labeled, "Make Choice The Rule." The rulers were distributed as a campaign gambit by pro-choice advocates, who urged recipients to mail them to Coleman headquarters in protest of his abortion position. "I called them my babies," says Kincaid, referring to the rulers.

Throughout the last week in October, Kincaid intensified her pressure. If Coleman did not make a commercial that dealt directly with abortion, she warned, there was no guarantee that even pro-life forces would hold firm. Finally, with the character ads fizzling, Boyd Marcus promised that an abortion ad would be scripted at the weekend retreat in McLean. Kincaid sent along several proposals.

On Monday she anxiously anticipated arrival of the finished product from Goodman's office in Baltimore. As she listened to Coleman's brief comments on rape and incest, teenage abortions, sex selection, rapists and wife abusers, Kincaid was appalled. "I got up and walked out of the room. I said, 'Is that all?'" she recalls. Kincaid believed that Goodman had "mixed apples and oranges" by putting abortion and spouse abuse in the same ad. The statement on rape and incest was not well-framed, she thought, given Coleman's support for such abortions in the primary. And she believed the candidate did not sound statesmanlike enough to pursuade voters. "I said, 'Take it away. It's better to have nothing.'"

Wilder and Greer had been waiting for such an ad. A day later, they bombarded the airwaves with a reponse ridiculing Coleman's television claim that he was "not going to restrict abortions for rape and incest." Quoting the *Fairfax Journal*, the *Roanoke Times*, and Coleman's own June 5 fund-raising letter, the ad asserted, "Marshall Coleman's not telling the truth about abortion, about Doug Wilder. And that's why we just can't trust Marshall Coleman."

The Coleman campaign canceled its abortion ad almost immediately, and with Kincaid and others urging a replacement, decided to produce a new commercial Wednesday night. "I said, 'Let me go. Let me be there,'" recalls Kincaid. Marcus agreed.

Bob Goodman remembers the filming session at Coleman's home as a "wild scene." When he and Adam Goodman, his son and colleague, arrived about 8:00 P.M., Kincaid and a pro-choice Republican woman were arguing loudly, he says. Marcus, Coleman, and the Goodmans adjourned to work on a script. Kincaid, who says she "never felt as persona non grata in my life," remembers listening to the four of them debate language for several hours in another room. At one point, Bob Goodman came back and asked her, "If Willie Horton raped you, and you became pregnant, what would you do?"

"I knew he was trying to discredit me," she says. "I said I would carry the child to term."

Sometime after 10:00 P.M., Adam Goodman returned to the room where Kincaid was waiting and presented a script for her approval. She had hoped that the language would mention improving health regulations at abortion clinics, but she was pleased that at least it did talk about birth-control abortions. The new commercial, filmed late that night and aired the next day, featured Coleman saying, "I'm Marshall Coleman. I've said many times that, as governor, I will not seek to outlaw abortion in cases of rape or incest. You know that, my opponent knows that. I stand with the majority of Virginians who take the very reasonable view that none of us want to see abortion used merely as a means of birth control. Let's stop spreading fear on abortion and start making sense. Let's stop using emotion to divide us and start using reason to unite us." For the first time since the Webster decision, Kincaid felt satisfied with a Coleman response on abortion.

NOVEMBER 2, 1989

If a single day could serve as a metaphor for the state of the Democratic and Republican campaigns in the final week of the race, it would be the Thursday that preceded the election.

The Wilder campaign had scheduled a routine student rally for midday at the College of William and Mary, the venerable Williamsburg institution that is the second oldest university in the nation, and whose alumni include three early presidents. Unbeknownst to schedulers, a group of college Republicans had stayed up most of the previous night preparing for his visit. As the candidate mounted the flagstone steps at the campus center, about a dozen angry hecklers tried to push to the front of the crowd of 150 and began chanting the taunts they had practiced. "No more lies! No more lies!" they screamed, holding aloft megaphones and signs reading, "You're a liar," "Keep Virginia Doug-Free," and "Wilder-gate, Let the Tapes Role." Wilder supporters, pushing back, chanted, "We want Wilder, We want

Wilder," as they attempted to block the negative signs with campaign placards.

Finishing his comments about abortion and Coleman's proposed cap on out-of-state enrollment at public universities ("By putting on a 10 percent cap, you might not be here," he quipped, pointing to one of the protesters), the candidate startled reporters by jumping right into the restless throng. Appearing amused rather than threatened by the scene, he shook hands and autographed one of the signs held by a college Republican. "I always do that," Wilder said later. "It disarms them. It gives them very little to say. It almost makes them embarrassed. I want them to know that it doesn't faze me one bit."

Meanwhile, Coleman was preparing to stage the most controversial performance of his campaign. Still looking for ways to stem the erosion of moderate and conservative voters to Wilder, the Coleman camp had several possible options. The right-to-work tape was a boon and would be emphasized until election day. They could also attack the *Washington Post*, a traditional target whose liberal columns and editorials infuriated the political right. The polls published by the paper were hurting Coleman, and a jab at the newspaper might both discredit the numbers and raise the adrenaline of campaign workers. And there was another possible way to stir enthusiasm. Both the candidate and many of his supporters believed that Wilder was benefitting from disproportionately favorable media attention, particularly in the national press, based largely on race and abortion. Why not accuse the press generally of applying a double standard?

For at least a day, Coleman and his advisers discussed whether to question the fairness of the coverage at a press conference slated for Thursday afternoon. Coleman had invited Wilder to meet him at the capitol to explain the right-to-work tape. When the Republican awoke that morning and saw the front page of the *Washington Post*, the decision was made. Two stories were packaged there. One was a positive look at the Wilder campaign as it approached what polls were showing might be a historic victory. The other was headlined, "Poll Firm That Irked Voters

Paid By Coleman: Research Group Used Leading Questions on Wilder in Phone Calls." It described a telephone research group that had irritated some voters by portraying Wilder's positions in a harsh light. *Post* reporters believed the Coleman campaign had tried to mislead them about who was paying for the calls. Inside the newspaper, on page A-37, was the *Washington Post's* first story about the right-to-work tape.

Facing the press at what staff members earlier in the day had promoted as "The Showdown at the OK Corral," Coleman unleashed his fury. "I don't think it matters how much history Doug Wilder's election on Tuesday would make. . . . I for one am not going to stand by and watch a person who is unfit . . . glide into office with a 'feel good, make history' message." He accused the *Washington Post* of acting like "an unofficial arm of the Wilder campaign," and he reiterated his list of complaints against Wilder, ranging from the Supreme Court reprimand to failure to disclose ownership of properties. "Any one of these things would disqualify me from high office. Any one of these things. . . . But for the most part, members of the news media have treated them like minor foibles," he said.

Pressed by reporters to say why he thought Wilder was getting special treatment, Coleman replied, "I've said, and I will repeat it; I think that a double standard applies to Doug Wilder. If the press wants to say why that is, it's up to the press."

The debate that followed focused on whether Coleman had deliberately injected race into the campaign as a means of rallying his troops, and on whether his complaints about a double standard were justified. If tapping racial sentiment was his intent, he had done so in a sophisticated, New South way. While polls show that most Southerners support the major advances of the civil rights era, there is substantial unhappiness among whites over affirmative action programs and the notion that blacks are sometimes treated by a double standard.

Frank Atkinson is among those Coleman advisers who acknowledge that race was a component of what the candidate was referring to when he spoke of a double standard. But he said abortion and conservative philosophy were also handicaps for Coleman in dealing with elements of the press. Coleman was not trying to whip up racial voting, he says, but was raising a legitimate question about the impact of several factors—including race—on the coverage of the campaign. "Race was injected into the campaign about a dozen ways" by both sides, he says. "It's awfully hard to decide what's a proper and an improper discussion."

Democrats had no difficulty assigning the "double-standard" press conference to the improper category. "He's bumping up against a line that we in the Wilder campaign have assiduously avoided," Laura Dillard told in-state reporters, as she labeled the remarks "cynical" and "ludicrous." But in talking to the *New York Times*, she was less circumspect. The comments were "offensive" and "will sicken the voters of Virginia," she predicted.

After the campaign Wilder and others indicated that they believe it was a mistake not to respond more forcefully to Coleman in the wake of the press conference. The Democrat was essentially pursuing a positive, feel-good approach to the final days, and decided not to be sidetracked. "We had a campaign plan many people never saw," Wilder says. "We were never off plan until the end, when we gave Coleman three or four days of hammering at us and we were good people." Wilder says he was inclined to respond, but listened to Frank Greer's advice that it was important to leave the voters with a positive feeling. "In the end, I think it hurt us," he says.

Two other events on the Thursday before the election were over-shadowed by the actions of the candidates.

Mason-Dixon released its latest polling figures to the news organizations which employed the firm, showing that Wilder entered the weekend with a 48 to 44 percent advantage over Coleman. Almost all of those still undecided were white, and to win the election, Coleman would need to capture an unlikely three out of four white votes, said Brad Coker, president of the firm. "The likeliness of this happening, while possible, appears to be remote," and "appears to hinge almost exclusively on a racial vote," he added.

Also that day, the National Right to Life Committee called a press conference to announce that eight Virginia television stations had rejected antiabortion ads the group had attempted to place. Meanwhile, most were showing a National Abortion Rights Action League (NARAL) ad featuring a Charlottesville-area physician who warned that Coleman would return Virginia women to the days of back-alley abortions.

The rejected ads were a harsh interpretation of Wilder's views, but no harsher than the NARAL commentary on Coleman's, spokesmen argued. "Do you think abortion should be allowed even in the late stages of pregnancy? Doug Wilder does," began one of the rejected ads. "Do you think fathers should be prohibited from having any rights whatsoever concerning the possible killing of their unborn child by abortion? Doug Wilder does. Do you think abortion should be allowed as a method of birth control? Doug Wilder does. Now whose position on abortion is extreme, yours or Doug Wilder's?"

NOVEMBER 5, 1989

With the election only two days away, yet another poll added its weight to the notion that Doug Wilder was about to become the first black man elected to head an American state. The *Richmond Times-Dispatch* informed its Sunday readers that Wilder was leading by 45 percentage points to 36. However, the poll also included an unusually large undecided group, 19 percent, and there was a notation, deep in the story, that Coleman had surged in the final two days of tracking. The poll was conducted between October 27 and November 1, the day the right-to-work tape had been released. The numbers did not register the effects either of the "double-standard" press conference or of front-page coverage throughout the state of a Friday campaign visit by President Bush.

On Saturday, the *Washington Post*, nervous about its earlier numbers, had released another poll which showed the 15-point gap closing slightly. Still, Wilder had a 52 to 41 margin. At GOP campaign headquarters, Marcus believed that Coleman approached the election trailing Wilder by about 3 percentage points. Wilder's own tracking showed him with about an 8-point advantage. If the entire block of undecided voters was awarded to Coleman, the result would be a 50 to 50 tie.

NOVEMBER 6, 1989

Finally, after hundreds of thousands of telephone calls and mailings and countless meetings with precinct organizers, Jill Alper's and Mike Thomas's moment in the spotlight had arrived. For four and a half months, the campaigns had belonged to the candidates and their managers. But the speechmaking was about to end, and all that would matter on the morrow was who could get their people to the polls.

A twenty-four-year-old organizational expert, Alper was in charge of the get-out-the-vote effort for the Wilder-Beyer-Terry joint campaign. Thomas, twenty-nine, who is a former director of the Virginia Society for Human Life and a veteran of voter-turnout efforts in several Republican campaigns, was Alper's counterpart in the Coleman organization. Alper and Thomas approached the election using similar tools—phone banks, computerized mailing lists, and poll watchers—but some different techniques.

The Democratic candidates had decided to pool resources for overlapping functions, including voter registration, field operations, direct mail, and election-day get-out-the-vote efforts. Working through the state party and in conjunction with the Virginia AFL-CIO, the joint campaign's overall budget topped $900,000. Each campaign supplied some money, as did the Democratic National Committee. Organized labor chipped in about $175,000, according to state labor officials. But the precise fund-raising figures are unknown because Virginia election laws do not require political parties to detail such spending. In effect, there is no accounting for hundreds of thousands of dollars in spending that benefitted Wilder and his Democratic ticketmates.

The AFL-CIO also conducted an extensive voter turnout effort on Wilder's behalf. About 200,000 union members and their families were surveyed by telephone. Those identified as favorable to Wilder received follow-up communications of various types. There was a massive program of leaflet distribution at plant gates. And just prior to the election, highly polarizing postcards were sent to several groups. Older union members, many of whom were skeptical about Wilder, received giant postcards picturing Franklin Delano Roosevelt and pledging that Wilder would continue Roosevelt's political tradition. About 60,000 individuals who were likely but uncertain Wilder voters got a card picturing a labor clash from the 1930s. "Those were the bad old days," the card said. "Marshall Coleman wants to bring them back." Pauline Fox Huffman, the regional director of the union's Committee On Political Education (COPE), estimates that labor's effort in cash and in-kind contributions added $600,000 to the Democratic effort.

Armed with lists of voters in the 1988 Democratic presidential primary, as well as membership rolls of such pro-choice groups as the Virginia Organization to Keep Abortion Legal (VOKAL), the joint campaign staff also conducted an elaborate program of identifying likely Wilder voters and pushing to get them to the polls on election day. Nowhere was the effort more concentrated or effective than in majority-black precincts across the state. As election day approached, the most ambitious plan ever attempted in Virginia for getting black voters to the polls was in place. Democrats have long realized that blacks are their most dependable voting group, and that areas of concentrated black housing are a gold mine of Democratic votes. Every person who can be gotten to the polls in a black precinct equals one likely Democratic vote. With that in mind, Chuck Robb in 1981 organized an operation in which "flushers," often college students hoping to pick up a few dollars for a day's work, went door-to-door in black precincts urging people to vote for him for governor. Democratic activist Moo Murray, who has worked on get-out-the-vote efforts for the last three Democratic candidates for governor of Virginia, recalls the early Robb effort as a haphazard one. "Basically, we sent a bunch of cash down to Tidewater and hoped it worked," she says.

By the time of Gerald Baliles's gubernatorial race in 1985 the operation was more sophisticated, and flushers operated in major cities throughout the state. For the 1989 race, Democrats were organized not only in predictable areas of cities such as Richmond, Norfolk, and Alexandria, but even in normally Republican precincts where there were pockets of black voters. Workers in many precincts were supplied with "card decks" listing known Democratic voters. In a typical drill, "flushers"—paid forty dollars a day—would make a morning run though a precinct, urging people to vote. During the day checkers at various polling places would identify spots where voting was off from previous years. Both phone bank callers and flushers would concentrate on those areas. By late afternoon, theoretically, Wilder's workers would have an idea of which individual Democrats had not yet voted.

"It's like magic," says Marian Tucker, who also acknowledged after the election that reality and theory did not always mesh. At one point on election day, flushers with whom she was working were following instruction packets that gave them ten minutes to sort through card decks of voters and return to the field. "I called up Moo and said, 'Have you read this thing?'" Tucker recalls. "She said, 'It worked in Minneapolis.' I said, 'They must be eating mushrooms in Minneapolis.'"

Blessed in only a few precincts with similar concentrations of known Republican voters, Thomas and the Coleman campaign relied on phone banks, grassroots workers, and impressive computerized voter lists long maintained by the state GOP to identify Coleman supporters. The June primary was a boon in that respect, automatically supplying a list of 400,000 likely backers. About 75 percent of them received either a telephone call or a visit from a Coleman volunteer, Thomas says. Unlike the Democrats, Coleman handled his get-out-the-vote efforts within his own organizational machinery, and there were such plans as a "Twenty-Five for Coleman" program, in which thousands of volunteers were urged to contact twenty-five people in Coleman's behalf. By Monday night, paid telephone workers reporting to Thomas were just finishing making 400,000 calls to pro-Coleman households. The next morning, they would begin redialing the list.

As the months of campaigning ended, both Wilder and Coleman spoke in victorious tones of the futures that awaited them. Through a six-city, thousand-mile wrap-up tour, Wilder repeated his challenge to "keep Virginia moving forward" and lapsed into references to "my administration."

"The fight for Virginia's future is about to begin. I am ready to be your governor," pledged Coleman, shrugging off the polls and looking not at all like a man in defeat.

At a rally on the steps of the state capitol, where a Democratic throng greeted Wilder as if he were already on the way to his inauguration, Mark Warner whispered, "It's going to be very close."

12

INTO THE MAINSTREAM

Not long after the polls closed at 7:00 P.M., the ballroom at Richmond's Marriott Hotel began filling with those anxious to know whether history would record the success or failure of a black Southerner in his unprecedented bid for high state office. All day, poll watchers had been seeing huge turnouts in Tidewater, in the Southside, in the Valley, and elsewhere. Anxious officials in both parties had been asking what it could mean. Were blacks rallying to elect one of their own? Was there an outpouring of closet racists unwilling to elect a black man to the Commonwealth's most revered position? Was the pro-life movement more unified than it had seemed? Were these voters women demanding a right to reproductive choice?

Within seconds of the poll closings, an answer of sorts appeared to have been provided. Television stations across the state reported that an exit poll conducted by Mason-Dixon Opinion Research, which four years earlier had proved the most accurate prognosticator of Virginia election results, had found Douglas Wilder winning by a landslide 10 percentage points. Jubilation and astonishment combined as Democrats, black and white, converged on the celebration site. "It signals a new beginning, a renaissance," proclaimed Larry Chenshaw, a telephone company manager and middle-class black voter, marveling at the polling report. "It means that Virginia, which rightly or wrongly is considered the capital of the Confederacy, in the last year of the decade of the eighties was able to elect a person based on merit rather than race."

Less than a mile away in a suite at another hotel, Boyd Marcus heard the same exit poll results about 6:30 P.M., a half hour before they were publicly announced. He was stunned. Forcing his usual composure, Marcus found Coleman in another room and reported the grim news. "I felt awful," he says. "It was not just that we were losing, but that I had miscalculated so badly. It called into my own mind, should I really be in this business?"

The candidate and his manager discussed the report for several minutes, and then Coleman summoned his sons, Billy and Sean, to a private room. About ten minutes later, he called in Marcus, Frank Atkinson, and Richard Cullen. "He was so good," recalls Marcus. "He said we'd all made decisions as a group, that nobody was to blame. He said we'd run the best campaign we could run, and that whatever we were doing with the rest of our lives, we could call on him to help out." But when Bob Goodman and his staff arrived from Baltimore and Goodman surveyed the glum group, he heard the explanation and laughed. "Exit polls," he said. "Don't believe them."

The Associated Press (AP) reported its first election returns at 7:16 P.M. The results, clearly meaningless, showed Coleman leading by 537 votes with 5 percent of the precincts counted. Surprisingly, an hour later the Republican was still in front. With a quarter of the vote in, he was leading by about 1,600 votes. Commentators noted that it was probably only a matter of time until Wilder surged ahead. The wire service's 8:39 P.M. report put the Democrat in front for the first time. His lead was slight, but apparently the rout had begun. By 9:00 P.M., the gap had jumped to 19,600 votes, and Wilder seemed comfortably on his way to becoming the first black ever to be elected governor of an American state.

For three-quarters of the next hour, he maintained a 20,000-or-more-vote lead. Then, after the 9:44 P.M. report, the stream of numbers from AP abruptly stopped, and almost forty-five minutes passed before a bulletin moved across the wires: "We have discovered an error in the statewide summaries of the Virginia races. A small number of precincts were tabulated incorrectly, weighing the vote in favor of Doug Wilder. The problem is being corrected . . . "

Several precincts had been counted twice. By the time the revised tabulation was filed, it was 10:37 P.M., and the corrected totals had sliced Wilder's lead by two-thirds. With 98 percent of the precincts reporting, the Democrat was ahead by only 6,473 votes, about four-tenths of one percent of the total vote.

Few of those Democrats who were gathered in the overcrowded Marriott ballroom were monitoring minute-by-minute results. Although television news reports were being flashed onto large screens at either side of the room, the crowd was too dense and the noise too deafening for many to see or hear. Still, as 11:00 P.M. approached, there was a growing sense in the room that something was awry. A few revelers, asked for comment on the election, were still celebrating Wilder's "historic landslide." But an edge of anger was creeping into the comments of others as the closeness of the tally became more and more apparent.

Adding to the growing dismay, particularly among black Democrats, was the realization that Don Beyer was winning the race for lieutenant governor by the landslide proportion projected earlier in the evening for Wilder. There was delight over Beyer's apparent victory, but the contrast between Wilder's and Beyer's vote totals was disturbing. Beyer had proven to be a personable and articulate campaigner in his race against Eddy Dalton. Yet the fact remained that Beyer had never held public office, had started the race 20 percentage points behind Dalton in the polls, and was now outperforming a sitting lieutenant governor with twenty years of public service.

Some of those in the Marriott ballroom thought they knew why, and the reason they cited was race. "It tells me race is definitely a factor still in Virginia," said Richmond councilman Walter Kenney, a member of that body since 1977 when a black majority was elected to lead city government. "Race is a lesser issue, but it's still an issue."

"I think it proves that black people can support white candidates, but white people still find it difficult to support black people," said Dr. Wilbert Wilson, a federal drug abuse researcher who had driven from Maryland for the Wilder victory party.

"There's no question in my mind this election should be over now."

Meanwhile, at Marshall Coleman's election-night retreat the despondency of the early evening had lifted, and each new total was being cheered. "It was like being snatched back from the jaws of death," says Boyd Marcus.

Doug Wilder and a handful of his closest associates had been following the returns from a suite at the Commonwealth Park Hotel, a luxury establishment at the foot of Capitol Hill. The Wilder children were there, as were Frank Greer, Paul Goldman, Joel Harris, Mike Donilon, Jay Shropshire, Mark Warner, and Pamela Harriman, a prominent Democratic fundraiser and widow of former ambassador W. Averell Harriman. The candidate himself seemed the calmest of the lot as he munched refreshments and moved from room to room. When a group in front of one television became too nervous, he repositioned himself at another set. Through the evening, he reassured anxious aides: "Don't worry. We're all right. We're all right."

Finally, shortly after 11:00 P.M., Wilder signaled to his state police bodyguard that it was time to go. Nothing had been heard from Coleman in the way of a concession statement, but with only a handful of precinct results still unreported, reversal of the Democratic candidate's several-thousand-vote lead seemed unlikely. Twenty minutes later, Wilder stepped onto a stage at the Marriott and—with dozens of news cameras and reporters from across the nation recording the pandemonium—pronounced his quest ended.

"I am here to claim to be the next governor of Virginia," said Wilder, as hundreds of people filling the room responded with shrieks of joy. Tears were streaming down the faces of some, and the candidate's own cheeks glistened with sweat as he praised the Virginia electorate and "many who are not even alive at this time." To murmurs of "amen" and a chorus of applause, he vowed, "We've come this distance because people prior to our coming believed in what we could do."

His election, he said, was no fluke. "No one can blame it on the weather. No one can say it was a single issue. No one can

say that notwithstanding a record turnout I could not be elected."
Wilder, who even at that euphoric moment seemed more com-
posed than most of those around him, also repeated the moving
lines he had uttered at certain rare occasions during the campaign. "As a boy when I would read George Mason and Thomas
Jefferson that all men are created equal, and endowed with certain inalienable rights, I knew it meant *me*. . . . I can't say any
more than to tell you how humble I am, and how proud I am to
be a Virginian."

Across town at the Omni Hotel, however, Coleman appeared
before supporters a few moments later and advised them not to
give up hope of winning. "This race is not yet over," he vowed,
typically summing up the roller-coaster events of the evening
with a quip. "I have made my biggest comeback— 10 points in
three hours," he said. Coleman said he would congratulate Wilder
if the Democrat proved to be the winner, but as for now, "we don't
yet know what the outcome is." Holding open the prospect of a
recount, he and his sons headed home to Northern Virginia.

Back at the Marriott, as Wilder rushed away to a series of
network television appearances and the crowd began to thin,
the NAACP's Jack Gravely stood in the emptying ballroom and
focused on the "landslide" that had eroded into a photo finish.
"It's a great night," he said. "Fifty-point-something percent of
Virginia voted its hopes and not its fears." More slowly, he added,
"Obviously something happened in those booths. The bugabear
got out. . . . But I'm not going to trash the victory. We'll take it
any way it comes."

The next day's unofficial results from AP showed Wilder winning by 5,533 votes. The United Press International put the number at 7,755. Either way, the outcome was closer than in any
Virginia gubernatorial race in modern times.

At a brief news conference Coleman said he would wait for
the official canvass by the State Board of Elections on November 27, and would seek a recount if the margin was within one-
half of 1 percentage point of the total vote, as it almost certainly would be. Introduced to a crowded news conference in
Richmond as the governor-elect, Wilder announced the forma-
tion of a transition team and set about establishing a govern-

ment. But references to his election were couched in the phrase "apparent winner," and some of the euphoria that should have accompanied so historic a victory seemed lost. Headlines in November 9 issues of the *Washington Post* and the *New York Times* acknowledged the sobering reality. "Black Democrats' Victories Clouded by White Defections," reported the *Post*. "Joy of Democrats Diluted in Virginia," concurred the *Times*.

Throughout the weeks that followed, teams of lawyers pored over lists of registered voters and election returns, preparing for the recount sought by Coleman after the official canvass. The canvass had shown that only 6,854 votes—less than four-tenths of 1 percent of the total cast—separated Coleman and Wilder. Not until December 20, twenty-four days before the scheduled inauguration, was the Wilder victory formally confirmed. At 8:30 P.M. that day, Richmond circuit court clerk Iva R. Purdy announced the final tally. The recount had subtracted 203 votes from Wilder's earlier total, and 90 votes from Coleman's. The final figures were 896,936 votes for Wilder, and 890,195 votes for Coleman. Both winner and loser had received more votes than any previous candidate for the state's highest office. Wilder's 6,741-vote margin, out of the record 1,787,131 cast, equated to fewer than three votes per precinct. Shortly before noon on December 21, Coleman telephoned his congratulations to Wilder.

In contrast, the November canvass showed that Don Beyer had won 54 percent of the vote in his race for lieutenant governor against Dalton. Mary Sue Terry, who had long been considered a shoo-in for reelection as attorney general, won 63 percent of the vote against GOP state senator Joseph Benedetti.

The voting patterns that produced Wilder's narrow victory varied substantially from those of previous Virginia elections. A state map shaded to show the geographic areas carried by Coleman and Wilder might give the impression that the Republican must certainly have won in a landslide, so great was the concentration of Wilder votes in urban areas. Wilder carried only twenty-two of Virginia's ninety-five counties. Among them were the populous suburban counties of Northern Virginia, a handful of localities near the epicenter of the coal strike, and several others in southern and eastern Virginia with large black populations. His votes came primarily from the cities, of which he won half, including all but one of the ten largest. Among the principal cities, Coleman held a majority only in Virginia Beach, the site of the Greekfest riot. Even there the margin of Wilder's loss was a mere 2,762 votes, representing an improvement over his 5,300-vote deficit in that city in his 1985 race for lieutenant governor.

A postelection analysis by Dr. Larry Sabato, a University of Virginia political scientist, and a leading authority on Virginia voting patterns, revealed that Wilder won 68.5 percent of the vote in the central cities, 47 percent of the suburban vote, and 45 percent of the vote in rural areas. His urban backing was up 4 percentage points from his 1985 race, due partially to a massive outpouring of black voters. But the gain was more than offset by a slight drop in suburban support and a 5-percentage-point loss among rural voters. Suburban and rural voters account for about three-fourths of the state's total. Wilder had made overt appeals to rural voters, including highlighting improved rural housing as one of three major goals. He also expected that the rape and incest portion of his pro-choice message on abortion and his tirades against real estate developers would have strong appeal in rural areas. But the strategy did not pay the expected dividends on election day. "It should have worked in the rural part of the state," says one of Wilder's advisers, "but it didn't because there was a more powerful message." The suggestion, of course, was that the problem was race.

Regionally, Wilder's victory was forged in Northern Virginia and Tidewater. He won five of the state's ten congressional districts—two in Northern Virginia (the Eighth and Tenth), two in Tidewater (the First and Second), and one in southeastern Virginia (the Fourth), which has the largest black population of any Virginia congressional district and is the most consistently Democratic district in the state. Wilder's margin in the Tenth District, where pro-abortion sentiment is strong, was unusually large for a Democrat. He won 59 percent of the ballots there, the highest portion for either candidate in any district. In contrast, even while carrying the Fourth District he did poorly there for a Democrat, winning just 52 percent of the vote in a strongly Democratic district where Old South attitudes still linger. In contrast, Don Beyer won 55 percent and Mary Sue Terry 72 percent of the Fourth district's votes.

Wilder's second most disappointing showing was in the Southwest's Ninth district. The area that had greeted him so warmly in 1985, and that is often a source of Democratic strength, was carried by Coleman by a 52 to 48 percentage-point margin. Wilder's total was 6 points off the mark set by Governor Baliles in 1985. The erosion was attributed by local residents to resentment in noncoal counties over the strike, and to racial attitudes. But the coal strike apparently did not affect the regional totals of the other Democrats. Beyer won 55 percent of the vote and Terry 64 percent of the vote in the Southwest.

Coleman won majorities in all of the central and western regions of the state, including the Southwest, the Valley, the Piedmont, the Richmond area, and the Southside. Charges of race-based voting were strongest in relation to the Southside's Fifth District, where whites once rallied for massive resistance to public school integration and the power of the old Byrd Organization was centered. Although Republicans usually do well in the district, Coleman's margin was a whopping 16 percentage points, 10 points higher than the gap in the 1985 governor's race. The erosion of support for Wilder in 1989, as compared with that for Gerald Baliles four years earlier, was greater in the Fifth than in any other district.

Voter turnout was up dramatically in every congressional district in 1989, and as might be expected in a state with a white population four times as large as that of blacks, a substantial majority of the new voters were white. Using his own calculations as well as exit polls conducted by Mason-Dixon Opinion Research and the CBS News/*New York Times* polling service, Larry Sabato projects that 17 percent of the electorate was black. By his tabulation, 73 percent of registered blacks voted, compared with 65 percent of whites. Black turnout was up 19 percentage points from 1985, a stunning testament to Wilder's strategy in the black community. The Sunday morning efforts of Matthews, the get-out-the-vote operation perfected by the joint campaign committee, and—probably most significant—the ties forged by Wilder during twenty years as the state's leading black politician, combined in a surge of support.

Sabato estimates that Wilder was the choice of 96 percent of the blacks who voted. The number of whites backing the Democrat he put at 41 percent, slightly higher than the 39 percent recorded by the CBS News/*New York Times* exit poll. Although down slightly from 1985, when Wilder received 44 percent of the white vote, the figure is also well ahead of the 30 percent of New York's white voters who supported Dinkins. The conclusion is obvious, and for anyone whose memory goes back a few decades, startling: in the year 1989 a notably larger percentage of whites in Virginia were prepared to vote for a black candidate for high office than was true in New York City.

Figures supplied by the exit polls and adjusted by Sabato to reflect actual results suggest that Wilder's and Donilon's demographic strategy worked. The Democratic candidate won largely by capturing the votes of blacks, younger white women, and to a lesser degree younger white men. Overall, Sabato says, 53 percent of women backed Wilder and 53 percent of men supported Coleman. Of voters in the eighteen to twenty-nine age range, 55 percent favored Wilder, while in the thirty to forty-four age group, 57 percent did. But older voters preferred Coleman. He won 54 percent of the votes of those in the forty-five to fifty-nine age range, and 62 percent of voters over sixty. Those responses seemed to confirm predictions that older voters would have more conservative views on abortion and race than younger voters.

As he awaited his January 13 inaugural Wilder deflected questions about the messages carried by his election, much as he had refused to speculate about the import of race during the campaign. "There isn't any lesson to learn from what we did in Virginia as a prototype relative to being a black candidate," he insisted at a packed news conference the morning after the election. As for abortion, he said later, "it didn't dominate the campaign the way people thought it did." The only reason the issue was even useful, he said, was that it illustrated the broad theme he was trying to convey—that Coleman was linked to the past.

"The lesson is that unless it [abortion] is connected with something else, it's nothing," he said.

Others, however, saw major implications for state and national politics in the results. In the area of campaign mechanics, the 1989 Virginia gubernatorial election raised troubling questions about the roles of public opinion polls and negative television advertising in elections. Of concern to Virginia voters, the contest produced an alarming rise in the cost of winning the governor's office, and it demonstrated once again weaknesses in the state's laissez-faire approach to regulating campaign finances. And most significantly, Wilder's remarks to the contrary, the election also told a remarkable story about evolving attitudes on two of the most fundamental issues of the century: abortion and race. It was perhaps no accident that the outcome was so close, suggesting that—even if there is not quite a hung jury —the debate on either issue is far from ended.

Among the losers in the gubernatorial race were political poll takers, whose reputation with voters was sullied, perhaps to a degree unfairly. The wide gap between what some polls showed late in the contest and what actually happened on election day no doubt reflected a degree of polling error. But the disparities may also have demonstrated that some usual polling techniques do not work in contests between a white candidate and a black candidate, less because of a failing of poll takers than because lingering racial sentiment skews the results. Certainly the Virginia elections were a warning to voters and newspaper editors to beware of putting too much emphasis on polls. Campaign managers and pollsters have long argued that the primary value of political polls is in uncovering trends, not in predicting the outcome of an election. The Virginia election bore that out.

Of the major preelection polls, Mason-Dixon's last survey came closest to matching the actual results. Brad Coker showed a 48 to 44 percentage point lead for Wilder five days before the election, and he observed that three out of every four undecided white voters would have to break for Coleman for the Republican to win. That is close to what happened. The *Richmond Times-Dispatch* poll, released two days before the election, showed Wilder with a nine-point lead, 45 percentage points to 36. The

Washington Post polls were furthest of all from the final mark. The October 29 survey, nine days before the election, showed Wilder with a seemingly insurmountable 15-point lead. In the *Post*'s poll six days later—three days before the election—the spread in Wilder's favor was still 11 percentage points. In addition, every preelection poll missed Don Beyer's dramatic surge at the end of the lieutenant governor's race. The surveys had consistently shown the gap between Beyer and Dalton narrowing, but Eddy Dalton was still comfortably ahead in the final polls.

Apart from the preelection surveys, the Mason-Dixon exit poll that showed Wilder winning in a landslide erred dramatically. Yet the firm correctly forecast Beyer and Mary Sue Terry's easy victories.

In the wake of the election, the Virginia political poll takers have undergone much self-examination, and their explanations, if not entirely satisfying, are illuminating. First, none of the preelection polls ever put Wilder's support higher than 52 percentage points. So the problems seem primarily to have been in measuring Coleman's backing, or in interpreting how undecided voters would break. Traditionally in black-white contests, support for the black candidate solidifies rapidly. Those voters who are still undecided as the election approaches are usually overwhelmingly white and, as numerous elections have shown, are likely to vote disproportionately for the white candidate. Some political scientists argue that the best rule of thumb is to assign every undecided voter in the final poll to the white candidate. By that standard, the last *Washington Post* poll would have reflected a 52 to 48 percentage-point Wilder lead, much closer to the actual mark.

Coleman's preelection numbers may have been further dampened by dissatisfaction with him among some likely Republican voters over abortion, his ousting of Trible and Parris in the primary, or other factors. On the other hand, the last week of the campaign, in which he produced the right-to-work tape, blasted the press for exercising a double standard, and confronted the abortion issue directly, may have belatedly given many Republican-leaning voters the reason they were seeking to come home. Within that context, it is plausible that the polling results in the governor's race were more accurate than they seemed.

Another factor that might have tipped the polls in Wilder's favor is the widely recognized difficulty of getting honest answers to racially sensitive questions when the race of the interviewer and the respondent differ. This is less a problem, poll takers say, when blacks are being questioned by whites. But there is a decided difference in the way whites respond to a white questioner and a black one on matters involving race. Apparently, many whites supply the answer they think the black interviewer wants to hear. Two University of Virginia professors, conducting a survey of 362 adult Virginians during the autumn, found whites less supportive of Wilder when the interviewers were white than when they were black. In addition, the poll takers say that some voters, particularly Democrats, who did not intend to vote for Wilder because of race may have lied, indicating either that they were uncommitted or that they backed the Democratic nominee. Coker believes such deception is the primary reason for the miscalculation in his exit poll.

Whatever the reasons for the preelection polling results, there is little doubt that they fostered an inflated sense of Wilder's strength, and that the numbers may have undermined Republican morale and boosted the spirits of Democrats at some critical moments.

Democrats concede that point, but they point out that polls showing Don Beyer trailing did not prevent him from winning the lieutenant governorship. And they argue that the art of campaigning is dealing with breaking events—good or bad. Coleman may have been saddled with bad polls and a poorly timed Supreme Court decision, but Wilder had to deal with a coal strike in the weakest part of his political base and a racially explosive episode in another. "The only double standard in this campaign," complained Laura Dillard, "is the claim that everything that went bad for them was unfair, and everything that went bad for us should have happened."

As much as any recent American election, the Virginia gubernatorial race demonstrated the extent to which negativism has come to dominate campaign advertising and television advertising has come to dominate campaigns. The view is widespread that a single television advertisement, tapping voter concerns about Paul Trible's fortitude, was the most important element in Coleman's primary victory. Ads attacking Wilder's character and Coleman's alleged desire to "take us back" dominated the fall fare. Indeed, fluctuations in the polls were generally interpreted by both campaigns as reflections of the success or failure of television advertisements being run when the poll was taken. The most successful ads seemed to be those that manipulated the four emotions once cited by Bob Goodman as the keys to voting—love, hate, fear, and hope. Right and wrong, as Goodman also noted, at times appeared considerably less important to the campaigns. Sadly, the huge turnout dispelled the popular theory that negative campaigning turns off voters and undermines political participation. If the Virginia election was any measure, "the rowdier the better" may well be the rule in American politics. Wilder's principal regret is that he did not hit harder at his opponent in the last week of the contest; Coleman's advisers say his key mistake may have been to devote two weeks in late September and early October to praising himself rather than attacking Wilder.

At the same time, the election results were not a mandate for unrelieved mudslinging. Just as voters rebel at being confronted with their racial prejudices, so they apparently dislike the notion of name-calling, and are likely to penalize the candidate most associated with it. Wilder's litany that "We just can't trust Marshall Coleman" was as negative as any single message delivered by Coleman. But he and his aide Frank Greer shrewdly framed every negative attack as a response. Polls showed that many voters, already predisposed to think of Coleman as a bulldog because of the primary, blamed him for the name-calling nature of the campaign. And indeed Coleman may have been responsible. From the opening round of the Republican primary at Ingleside in late 1988 onward, Coleman signaled that he intended to make an aggressive assault on Wilder.

The election results also suggested that a candidate who focuses too exclusively on negative factors does so at his peril.

Many analysts have argued that Coleman erred by not building a fuller and more positive portrait of himself for voters. For several weeks in the summer, Wilder ran a biographical advertisement that draped the candidate in images of Monticello and the American flag. Coleman, apparently believing that he was already well enough known, never put forward a similar ad. Nor did he develop a theme that rivaled the "New Mainstream . . . New Extremism" slogan adopted by Wilder. The Republican tagline—"Leaders We Can Trust"—said nothing about Coleman's vision for the state, and seemed another extension of negativism. Even so, the closeness of the election indicates that many voters were influenced by the portrait of Wilder drawn by Coleman. One of the challenges Wilder faces as Virginia's governor is to dispel fears that he is a lax manager and a politician not given to total candor.

For Virginians themselves, the election raised several danger signs. Spending in the general election and primary approached $24 million, making the race one of the costliest governor's races in the nation's history. (Texans spent $33.5 million on their 1986 race, while the tab for electing Florida's governor that year was $24 million.) The Virginia contest was even more expensive than the 1986 California race, which cost $22.5 million. Equally shocking was the comparison between 1985 and 1989 campaign expenditures. Four years earlier, the Virginia governor's race had cost $8.3 million. In 1989, each side produced a record number of contributors—1,393 for Wilder, 1,320 for Coleman—but large portions of the totals came from single individuals. The continued absence of limits on allowable contributions in Virginia campaigns remains questionable public policy. Massive donations to Coleman from Dwight Schar became an issue, primarily because Coleman's personal and political financial portfolio was so tied to one person. Yet both candidates received gifts well beyond the capacity of all but a few of the state's wealthiest citizens.

Also questionable is state policy that allowed the Democratic party to spend a reported $900,000 on joint campaign activities, without having to account publicly either for contributions or expenditures. Such items as telephone banks, massive mailings, and election day get-out-the-vote operations handled through state party headquarters went undocumented in campaign spending reports.

The 1989 governor's race added to the growing sense that there are now two Virginias—one fast-paced and urban, scrambling pellmell toward the twenty-first century, consumed by the challenges and problems of growth, freed of the restraints of the past; the other, slower, more wedded to tradition, uneasy about change, satisfied that the institutions and values that have defined Virginia for years are, if not perfect, at least the proper guideposts to the future. The campaigns waged by Doug Wilder and Marshall Coleman did not fit neatly into the schism. Each man voiced themes and positions designed to bridge the groups at various points. But in the end, when the votes were counted, it was the new Virginia that had elected Wilder, and the old that had failed—narrowly—to install Coleman.

While race and abortion commanded the lion's share of attention, they were not the only themes on which Virginia's 1989 race for governor turned. Any election outcome is a mosaic assembled from dozens of issues, interest groups, and personalities. Any group that gave Douglas Wilder as many as seven thousand votes might make a legitimate claim to having decisively affected the outcome. Critical issues included experience, character, crime, developers, and the state of the economy, as well as race and abortion.

For instance, a key to Coleman's defeat was his inability to make a persuasive case for change in the Democratic party's control of state government. The problem was not a lack of trying: that he did mightily. He introduced a host of ideas for fighting drugs, addressing transportation problems, and adjusting educational policies. Almost certainly he was more aggressive than either of his primary opponents would have been in arguing for shifting directions. The only problem was that change did not seem to be a priority in a state where the economy and government were viewed as performing well. The absence of a compelling reason for change was cited by many of the editorial writers who supported Wilder. Their backing in turn helped solidify Wilder's credentials in the minds of voters. He won the support of the bulk of the state's newspapers, including the *Virginian-Pilot/Ledger-Star*, the *Roanoke Times & World-News*, the *Washington Post*, the *Fredericksburg Free-Lance Star*, the *Charlottesville Daily Progress*, and the *Lynchburg News*. The only major papers backing Coleman were the *Richmond Times-Dispatch*, the *Richmond News Leader*, and the *Washington Times*.

Had Paul Trible or Stan Parris won the Republican gubernatorial nomination instead of Coleman, it is possible that either might have been able to portray himself, in contrast to Wilder, as the true candidate of continuity. But that was not a mantle that fit easily on the shoulders of Coleman, a born maverick always searching for innovative approaches to government.

If there were multiple reasons for the outcome, however, none carry wider or more important implications than race and abortion. Immediately after the balloting, worried national Republicans began sifting through the results, looking for clues about how *not* to respond to abortion questions in the 1990 elections and beyond. The assessment of Coleman campaign veterans such as Bob Goodman is hardly reassuring. "Abortion could become to the Democrats what Social Security was in the 1930s," the GOP media strategist suggests. Even if that is an overstatement, Democrats clearly believe the issue can help them reverse one of the most troubling trends they face—the tendency of younger voters in the 1980s to cast their lot with the Republican party.

That abortion was the silver bullet in Wilder's arsenal is indisputable. For a campaign that intended to emphasize a past-versus-future theme, the timing of the Supreme Court decision could scarcely have been better. Wilder might have won without abortion, but looking at polling results alone, it is hard to see how. He would have had to rally an outpouring of support among Republican-leaning, younger white women in some other way, or else construct a very different demographic strategy.

Yet the abortion decision was not necessarily a fatal blow to the Coleman campaign. One could argue that it was a stroke of luck for the Republican when the court decided to open the door to a state's right to limit abortions, rather than to strike down *Roe v. Wade* altogether. One could also claim, as many do, that there would have been another result if Coleman had handled the issue differently.

Among political consultants it has become an article of faith that a charge ignored by a candidate is a charge accepted by voters. Hence, when Michael Dukakis failed to respond to George Bush's portrayal of him as unpatriotic and soft on crime, the claims supposedly became the basis on which impressions of the Democratic presidential nominee were formed. In the same way, Coleman's decision to ignore abortion for weeks is thought to have produced a free fall in the polls, which stopped only when he began to challenge Wilder's commitment to women and, finally, proceeded to address the abortion issue directly. Had he done either or both earlier, the final result could have changed, according to political analysts.

Future Republican candidates who oppose abortion can consider two options that were untested by Coleman. One is to run more aggressively on the abortion issue. The other is to run from a more moderate position. Particularly in the South, even Democrats acknowledge that the balance between pro-life and pro-choice forces is far from one-sided. Ambivalence on the issue abounds. A CBS News/*New York Times* election-day exit poll found 32 percent of Virginia voters saying that abortion mattered more to them than any other issue. Education was in second place, 10 percentage points behind. Of the group citing abortion as the most important issue, 55 percent preferred Wilder, and 43 percent voted for Coleman. However, when voters were also asked which of three views on abortion came closest to their own, there was a virtual tie between those who would restrict the practice and those who would not. Forty-seven percent of the voters said "abortion should be generally available to those who want it." Thirty-one percent believed "abortion should be available, but under more strict limits than now." And 17 percent said "abortion should be prohibited."

Such numbers offer strong evidence that Coleman stood to gain by challenging Wilder at the fringes of the pro-choice argument. "Abortion on demand," which Coleman seldom said loudly, has an ugly ring to voters, much as does "refusal to allow abortions in cases of rape and incest." Both Anne Kincaid and Bob Goodman prepared television spots emphasizing weak points for the opposition: third-trimester abortions, abortion as a means of birth control, multiple abortions by the same woman, or abortion because the sex of the fetus is not what the parents want. One of Goodman's ads, which was never used, showed a young child teetering across the floor as its mother watched. "A child's first step is a remarkable thing," the announcer said as gentle music played in the background. "But it would never happen if those who hold an extreme view on abortion have their way. The extreme view that abortion for any reason is all right. The extreme view that permits a parent to abort a child because it happens to be a girl and not a boy. Doug Wilder holds this extreme view. Thank goodness Virginia asks for something a lot more reasonable." The consensus of Coleman and Marcus was that such advertisements called too much attention to a subject they wanted to ignore.

During the campaign the National Right to Life Committee attempted to air ads stressing just such themes, but was turned down by most of the television stations it approached, partially because of fears that the ads were slanderous. That may have been a stroke of luck for Wilder. His blanket statement—"I trust the women of Virginia to decide"—allows for a variety of abortions that are apparently repugnant to many voters.

A candidate who decided to hammer at such themes would do so at some risk, however. Had the pros and cons of abortion been fully aired, Coleman would have had to deal more forthrightly with barbed questions such as this: how precisely does government weed out those abortions that it believes are improperly motivated—those for sex selection, for instance? And what are the penalties for women who have violated antiabortion laws? The reponses might well have cast Coleman in an unfavorable light among voters who distrust inquisitional procedures by their government.

Much postelection commentary to the contrary, it is by no means certain that Coleman would have won those debates, just as it is unclear that keeping a spotlight on abortion was in his best interests, given the extremity of his antiabortion views. If polls show that most voters are unsure of abortion generally, they also show widespread opposition to two ideas: a constitutional amendment banning the practice, and a ban on abortions in cases of rape and incest. Coleman had endorsed both in the primary. Any time that he tried to paint Wilder as the extremist on abortion, the Democrat had only to strike back by spotlighting those positions. Indeed, in the final week of the campaign, when Coleman finally did address abortion on television, Wilder immediately responded with a rape-and-incest ad.

If the Wilder-Coleman election is any indication, probably the safest political advice for both Democrats and Republicans, particularly in moderately conservative states such as Virginia, is to avoid the extremes of the issue. Wilder took heat from pro-choice activists for his advocacy, beginning in 1985, of parental notification for girls under eighteen, but the position did protect him from being portrayed as a pure abortion-on-demand candidate. Had he not been saddled with opposition to abortion in cases of rape and incest, Coleman would have faced a far easier task in trying to shift the charge of extremism from himself to Wilder. Wilder's framing the issue as a libertarian question, rather than a debate on the merits of abortion, was also a winning tactic certain to be repeated in contests nationwide. The fact that it is politically perilous to oppose abortion in cases of rape and incest does not mean that it cannot be successfully done. But the view may best be advanced by a candidate with much personal warmth who enjoys considerable trust among the electorate.

Even the messages involving abortion, however, paled in importance beside those relative to race. The historically momentous result of the 1989 Virginia governor's race was that a black man had been elected chief executive of an American state, and that the breakthrough had come in what had long been considered the nation's most racially discriminatory region, the South. At a minimum the results, compared with those in the New York mayoral race, seemed to suggest that the stereotype of the South as the most racially unenlightened section of the country was outdated.

The victory, however narrow the margin, once again placed Virginia at the forefront of national change. To the names of those native sons who had helped propel the nation in revolutionary directions — George Washington, Thomas Jefferson, Patrick Henry, George Mason, Robert E. Lee, and Harry Byrd, Sr. — was added Douglas Wilder. For black Americans and others denied a birthright claim to equality of opportunity under the law, the victory constituted a historic milestone in the ongoing quest for realization of the American dream. The victory was made brighter yet by the successes of other black politicians on election night. In New York City; Seattle, Washington; Durham, North Carolina; and New Haven, Connecticut, majority-white constituencies elected black politicians to lead them.

Significantly those winners, like Wilder, had pursued a different route to power than many of the prominent black politicians who preceded them. Their public careers were supportive of the civil rights movement, but not identified with it. None had leaped to the top overnight. All had toiled in the political vineyards for years, and had positioned themselves as mainstream candidates appealing to middle-class values and goals. Thus black Americans were now mayors of some of the nation's major cities. But only the Commonwealth of Virginia had chosen a black man to be its governor.

What the election results, particularly Virginia's, said was that color alone was no longer an absolute bar to election, no matter what the makeup of the citizenry or the prestige of the office. Those African-Americans who primarily made mainstream, nonracial appeals to the electorate could win even when the overwhelming majority of the voters was white. Such black candidates could not ignore black constituencies, but years of prior service in which they presumably worked to better the lot of African-Americans made the balancing act at election time less difficult. Candidates such as Wilder had already earned black support, and did not have to make many overt appeals to rally it.

Even so, the Wilder victory, as well as that of David Dinkins for mayor of New York, left little doubt that the ideal of a totally color-blind electorate remains only that. In voting patterns, there was too much evidence that many Virginians remained unable to distinguish the book from its cover. A sitting lieutenant governor, once voted among the most effective members of the state senate, unopposed for the nomination, inheriting a Democratic legacy of record low unemployment and a thriving state economy, was unable to win the governorship by more than a fraction of the vote, even though during the campaign he dominated the debate on an issue—abortion—that rivaled race in its emotional power. To a degree, Douglas Wilder's problems with the electorate were a result both of his own making and of Coleman's negative campaign tactics. But by no means entirely. For Wilder ran unusually poorly for a Democratic gubernatorial candidate in rural areas, and better than ordinarily in urban areas. That both results were in part race-related seems clear.

It would be a mistake to assume that most, or even a substantial majority, of those who voted for Marshall Coleman did so with racist intent. Nor did the Republican candidate try to exploit race in ways that he might have, or that had been tried in some past campaigns. He did not sanction a television advertisement highlighting Greekfest, as some advisers wanted him to do. He did not authorize a Willie Horton–type ad, such as George Bush used against Michael Dukakis in the 1988 presidential race, although the failure of Wilder to report the Louisa County land given him by Curtis Poindexter's family was a perfect opportunity. He did not follow Stan Parris's route in the GOP primary of trying to link Wilder to more militant black figures, although it is standard Republican rhetoric against white Democrats in state elections to lambaste "the party of Jesse Jackson." Some Wilder partisans do argue that Coleman's tough attacks on Wilder's character were racially inspired, but given Coleman's vigorous assaults on Trible and other white opponents in the primary, that would be a hard case to prove.

How much credit Coleman deserves for such constraint, as a manifestation of personal attitude rather than strategic calculations, is a matter of opinion. Certainly the GOP candidate knew very well that comments viewed as having racist overtones had caused problems for the Virginia Republican party in the 1981 and 1985 races for governor. With dozens of state and national news reporters focusing on the contest, any hint that race was being exploited was certain to be fully aired. Given that knowledge, and the extreme sensitivity of the Coleman camp to other racial matters, it is inconceivable that they did not foresee the consequences when late in the campaign Coleman declared that a double standard was being applied to Wilder. Had they not wanted the public and press to focus on a racial double standard, they could easily have ascribed the difference in treatment to conservatism, abortion, or some other issue. Instead, Coleman left open the question of what was causing the double standard, ensuring that race would be raised.

There are two basic views of what Coleman was doing with the double-standard speech. The most sympathetic view, and not surprisingly the one voiced by Coleman's strategists, is that Wilder was truly being treated more gently than Coleman by reporters and the public, and that the reasons for it were a legitimate area of public inquiry. The other is that Coleman was making a direct appeal to whites inclined not to vote for Wilder because of race, and specifically to the substantial number who, public opinion polls have shown, believe that blacks are unfairly coddled by affirmative action programs. Although Coleman's specific request was *not* to let race matter, in the view of critics the historical context of the state in which the words were being spoken ensured that the larger, unspoken message would be this: "*do* remember that my opponent is black." After all, for many years race had been a key issue, and at times *the* key issue, in Virginia politics.

"[Coleman] got caught in a vortex," says Scott Reynolds of the AFL-CIO, who is of the second school of thought. "He had to sell out. He kept saying that he was not going to inject racism, and yet at the end, he couldn't help himself." Adds Laura Dillard, "They held a press conference and they flat out tried to appeal to the absolute worst in people."

Coleman partisans offer several defenses. They point out that two slogans from the Democratic camp—"Let's Make History" and "We've Come Too Far to Turn Back Now"—indeed contained implicit racial messages. White voters were being urged to vote for a black candidate as a way of showing that race no longer mattered. Although the Wilder campaign itself avoided references to history-making, the joint campaign committee, working partially with Wilder funds, distributed in the final days of the election an appeal in an envelope marked, "You can help make history!" That positive racial message stirred little press comment. By contrast, had Coleman adopted slogans with negative racial overtones, he almost certainly would have been skewered. And yet, there was a subtle difference in the two types of racial appeals. The former was ultimately an appeal to take race *out* of politics; the latter would have been urging voters to *let* race matter.

Coleman also complained specifically about his treatment in the *Washington Post* during the last two weeks of the election. The newspaper's own ombudsman acknowledged that he may have been treated unfairly. The principal damage lay in the *Post*'s polls, and the impression they created that Coleman's cause was floundering. But Coleman also received a couple of tough breaks in news judgments. The right-to-work story in the final week was buried inside the newspaper, and President Bush's visit to the state on the final Friday of the campaign merited only three paragraphs. Of such episodes the *Post* ombudsman Richard Harwood later wrote, "Little things like that, combined with the collective weight and thrust of the *Post*'s coverage in the most crucial period of the campaign, are enough to raise non-paranoid questions about the disinterested nature of the coverage." Still, aside from the polls, Coleman quite possibly gained as much or more by using the *Post* as a whipping boy to rally conservatives in the final hours of the campaign than he may have lost by having a few stories underplayed.

On the argument that Wilder's flaws were ignored, Republicans seem on less solid ground. Wilder himself is particularly agitated by the suggestion. "I was the most ventilated candidate in Virginia history," he says, citing extensive probes of his personal and professional affairs in books and articles. "To say that someone was using a double standard was mind-boggling." Numerous articles detailing his various problems were written during the campaign, and the *Washington Post*, a particular object of Coleman's scorn, broke several stories involving the gaps in Wilder's financial disclosures. The evidence is less that voters had never heard of the difficulties, than that a substantial number had judged them unimportant. The closeness of the final tally would suggest that many others did indeed care.

Wilder gained substantial advantages in the 1989 race from being black: among them, a clear road to the Democratic nomination, an extraordinary amount of mostly positive national press attention, and the ability to run as both the candidate of change and that of continuity. But there can be little doubt that he also endured closer personal scrutiny than previous gubernatorial candidates, and both poll takers and political scientists agree that thousands of votes were denied to him on election day because of color.

Precisely how many ballots Wilder lost or gained because of race will never be known. Some of the best clues lie in exploring the shifts in voting patterns of those groups and regions (central cities and the Fourth and Fifth districts, for instance), that have shown special interest in racial matters in the past. There was also subjective evidence of race-based voting in numerous public comments reported by newspapers in the days leading up to the election.

For instance, Chris Nolen, the GOP chairman in a western Virginia county, told a *Washington Post* reporter shortly before the election that race was an issue in his area. "It's not talked about openly, even in families, but it's understood," he said. Similarly, eighty-four-year-old F. O. Clarke of Suffolk told the *Virginian-Pilot* that "anybody eighty-four years old, raised in the South has a prejudice. Most of the people I've talked to have the same feeling I do." Clarke was a Coleman voter. In the same way Gloria Jennings, a thirty-five-year-old black woman living in the same precinct as Clarke, was equally aware of race in deciding to vote for Wilder. Asked why she supported the Democrat, Jennings replied: "He's black." If Larry Sabato's estimate that 96 percent of all black votes went to Wilder is correct, he might seem to have benefited considerably from racially motivated voting. But it must be kept in mind that white Democrats also receive overwhelming black support, and that for every black vote cast in the election, there were about four by whites.

Opinion polls provided relatively little help in assessing the import of race, and in some cases only added to the confusion. It is notoriously difficult for poll takers to elicit honest answers about the relationship between color and voting, in part because for many the impact may be more subconscious than conscious. Numerous polls have documented a general softening of racial attitudes in the last three decades, and those shifts doubtless helped pave the way for Wilder's acceptance. According to the National Opinion Research Corporation at the University of Chicago, the number of Americans who would reject a qualified black person for president, even if nominated by his or her party, has dropped from 63 percent in 1958 to 17 percent in 1989. In the South as a whole, the figure is 25 percent, according to the survey.

Asked in the CBS News/*New York Times* exit poll to choose the issues that most affected their decision, 9 percent of voters cited "race relations." Two-thirds of that group said they voted for Wilder; one-third for Coleman. Mason-Dixon's Brad Coker believes that some of the best evidence of racial voting was found in his exit poll. The survey correctly captured voter sentiment in the victories of Don Beyer and Mary Sue Terry, but erred greatly in forecasting the outcome of the gubernatorial race. Noting similar failures in exit polls involving black-white contests in New York City, Philadelphia, and California, Coker argues that some voters simply lied. A shift of only 5 percent of those surveyed would have closed the 10-point gap that Coleman supposedly faced to an even race, and Coker attributes about 4 of that 5 percent to Democrats who claimed to have voted a straight party ticket when in fact they backed Coleman for governor. Those influenced by race may have been unwilling to indicate bias by admitting to an interviewer that they voted for Coleman, Beyer, and Terry, Coker believes.

Coker's conclusion, however, is questioned by the woman who directs surveys for CBS News in New York. Kathy Frankovic says that "absolutely, of course" there was some racial voting in the Virginia contest. But she argues that a polling error by Mason-

Dixon may have also played a role in the discrepancy. For instance, she says, Coker might have gotten better numbers had he allowed voters to privately fill out a questionnaire, rather than interviewing them in person. "I think one should not blame the voters when the fault might lie elsewhere," she said. Still, if the interviewing technique was Coker's problem, the question remains: why in the Wilder-Coleman race alone would personal interviews have caused problems?

Adding to the debate are the results of two other exit polls. One, conducted in-house for the Coleman campaign, projected Coleman to be the winner by 50.4 to 49.6 percent. Unlike in the detailed Mason-Dixon and CBS News/*New York Times* surveys, voters were asked only three questions by interviewers: Did you vote for governor? Did you vote for Marshall Coleman or Doug Wilder? Did you vote in the Republican primary in June? According to Frankovic, the CBS News/*New York Times* survey showed Wilder winning by about 52 percent of the vote, a much narrower margin than that recorded by Mason-Dixon. Both Sabato and Coker insist, however, that they were told separately by several sources at the *New York Times* that as late as 6:00 P.M. on election night, the survey was reflecting a gap similar to Coker's. Coker implies that the final numbers, not made public until Wednesday, were adjusted to reflect the actual results. Frankovic denies that charge.

In any event, there are two points of agreement among all the poll takers and analysts: (1) race did matter in the Virginia election; but (2) it counted for less than it would have ten, or perhaps even five years ago, because it did not prevent the black candidate from winning. Thus, an important threshold had been crossed. While race is a factor in American politics, it need no longer be the determining one.

As his term as governor of Virginia began, some analysts were predicting that Douglas Wilder's attention would be diverted by a national, and even international, audience anxious to hear the story of his success and ready to propel him into a larger political arena. As a history-maker and the nation's highest black elected official, such a role is probably his for the asking. Wilder downplays any notion of rivalry with Jesse Jackson, but there will be many urging him forward, both for his own sake, and as a way of mitigating Jackson's divisive role in the Democratic party. Wilder's political instincts may tell him that his future is best served by tending the home fires well, but he is nothing if not competitive and ambitious. Jackson may be too tempting a target to ignore.

Already, as Wilder took office, black leaders were cautioning African-Americans about expecting too much change in state policy as a result of installing a black man as governor. Indeed, if his first weeks in office were a gauge, he intended to be as fiscally cautious as the state's Republican governors of the 1970s. As delegate William P. Robinson, Jr., of Norfolk, chairman of the legislature's Black Caucus, declared, "his election raised expectations, but the realities of short revenues will unquestionably cause him to be less aggressive in initiating some of his personal concepts. What all of us must do is to articulate to the black community in particular that without the money he is very much constrained in what he can do."

The primary legacy of Wilder's victory, prominent blacks were asserting, might simply be the proof that it is possible for a black politician to emerge from within a political system dominated by whites. With an ever-dwindling number of exceptions, most of those political offices open to black candidates by virtue of a heavily black electorate have been filled. The challenges for the 1990s will come in districts where blacks can win only by claiming the votes of significant numbers of whites. Wilder's campaign offers a formula, albeit not an easily followed one, for doing that.

Still, there should be no illusions from the election of a single black governor about the ease of crossing the racial divide in American politics. Wilder's victory leaves the nation with one black governor out of fifty, no black U.S. senators, and only two dozen blacks in the 435-member House of Representatives. And it is also true that just as Wilder's race *was* undeniably a factor in the election, so his performance as governor will almost certainly be viewed by many at least partly in racial terms. As a politician Wilder has consistently shown an aptitude, sometimes from necessity, sometimes not, for creating his own rules rather than playing by those of others. It may be that the innovative instincts that guided his unprecedented political journey over racial barriers will serve him equally well in the job that he faces as the first elected black governor of an American state. If so, the election of this black Virginian will indeed have assured that, for all those who follow, a mighty mountain will be less steep. For one man at least had climbed that mountain.

In a constituency with four white voters for every black voter, a black candidate had been elected governor of an American state. Regardless of how narrow the margin of victory, or of what the particular issues were that confronted the electorate, that much had happened, and for the first time ever. It had taken place in Virginia, for a man named Douglas Wilder. Once more the Virginians had made American history.

STATE OF VIRGINIA ELECTION RESULTS

CONGRESSIONAL DISTRICT	1989 GOVERNOR		1989 LIEUTENANT GOVERNOR		1989 ATTORNEY GENERAL		1985 LIEUTENANT GOVERNOR	
	Wilder (D)	Coleman (R)	Beyer (D)	Dalton (R)	Terry (D)	Benedetti (R)	Wilder (D)	Chichester (R)
1	97,445 51.1%	93,230 48.9%	95,662 52.9%	85,077 47.1%	123,124 67.8%	58,445 32.2%	73,291 53.0%	64,877 47.0%
2	79,658 55.4%	63,809 44.4%	79,179 57.0%	59,706 43.0%	99,261 70.8%	40,817 29.1%	58,393 55.5%	46,750 44.5%
3	104,949 48.2%	112,450 51.6%	113,154 53.3%	98,895 46.6%	120,561 56.3%	93,325 43.6%	80,767 47.3%	90,044 52.7%
4	95,278 52.2%	87,218 47.8%	94,992 55.4%	76,595 44.6%	125,254 72.0%	48,799 28.0%	78,652 55.2%	63,747 44.8%
5	72,228 42.1%	99,251 57.9%	76,503 48.0%	82,995 52.0%	102,849 63.0%	60,446 37.0%	62,978 48.6%	66,563 51.4%
6	77,189 45.9%	90,723 54.0%	81,877 50.1%	81,428 49.9%	99,135 60.3%	65,225 39.7%	61,802 50.8%	59,793 49.2%
7	77,962 42.7%	104,472 57.2%	84,972 47.9%	92,273 52.0%	98,064 55.4%	79,091 44.6%	57,566 44.9%	70,762 55.1%
8	102,225 55.5%	81,441 44.2%	107,694 59.2%	73,949 40.7%	111,607 61.8%	69,006 38.2%	65,795 54.3%	55,448 45.7%
9	70,997 48.2%	76,319 51.8%	77,658 54.5%	64,689 45.4%	90,509 63.6%	51,706 36.4%	66,197 54.4%	55,552 45.6%
10	119,208 59.3%	81,372 40.5%	122,686 61.8%	75,756 38.2%	125,731 63.8%	71,264 36.2%	79,888 55.8%	63,159 44.2%
TOTAL*	897,139† 50.1%	890,285 49.8%	934,377 54.1%	791,360 45.8%	1,096,095 63.2%	638,124 36.8%	685,329 51.8%	636,695 48.2%

* Source: Virginia State Board of Elections.

† This compilation is based on the official results as certified by the State Board of Elections at its November 27 canvass. These figures could not be adjusted after the December 20, 1989, gubernatorial recount since the recount was not done by congressional districts.

SUGGESTED READING

Baker, Donald. *Wilder: Hold Fast to Dreams*. Cabin John: Seven Locks Press, 1989.

Barnes, Fred. "Republicans Miscarry Abortion." *American Spectator*, January 1990, pp. 14–15.

Buni, Andrew. *The Negro in Virginia Politics, 1902–1965*, Charlottesville: University of Virginia Press, 1967.

Cavanagh, Thomas E., ed. "Race and Political Strategy: A JCPS Roundtable." Washington: Joint Center for Political Studies, 1983.

Chesson, Michael B. *Richmond After the War 1865–1890*. Richmond: Virginia State Library, 1981.

Coker, Brad. "Not All Polls Are Created Equal." *Washington Post*, November 18, 1989, A23.

Dabney, Virginius. *Virginia: The New Dominion*. New York: Doubleday & Co., 1971.

Governor's Commission on Virginia's Future. "Toward a New Dominion: Choices for Virginians." Charlottesville: University of Virginia Institute of Government, December 1984.

Harwood, Richard. "Tilt! Tilt!" *Washington Post*, November 19, 1989, D6.

Johnson, Steven. "Coleman Aides' Postmortem Cites Missed Opportunities," *The Daily Progress*, November 23, 1989, A1.

Key, V. O., Jr. *Southern Politics in State and Nation*. New York: Random House, 1949.

Lawson, Steven F. *Black Ballots, Voting Rights in the South, 1944–1969*. New York: Columbia University Press, 1976.

———. *In Pursuit of Power: Southern Blacks and Electoral Politics, 1965–1982*. New York: Columbia University Press, 1985.

MacPherson, Myra. "Douglas Wilder: Winning the Waiting Game." *Washington Post*, February 2, 1986, G1–G4.

Morin, Richard. "We Pollsters Had It Coming." *Washington Post*, November 13, 1989, A13.

Pettigrew, Thomas F., and Denise Alston. "Tom Bradley's Campaigns for Governor: The Dilemma of Race and Political Strategies." Washington: Joint Center for Political Studies, 1988.

Rabinowitz, Howard N., ed. *Southern Black Leaders of the Reconstruction Period*. Urbana: University of Illinois Press, 1982.

Sabato, Larry. "Virginia Votes 1983–1986." Charlottesville: University of Virginia Institute of Government, 1987.

———. "Virginia's National Election for Governor—1989." Draft chapter to be published in future edition of *Virginia Votes*.

Wilder, Douglas. Interview, March 15, 1974. Southern Oral History Project, University of North Carolina.

Wilkinson, J. Harvie III. *Harry Byrd and the Changing Face of Virginia Politics 1945–1966*. Charlottesville: The University of Virginia Press, 1968.

Yancey, Dwayne. *When Hell Froze Over*. Dallas: Taylor Publishing Company, 1988.

INDEX